Common Prayer

		¶ Psalmes	Matins.		Euensong,	
			i. Lesson,	ii. Lesson,	i. Lesson,	ii. Lesson
c	kalend	i				
d	iii. No	ii	Jere. xii	Jhon. xx	Jere. xiii	Hebre. iiii
e	vi. No,	iii	xiiii	xxi	xv	v
f	Pri. No	iiii	xvi	Actes, i	xvii	vi
g	Nonas	v	xviii	ii	xix	vii
A	viii. Id	vi	xx	iii	xxi	viii
b	vii. Id	vii	xxii	iiii	xxiii	ix
c	vi. Id	viii	xxiiii	v	xxv	x
d	v. Id	ix	xxvi	vi	xxvii	xi
e	iiii. Id	x	xxviii	vii	xxix	xii
f	iii. Id	xi	xxx	viii	xxxi	xiii
g	Pri. Id	xii	xxxii	ix	xxxiii	Jacob. i
A	Idus	xiii	xxxiiii	x	xxxv	ii
b	xix. kl	xiiii	xxxvi	xi	xxxvii	iii
c	xviii. kl	xv	xl	xii	xli	iiii
d	xvii. kl	xvi	xli	xiiii	xliii	v
e	xvi. kl	xvii	xliiii	xv	xliiii	i. Peter, i
f	xv. kl	xviii	xlvii	xvi	xlviii	ii
g	xiiii. kl	xix	xlix	xvii	l	iii
A	xiii. kl	xx	li	xviii	lii	v
b	xii. kl	xxi	xxi Lament, i	xix Lament, ii		ii. Peter, i
c	xi. kl	xxii	xxii	iii	xx	iiii
d	x. kl	xxiii	xxiii	v	xxi Ezech, ii	iii
e	ix. kl	xxiiii Bart ap	xxiiii Ezech, iii	xxii	vi	i. Jhon, i
f	viii. kl	xxv	xxv	vii	xxiii	iii
g	vii. kl	xxvi	xxvi	xiiii	xxiiii	iii
A	vi. kl	xxvii	xxvii	xxxiii	xxv	xxxiiii	iiii
b	v. kl	xxviii	xxviii Dani, i	xxvi Dan, ii		v
c	iiii. kl	xxix	xxix	iii	xxvii	iiii	ii. iii. Jhon
d	iii. kl	xxx	xxx	v	xxviii	vi	Jude, i
A	ii. kl	xxxi	xxxi	vii Math, i	viii	Roma, i

"The Ordre how the rest of the holy Scripture (besyde the Psalter) I appointed to be redde [August]." From the Book of Common Prayer (London, 1549). By permission of the Houghton Library, Harvard University.

Common Prayer

THE LANGUAGE OF PUBLIC DEVOTION

IN EARLY MODERN ENGLAND

Ramie Targoff

THE UNIVERSITY OF CHICAGO PRESS
chicago and london

Ramie Targoff is assistant professor of English at Yale University. Her
articles and essays have appeared in journals such as *Word and Image*,
English Literary Renaissance, and *Representations*, as well as in edited collections.
This is her first book.

The University of Chicago Press, Chicago 60637
The University of Chicago Press, Ltd., London
© 2001 by The University of Chicago
All rights reserved. Published 2001
Printed in the United States of America
10 09 08 07 06 05 04 03 02 01   1 2 3 4 5

ISBN: 0-226-78968-3 (cloth)
ISBN: 0-226-78969-1 (paper)

Library of Congress Cataloging-in-Publication Data

Targoff, Ramie.
Common prayer : the language of public devotion in early modern
England / Ramie Targoff.
p.   cm.
Includes bibliographical references and index.
ISBN 0-226-78968-3 (alk. paper) —
ISBN 0-226-78969-1 (pbk. : alk. paper)
1. English literature—Early modern, 1500–1700—History and
criticism.   2. Christianity and literature—England—History—
16th century.   3. Christianity and literature—England—History—
17th century.   4. Public worship—England—History—16th century.
5. Public worship—England—History—17th century.   6. Prayer—
England—History—16th century.   7. Prayer—England—History—
17th century.   8. Reformation—England.   9. Prayer in literature.
I. Title.
PR428.C48 T37   2001
820.9'3823'09031—dc21   00-060729

For Stephen

Contents

Illustrations

Acknowledgments

In a study preoccupied with the ways in which the private and individual voice is shaped by the public and collective forms that surround it, I am eager to express my gratitude to the wide range of voices that have informed this book. First, my research has been generously supported by grants from the Mellon Foundation and the Townsend Center for the Humanities at the University of California, Berkeley; a year-long dissertation grant from the National Endowment for the Humanities; a Visiting Fellowship at the Wissenschaftskolleg zu Berlin; and, above all, two Griswold Faculty Research Grants and a Morse Fellowship from Yale University. I have also benefited tremendously from the wonderful collections and librarians at the Beinecke Library at Yale, and the Houghton Library at Harvard University. This book could not have been written without access to the primary materials that these libraries made available.

Second, I am equally if not more indebted to a wide range of friends, colleagues, and teachers who have contributed intellectual energy and support to this project. Jeffrey Knapp has read my work with unprecedented attention and care from its inception. Annabel Patterson generously read the entire manuscript twice, and has offered incisive and immensely helpful advice throughout. Debora Shuger has been a rigorous and fine reader at every stage of this project, and her extensive feedback has guided my revisions in ways too numerous to list here. I have received important suggestions and valuable criticism from Paul Alpers, Sacvan Bercovitch, David Bevington, William Bouwsma, Sarah Cole, Philip Fisher, Mary Floyd-Wilson, Donald Friedman, Traugott Lawler, Lee Patterson, Richard Rambuss, Catherine Robson, John Rogers, Elaine Scarry, Michael Schoenfeldt, Richard Strier, and Gordon Teskey. Nathan Ewer, Julie Khoury, Amy Robinson, and above all Gustavo Secchi have been scrupulous and attentive research assistants. I thank also Alan Thomas, Randolph Petilos, and Sandra Hazel at the University of Chicago Press, as well as the readers who read this book in manuscript.

My parents, Cheri and Michael Targoff, and my grandparents, Phyllis and Alfred Kamen and Terry Targoff, have sustained and supported me with the utmost generosity.

My deepest thanks I owe to my husband, Stephen Greenblatt, whose personal and intellectual bounty knows no limits.

An earlier version of the introduction was published as "The Performance of Prayer: Sincerity and Theatricality in Early Modern England," in *Representations* 60 (fall 1997): 49–69. Copyright © 1997 by The Regents of the University of California. An earlier version of chapter 4 appeared under the title "The Poetics of Common Prayer: George Herbert and the Seventeenth-Century Devotional Lyric," in *English Literary Renaissance* 29, no. 3 (autumn 1999): 468–90. Copyright © 1999 by *English Literary Renaissance*. Several pages from the final section of chapter 4, "Printed Matter," appeared in an article on the publication history of Donne and Herbert, "Poets in Print: The Case of Herbert's *Temple*," in *Word and Image* 17, nos. 1 and 2 (2001): 142–54. Copyright © 2001. I am grateful to the editors and the presses involved for permission to reprint these materials here.

Author's Note on Spelling and Editions

Although I have used original editions for the texts in this book whenever possible, I have chosen to modernize all spelling, with the exception of sixteenth- and seventeenth-century verse, whose original spelling is not nearly so difficult to read as many prose works of that period, and offers compensatory pleasures. In the case of medieval verse, I have modernized and translated difficult passages except when the translation affects the rhyme.

The Performance of Prayer

The villain Claudius in act 3 of Hamlet struggles to pray. Secretly observing his uncle in an unexpected posture of devotion, Hamlet refuses this opportunity to take his revenge for fear of sending Claudius straight to salvation: "Now might I do it pat," he says, "now a is a praying / And now I'll do't—And so a goes to heaven . . . / And am I then revenged / To take him in the purging of his soul / When he is fit and seasoned for his passage?" (3.3.73–74, 84–86)[1] No sooner does Hamlet exit the stage, however, than Claudius announces to the audience the failure of his prayer. Despite his efforts to align his internal state with his external gestures of piety—"Bow, stubborn knees;" he commands, "and heart with strings of steel / Be soft as sinews of the new-born babe"—Claudius's heart, like that of the Old Testament pharaoh, remains hardened (3.3.70–71).[2] The scene concludes with Claudius's announcement of the irreconcilable discrepancy between his "thoughts" and his "words": "My words fly up, my thoughts remain below / Words without thoughts never to heaven go" (3.3.97–98).

For centuries of literary critics, this scene has primarily been registered as an important example of Hamlet's tendency toward procrastination and delay. As A. C. Bradley observes: "[T]his incident is, again, the turning point of the tragedy. So far, Hamlet's delay, though it is endangering his freedom and his life, has done no irreparable harm; but his failure here is the cause of all the disasters that follow."[3] Samuel Johnson recognizes the scene's significance within the structure of the plot, but finds Hamlet's decision to spare Claudius in order to assure that "[Claudius's] soul may be as damn'd and black / As hell, whereto it goes" to be a sentiment "too horrible to be read or to be uttered."[4] What critics of all persuasions have largely ignored, however, and what a Renaissance audience would certainly have been alert to, is the actual content of this scene: its detailed exploration of the devotional process that fails to produce a sincere state of contrition. In addition to its pivotal location in the narrative's unfolding, this incident speaks directly to the play's preoccupation with the relationship Claudius later refers to between "th'exterior [and] the inward man" (2.2.6)—

a preoccupation, not coincidentally, that lies at the heart of early modern debates about devotional performance.

According to most historians of early modern England, the dominant model for understanding the relationship between external practice and internal belief in the Elizabethan church was neatly summarized by Francis Bacon's assessment that the queen did not "make windows into men's hearts and secret thoughts."[5] Because rigid laws governing church attendance were rarely accompanied by probing inquiries into personal faith, so long as worshippers came to services on Sunday, they were free to believe whatever they chose. Hence Patrick Collinson, for example, explains:

> As every schoolboy used to know, what was enforced in the Elizabethan Church was not very much. Contrary to what the schoolboy was taught, it was Francis Bacon and not the Queen herself who spoke of her reluctance to make windows in men's souls, but the famous aphorism accurately encapsulates the limited aims of Elizabethan Church policy, seeking outward submission to the legally established religion rather than a willing, knowledgeable and conscientious assent to its propositional content.[6]

The vision of selfhood that emerges from this narrative depends upon a deliberate dissociation of the individual's private life from his or her public one: not only Catholic recusants and Puritan resistors, but middle-of-the-road English subjects were capable of sustaining a pretense of conformity that successfully masked their unreachable inwardness.

Within the context of English literary history, the *locus classicus* for the division of the self between sincere and theatrical roles is Shakespeare's *Hamlet*. Early in act 1, in response to Gertrude's request that he "cast [his] nighted colour off," Hamlet replies:

> 'Tis not alone my inky cloak, good-mother,
> Nor customary suits of solemn black . . .
> Together with all forms, moods, shapes of grief
> That can denote me truly. These indeed "seem,"
> For they are actions that a man might play;
> But I have that within which passes show—
> These but the trappings and the suits of woe. (1.2.77–86)

By drawing attention to the secret and impenetrable self underneath his "forms, moods, shapes of grief," Hamlet seems both to anticipate and to confirm our assumptions of a privileged and opaque interiority.[7] From this early moment in the first act through the introduction in act 5 of the courtier Osric—whose exceedingly deferential behavior Hamlet mocks as insincere—the play seems to draw our attention to Hamlet's ability to separate insides from outsides, seeming from being.

Hamlet's failure to consider the possible discrepancy between Claudius's inward and outward state of devotion threatens to undermine the critical consensus about his ability to penetrate the insincere. Claudius confesses not only his failure to pray, but also his guilt in his brother's murder in the first lines of his lengthy soliloquy:

> O my offense is rank! It smells to heaven,
> It hath the primal eldest curse upon't,
> A brother's murder. Pray can I not,
> Though inclination be as sharp as will,
> My stronger guilt defeats my strong intent,
> And, like a man to double business bound
> I stand in pause where I shall first begin,
> And both neglect. (3.3.36–43)

These frank admissions are announced to the theatrical audience, but fatefully go unheard by Hamlet, who enters the scene only after Claudius has assumed his kneeling position of piety. And yet, Hamlet's willingness to accept the sincerity of Claudius's prayer on the basis of his external posture does not simply or even primarily reflect an unusual flaw in Hamlet's skills of perception. Instead, it represents an explicit grappling on Shakespeare's part with one of the central issues surrounding devotional performance in early modern religious culture. For what is strikingly, and mistakenly, absent from our accounts of the Elizabethan settlement is precisely what the play interrogates in staging Claudius's prayer: the belief that external practices might not only reflect but also potentially transform the internal self.

Although Shakespeare makes it abundantly clear that the prayer Claudius performs at the end of his tortured soliloquy does not actually produce an internal state of contrition, its convincing façade seems to have an impact upon Hamlet. In the scene that immediately follows, Hamlet does not, as we might expect, consider the discrepancies he articulated at the beginning of the play between "actions that a man might play" and "that within which passes show," nor does he return to his earlier perception of Claudius's capacity to "smile, and smile, and be a villain" (1.5.109). Instead, he advises Gertrude:

> Assume a virtue if you have it not.
> That monster custom, who all sense doth eat,
> Of habits devilish, is angel yet in this:
> That to the use of actions fair and good
> He likewise gives a frock or livery
> That aptly is put on. Refrain tonight,
> And that shall lend a kind of easiness
> To the next abstinence, the next more easy—
> For use almost can change the stamp of nature. (3.4.151–151.8)

The proximity of these two moments in the play is not coincidental: Hamlet's advice to his mother offers an important explanation for his willingness to accept Claudius's devotion as sincere. In each of these scenes, that is, Hamlet adheres to the possibility that external practice might serve as both a criterion of outward judgment and a vehicle of inward change.

Within the context of *Hamlet*, the potential for a causal relation between outward performance and inward change is neither confirmed nor entirely denied; the play does not pursue any further the state of Claudius's mind, nor does it burden Hamlet with discovering the folly of his misreading. And yet, however ambivalent *Hamlet* may ultimately be about the transformative capacity of external behavior, the Church of England was firmly aligned behind it.[8] There were no absolute divisions between sincerity and theatricality, inwardness and outwardness within the early modern English church. Although established churchmen recognized the potential for externally convincing but internally empty acts of devotion, they tended to minimize the threat that such dissembling posed either to the dissemblers themselves or to the congregation of eyewitnesses.

This position stemmed not from a cynical indifference to the worshipper's inner state, but instead from an affirmative belief in what Aristotle describes as the efficacy of "habit." Hamlet's advice to Gertrude—"assume a virtue if you have it not"—originates from the behaviorist philosophy outlined in the *Nicomachean Ethics*, which posits a causal link between ethics (*ethike*) and habit (*ethos*). "Moral virtue," Aristotle declares, "comes about as a result of habit. . . . For the things we have to learn before we can do them, we learn by doing them . . . we become just by doing just acts, temperate by doing temperate acts, brave by doing brave acts."[9] This understanding of habitual practice helps to explain how the religious establishment could simultaneously seem uninterested in private belief and yet demonstrate repeatedly its desire to subsume private devotion within the public liturgy of the church. Indeed, what appears to be a simple request for an untaxing and potentially unmeaningful participation in a weekly service turns out to be a strategy to transform the worshipper's soul.

The crucial vehicle for implementing this strategy was common prayer. From its initial construction in 1549, the Book of Common Prayer collapsed the distinctions between personal and liturgical worship by introducing a single paradigm for devotional language. For early modern churchgoers, common prayer had two important aspects. First, it was a standardized devotional practice, a public activity in which all English subjects were required to participate weekly. Second, in the form of the Prayer Book, it was a collection of premeditated texts, whose very formalization ensured, in the view of the established churchmen, a devotional efficacy that could not be attained with spontaneous and original prayers.

In keeping with this dual thrust, I have divided this study in roughly two parts. The first chapters examine questions primarily related to common prayer as cultural practice. Here I mean to challenge one of the governing premises of our understanding of early modern religious culture: that the private sphere fostered by the Protestant Reformation represented a powerful alternative to the superficial and depersonalized practices of the medieval Catholic Church. What gets overlooked by this argument, as I argue in chapter 1, are two crucial features of late medieval and early modern devotional life that vastly complicate the binary between Catholicism and publicness on the one hand, and Protestantism and privacy on the other. First, the Catholic Church actively encouraged a private experience of its liturgy for its worshippers, whose most effective practice of prayer depended upon a strict isolation from the performance of the priest. Second, in designing the Book of Common Prayer, Thomas Cranmer and his fellow reformers actively sought to create a liturgical practice that did not accommodate personal deviation. By tracing the transition from the pre-Reformation Catholic service, in which the congregation was not meant to understand or follow the Latin prayers of the priest, to the Protestant service, which was designed to enable the laity's full comprehension and participation, I consider the ways in which common prayer fundamentally reconceived the relations between the individual worshipper and the public devotional sphere.

Chapter 2 moves from the initial articulations of common prayer in the 1540s and 1550s to the first serious attacks on the Prayer Book from within the Protestant Church in the 1570s, attacks that focus on the devotional limitations of reading rather than spontaneously composing one's prayers. The charges leveled by non-conformists against the liturgy for its imposition of a mechanical and artificial practice that inhibits devotional freedom are powerfully met by the clergyman Richard Hooker, who offers the first thorough defense of the establishment's practice of common prayer. Far from imagining liturgical spontaneity as a liberation, Hooker offers a novel account of devotional freedom as an enormous burden upon the individual's psychic well-being; formalized language becomes in this account a crucial safeguard against the natural weaknesses of human devotion.

The second part of this study views the ways in which the language of common prayer influenced the shape of early modern devotional poetry. The phenomenon that these chapters describe depends upon perhaps the most significant change that the Prayer Book brought to the status of the English language: after centuries in which the vernacular served a secondary role as the vehicle for lay edification and devotion but not for liturgical prayer, English emerges as a sacred tongue deemed worthy of communicating formal petitions to God. The particular properties of common prayer—its emphasis upon premeditation rather than spontaneity; its insistence upon the interchangeability of

first-person singular and plural pronouns; its preference for simultaneously eloquent and reiterable texts over complex and difficult models of language—
played an important role, I argue, in determining the poetic forms that seemed
most effective for acts of personal as well as collective expression.

In chapter 3, I trace the history of English devotional verse from its central
and unselfconscious position in medieval lay worship, where it was used primarily as a mnemonic and didactic tool, to its status as a separate but compatible
form of prayer in the late sixteenth century. This transformation turns on the
role of the metrical Psalms, whose recognition by Philip Sidney, among others,
as not only prayers but also poems helped to legitimize a place for poetry within
the church. Chapter 4 examines the lyrics of George Herbert, which splendidly
merged poetry with prayer in a manner that Sidney had imagined exclusively in
relation to the Psalms and scriptural verse. Although specifically focused on Herbert, I mean here to suggest more broadly an approach to the seventeenth-
century lyric that recognizes the powerful ways in which this body of literature
was inspired by public and liturgical, as well as private and meditative, models
of language. In my conclusion, I turn from England in the 1630s to New England in the 1640s, where we find an unexpected confirmation of the new position that poetry had assumed within Protestantism as an exceptional category
of prayer in John Cotton and his fellow Puritans' justifications of the Bay Psalm
Book.

Before I begin my inquiry into the innovations and complications of common prayer that developed over the course of the sixteenth and seventeenth
centuries, I want to consider one of the first questions that seems to have con-
fronted the Protestant reformers in justifying their commitment to public worship: how can the outward performance of prayer be relied upon to heighten
the worshipper's experience of inward faith? Or, to put the question in terms
that we have already seen in relation to *Hamlet*, what is the persuasive power of
either enacting or witnessing external displays of piety? The following pages are
meant to introduce the period's overriding concern with determining the opti-
mal conditions for the performance of prayer, a concern that connects nearly all
of the authors and materials that subsequent chapters will examine. As we shall
repeatedly observe, what emerges in the aftermath of the Reformation is less a
triumphant embrace of the individual's private and invisible self than a con-
certed effort to shape the otherwise uncontrollable and unreliable internal
sphere through common acts of devotion.

"BODILY REVERENCE"

For English reformers interested in subsuming rituals of private confession and
prayer within the public service of the church, the Christian tradition posed a

series of formidable obstacles. First, they had inherited from Augustine a profound sense of how difficult it was to gauge sincerity in the act of worshipping God. In book 10 of the *Confessions*, Augustine announces his indifference to the hypothetical human audience who witnesses his prayer: "What does it matter to me whether men should hear what I have to confess. . . . When they hear me speak about myself, how do they know whether I am telling the truth, since no one knows a man's thoughts, except the man's own spirit that is within him?"[10] This notion of an internality that is entirely inaccessible to anyone outside the self emerges from an earlier, more forceful injunction against externalized devotion. In his Sermon on the Mount, Christ explicitly connects the public practice of prayer with hypocrisy:

> And when thou prayest thou shalt not be like the hypocrites. For they love to stand and pray in the synagogues, and in corners of the streets, that they might be seen of men. . . . Thou therefore, when thou prayest, go into thy chamber, and shut thy door, and pray to thy Father which is in secret. (Matt. 6:5−6)[11]

What renders public prayer hypocritical, Christ seems to suggest, lies specifically in its performative nature: the worshipper caters to a visible and earthly rather than an invisible and divine audience. According to this logic, sincere devotion depends upon "shutting" off the public world and turning "in secret" toward the internal realm that is viewed only by God.

Faced with this notion of external devotion as at best an opaque, at worst a misdirected or fraudulent performance, English Protestants were challenged to construct a theological justification for the efficacy of public worship. The earliest example of such an account surfaces in the work of the Henrician martyr and Lutheran, William Tyndale, whose *Exposition of Matthew* (1533) systematically reverses both Augustine's and Christ's privileging of private over public devotion. In his commentary on the Sermon on the Mount, Tyndale replaces a literal with a metaphorical interpretation of Christ's instructions:

> Of entering into the chamber and shutting the door to, I say as above, the meaning is that we should avoid all worldly praise and profit, and pray with a single eye and true intent according to God's word; and it is not forbidden thereby to pray openly. For we must have a place to come together, to pray in general, to thank and to cry to God for the common necessities.[12]

In place of the scriptural emphasis on privacy, Tyndale stresses the necessity of "open," "general," and "common" petitions. The biblical rule now becomes the exception: the "secret place" of prayer is required only to accommodate the exceedingly devoted worshipper, whose fervent manner of prayer extends beyond the normative standards of the public realm.

If Tyndale's interpretive strategy in these passages is to shift Christ's definition of hypocrisy away from its association with "open" prayer, the task remains for him to provide an alternative method for identifying fraudulent as well as faithful performances within the public sphere. The solution Tyndale proposes is to suggest an evaluative system that does not depend simply on the invisible state of the soul, but also on its visible manifestations in the body. In response to Christ's injunction in verse 7, "when ye pray babble not much as the heathens do," Tyndale interprets "babbling" to mean a false kind of physical, not verbal, praying, and in a lengthy digression from the biblical chapter which moves directly to Christ's delivery of the Lord's Prayer, Tyndale considers the behavioral signs the worshipper ought and ought not to demonstrate during an act of devotion.

The primary distinction Tyndale draws between true and false prayer relies entirely upon two different affective states of the body:

> As before [Christ] rebuked their false intent in praying . . . even so here he rebuketh a false kind of praying, wherein the tongue and lips labor, and all the body is pained, but the heart talketh not with God, nor feeleth any sweetness at all . . . with their false intent of praying, [they] have turned it into a bodily labor, to vex the tongue, lips, eyes, and throat with roaring, and to weary all the members; so that they say (and may truly swear it) that there is no greater labor in the world than prayer. (258)

This description is surprising less for its association of painful exertion with fraudulent devotion than for its insistence on the bodily pleasure of true prayer: "But true prayer," Tyndale continues, "would so comfort the soul and courage the heart, that the body, though it were half dead and more, would revive and be lusty again, and the labor would be short and easy" (258). It is not only the soul and heart but also the body that experiences the effects of sincere devotion.

If we compare Tyndale's commentary on this verse to Martin Luther's, which served here as elsewhere as his primary source, Tyndale's somatic emphasis becomes more pronounced. Luther remarks that when "the heart is not involved and the body has to do all the work," then prayer certainly involves physical labor. "But," he adds, "on the other hand, if the heart is cheerful and willing, then it does not even notice the work." For the Christian who is earnest in his devotion and takes pleasure in praying manifests no bodily response whatsoever: "he simply looks at his need, and he has finished singing or praying the words before he has a chance to turn around."[13] Although Luther describes the labor involved in feigning devotion—"when the heart is not involved and the body has to do all the work"—he imagines no comparable state of bodily pleasure for the faithful. Whereas Tyndale describes the "lusty" body renewed by its devotion, Luther's true worshipper is characterized by an absence of all physical symptoms.

Tyndale's *Exposition of Matthew* marks the initial articulation in English Protestantism of an evaluative model that relies upon the external body for determining sincerity and hypocrisy at prayer. Within the context of public prayer, the worshippers' physical posture, the tone of their words, and the nature of their expressions were frequently seen as reliable indicators of an otherwise invisible devotional state. By the early seventeenth century, to pray in the English church was always to perform. In a sermon on Matthew, chapter 7, verse 7—"Ask, and it shall be given to you; seek, and ye shall find; knock, and it shall be opened to you"—Lancelot Andrewes, the prominent court preacher and eventual bishop of Winchester (1619), explains:

> They that are suitors for any earthly benefit do occupy not only their tongue in speaking, but their legs in resorting to great persons; they that seek do occupy not only their legs in going up and down, but their eyes to look in every place; and they that knock, as they use other members, so especially they use their hands. But when our Saviour enjoineth us the use of prayer, He expresseth it not in one word but in three several times, to teach us that when we come to pray to God the whole man must be occupied, and all the members of the body employed in the service of God.[14]

Here making literal Christ's metaphoric injunction to ask, seek, and knock, Andrewes imagines the act of prayer as both a physical and spiritual practice. Enlisting examples from both the Old and New Testaments, Andrewes concludes that words alone are insufficient in the service of God:

> Solomon prayed upon his knees; Daniel fell down upon his knees: so did St. Peter, so Paul; and not only men upon earth but the glorious spirits in heaven cast themselves and their crowns down before Him. . . . He that having prayed sit[ting] still without adding his endeavour, shall not receive the thing he prays for, for he must not only *orare* but *laborare*. (329)

"He must not only *orare* but *laborare*": the Augustinian model of praying privately and quietly is here cast aside as an inferior manifestation of faith.

Andrewes's belief in the efficacy of external labor as a crucial tool for exercising our devotion represents a seventeenth-century High Church response to prevalent theological concerns of many Tudor Protestants. During the reign of Edward VI, English reformers worried openly about the desirability of encouraging physical signs and gestures as part of the worshipper's practice of prayer. Thomas Becon, one of Cranmer's chaplains and a prolific author of Protestant devotional manuals, asserts in his *New Catechism* (1547) that "the outward speaking or singing of prayers, the kneeling or prostrating of ourselves, the lifting up of hands and eyes, the knocking of the breast, and such other like gestures in praying, are not discommendable, so long as they spring of the fervent action of the mind."[15] Becon's hesitancy to embrace the externalized performance of prayer further manifests itself in his anxiety about the potential disjunction between the worshipper's mind and body:

> To pretend outwardly an holy manner of praying, and yet not pray in deed in our hearts, is double iniquity, and increaseth much damnation unto us. . . . But let us hear what St. John Chrysostom saith: " . . . Their lips are moved only, but their mind is without fruit, and therefore are the ears of God deaf. . . . I have bowed, thou sayest, my knees. Thou hast bowed indeed thy knees within, but thy mind wandereth abroad. Thy body is within, but thy thought is without." (135)

For Becon, what is particularly blasphemous about what he terms "feigned holiness" is its opacity to the human eye: the ostensibly convincing performance of prayer never precludes the very real possibility of physical dissimulation.

By the seventeenth century, however, the concerns raised by early reformers such as Becon were met with increasingly elaborate accounts of the involuntary correspondence between external and internal states of devotion. Among other examples, the minister Robert Shelford declares in a sermon published in 1635 that "it cannot be, that these actions of the body accompanying those of the mind, should from their end be otherwise than spiritual duties." Citing a passage from Aquinas, Shelford concludes that bodily worship is performed in spirit "inasmuch as it proceeds from spiritual devotion, and is ordered to it. And because by our sense we cannot attain unto God, yet by sensible signs our mind is incited to tend towards him."[16] "By sensible signs": the body now not only reflects, but also helps to "incite" the mind's inclination toward God. In his 1639 tract, *Gods Holy House and Service*, the Norwich divine Foulke Robarts similarly argues for "such correspondency, and sympathy between the soul and the body," so that they "accord one with another, like those creatures and wheels, mentioned by the Prophet *Ezech. when those went, these went; when those stood, these stood: when those were lifted up, these were lifted up: for, the spirit of the living Creatures was in the wheels.*" "And do we not perceive plainly," he asks, "that when we betake our selves to our knees for prayer; the soul is humbled within us, by this very gesture?"[17] And in his 1636 tract, *Concerning Publicke-Prayer; And the Fasts of the Church*, John Browning declares that just as the body receives life and motion from the soul, so "it returneth also a further life by motion to it again: as *strings* touched in the same instrument, move one another; or as the body's warmth warms the *clothes*, which reciprocally preserve, and return the body's warmth again."[18]

These descriptions of the mutual dependence of body and soul in generating pious devotion, likened in Browning's tract to the exchange of heat between the skin and its woolen clothing, vividly convey what I have already described as the period's Aristotelian belief in the power of external gestures and habits to stimulate internal change. So Thomas Browne declares in his idiosyncratic, confessional treatise *Religio Medici* (1642): "At my devotion I love to use the civility of my knee, my hat, and hand, with all those outward and sensible motions which may express or promote my invisible devotion."[19] The potential for "invisible devotion" to be enhanced by the process of its externalization—a potential that lies in the distinction between the two verbs "express" and "promote"—motivates John Bulwer's explanation of the universal reliance upon the hands in the performance of prayer. In his 1644 encyclopedia of gestures, *Chirologia*, Bulwer claims that "we stand in need of some outward help to declare the ascension of our inward zeal which we reveal by the extension of our hands which supplying the place of wings help our hearts in their flight upwards."[20] For Bulwer, as for Browne, the invisibility of the heart is less a benefit—a means of assuring, as Augustine imagines, that only God will have access to one's thoughts—than a fault in need of compensation.

One of the primary advantages offered by praying in the presence of others was the possibility it provided for imitation. Once again, Augustine's reaction to an external and witnessed performance of prayer runs counter to the position cultivated by the English church. I refer here to an episode in the final book of *The City of God*, in which Augustine describes his reaction of total impotence in the face of a startling devotional act at the home of Innocentius, a wealthy citizen in Carthage. Innocentius, who was gravely ill with fistulas (which, we are told, "were numerous and complicated in the lowest part of his body behind"), was believed to be near death after exhausting all possible medical treatments. The whole household including Augustine began to pray for God's intervention, and Innocentius himself "fell down to the earth as if someone had struck him down." "Who will ever find words," Augustine asks, "to relate how he prayed—with what feeling, with what emotion, with what a flood of tears, with what groans and sobs that shook all his limbs and almost cut off his breath?" And yet, far from moving Augustine to pray with increased if not commensurate passion, he becomes paralyzed by Innocentius's example: "Whether the rest continued to pray, or had their attention diverted by all this, I do not know. For my part," he confesses, "I was quite unable to pray, but said in my heart only those few words: 'Lord, what prayers of thy people dost thou hear, if thou dost not hear these?'"[21]

Whereas Augustine's impulse is not to imitate but simply to observe or admire, early modern accounts emphasize the contagious power of watching a convincing act of prayer. Hence Robarts exclaims to the reader: "How doth the visible and expressive devotion of one Christian, beget and increase the same in an other? And how powerfully shall the reverend behaviors and gestures of an whole Congregation together work one upon another?"[22] Likewise, Browning explains that when the apostle instructs us to "teach and admonish one another, in Psalms, and Hymns, and Spiritual Songs," he means that by watching one another sing we shall heighten our own devotion: "Is it not by that cheerfulness, by that devotion they see in one another?" So, too, he continues, now addressing the performance of prayer in his contemporary church, "doth not the *reverent entrance* of one that entreth, as he should, stir up the fainting devotion of them that pray? Doth not the *devout kneeling* of those that are about us, put us also in mind of the duty, and earnestness of our prayers, we are about?" For, he concludes, "whereas the Priest preacheth to the ear only, every one in this his devotion, and by his example (which is most forceable) preacheth to each other's eye."[23]

Browning's notion that worshippers are capable of preaching to one another's eyes through the medium of what he terms "bodily reverence" not only resonates throughout late sixteenth- and seventeenth-century devotional texts but also has a significant literary precedent.[24] In his prose fiction, *The Countess of Pembroke's Arcadia*, Sidney describes the (albeit temporary) effect of the virtuous maiden Pamela's prayer on the wicked atheist Cecropia:

> But this prayer sent to heaven from so heavenly a creature, with such a fervent grace as if devotion had borrowed her body to make of itself a most beautiful representation; with her eyes so lifted to the skyward that one would have thought they had begun to fly thitherward to take their place among their fellow stars; her naked hands raising up their whole length and, as it were, kissing one another . . . all her senses being rather tokens than instruments of her inward motions altogether had so strange a working power that even the hardhearted wickedness of Cecropia, if it found not a love of that goodness, yet it felt an abashment at that goodness.[25]

This near-ecstatic passage not only describes the source of Pamela's "working power" on Cecropia, but also reveals Sidney's own rhetorical enthusiasm in conjuring up what Tyndale would no doubt describe as the bodily pleasures of true prayer. Far from questioning the relation between her "inward motions" and outward signs, the staunchly Protestant author insists on the expressive capacity of Pamela's "fervent grace."

THE ROYAL ACTOR

Cecropia's reaction to Pamela's prayer pales in comparison to a second, later response by King Charles I. On the eve of his execution at the hands of the English Puritans in 1649, Charles is said to have recited Pamela's words from the *Arcadia*. Pamela's prayer is the first of four prayers purportedly handed to the bishop of London, William Juxon, as Charles approached the scaffold; these texts were appended to *Eikon Basilike*, a posthumous book of Charles's meditations that aroused such unexpected sympathy that thirty-five editions were published in the year following the king's execution. Entitled "A Prayer in time of Captivity," the version of Pamela's prayer printed in *Eikon Basilike* is unaltered from Sidney's original text with only one exception: Pamela's final petition to an unspecified "Lord" to save her lover, Musidorus, is replaced with Charles's appeal to Christ for heavenly mercy.

The king's choice in prayers was not well received by the polemicist John Milton, who heaped scorn upon Charles for using so unsacred a text in his time of greatest devotional need. Thus Milton exclaims in *Eikonoklastes*, his 1649 prose tract responding to *Eikon Basilike*, that the king shamefully stole his deathbed prayer "word for word from the mouth of a heathen fiction praying to a heathen God":

> What greater argument of disgrace & ignominy could have been thrown with cunning upon the whole Clergy, than that the King among all his Priestery, and all those numberless volumes of their theological distillations, not meeting with one man or book of that coat that could befriend him with a prayer in Captivity, was forced to rob Sr. Philip and his captive shepherdess of their heathen orisons?[26]

For Milton, as we shall see in chapter 2, there was nothing more devotionally fraudulent than praying in set forms, let alone those of a heathen shepherdess. Within the terms of the Protestant establishment, however, Charles I's memorization and recitation of Pamela's words before his beheading spectacularly confirm the church's insistence on the ways in which premeditated prayers could penetrate the inner self, shape personal voice, and inscribe the printed words on the page upon the innermost parts of the spirit. Moreover, that this final display of faith involved the substitution of literature for liturgy reflects the slow but ultimately triumphant evolution of poesy from an unrecognized and often suspicious form of language into a compelling medium of prayer. In this single moment of textual resonances—the desperate and pious king's decision to frame his last spiritual performance within the context of a fictional performance from Sidney's *Arcadia*, and Milton's profound disapproval recorded in a treatise written against not only Charles, but also the Book of Common Prayer—lies the rich intertwining of devotional, political, and literary practice that this study means to recover.

CHAPTER ONE

Common Prayer

*I*n 1547, the first year of Edward VI's rule and the start of a short but intense period of Protestant reform unthinkable under Henry VIII, the archbishop of Canterbury, Thomas Cranmer, received a letter of complaint from Stephen Gardiner, the conservative bishop of Winchester. Not so secretly a Catholic at heart, Gardiner sought to obstruct Cranmer's plans to introduce a vernacular liturgy into the Church of England. Arguing that "in times past, when men came to church more diligently than some do now, the people in the church took small heed what the priest and the clerks did in the chancel, but only to stand up at the Gospel and kneel at the Sacring," he boldly declared that the prayers of the priest were never intended to be either heard or understood by the laity.[1] For Gardiner, the very notion of "hearing" the service belies traditional practice—"it is in speech so called hearing, but in deed nothing so practiced, nor never was." The worshippers could not have heard, let alone understood, all that the priest spoke, for this would have required the priest to turn his body toward the congregation throughout his prayers, and concern himself with keeping the worshippers occupied (so that they "hold their peace") instead of focusing his attention on the liturgy. Therefore, Gardiner concludes, it was never intended that the people should hear either matins or the Mass, but only that they be "present there and pray themselves in silence."[2]

What Gardiner intends here as a positive account of the traditional Catholic service could with few adjustments be taken as scathing critique: a liturgy performed largely inaudibly by a priest whose prayers neither address nor engage the congregation neatly encapsulates the Protestant attack on the late medieval church during the English Reformation. Whereas Protestants sought to break down the auricular barriers between the clergy and the congregation, Catholics insisted that these barriers were actually conducive to a genuine devotional practice. For sixteenth-century Catholics, the challenge of public devotion was not to promote a shared and collective liturgical language, but instead to encourage the worshippers to perform their own private devotions during the priest's service. So John Christopherson, the dean of Norwich under the new

Catholic monarch, Queen Mary, remarks in 1554 that the congregation should not aim to understand the priest's prayers, but instead should "travail themselves in fervent praying, and so shall they highly please God." For, he continues,

> it is much better for them not to understand the common service of the church, because when they hear others praying in a loud voice, in the language that they understand, they are letted from prayer themselves, and so come they to such a slackness and negligence in praying, that at length as we have well seen in these late days, in manner pray not at all.[3]

How is it, we might ask, that understanding the priest's words would actually provoke only "slackness and negligence" in the worshippers? Although this position might seem counterintuitive, within the devotional framework of sixteenth-century Catholicism it makes perfect sense: if the worshippers attend to the words of the priest, they are distracted from generating their own prayers. As Christopherson reflects upon the Book of Common Prayer, now rejected by the Catholic regime: "I have oftentime much marveled at us Englishmen of late that we came to the church at the time of our English service *to hear only and not to pray ourselves.*"[4]

If for Christopherson the vernacular liturgy threatens to diminish the congregation's incentive to pray, for his fellow Catholic Thomas Harding, the prebendary of Winchester, the dangers of using a vernacular prayer book lie in the opportunities that it provides for worshippers to develop their own misguided interpretations of the priest's service.[5] In his vitriolic debate with the Protestant bishop of Salisbury, John Jewel, over "prayers in a strange tongue," Harding argues that "whereas of the service in the vulgar [vernacular] tongue the people will frame lewd and perverse meanings of their own lewd senses: so of the Latin service they will make no constructions either of false doctrine or of evil life." "Lewd senses," "lewd and perverse meanings": for Harding, the minds of the laity are so easily corrupted that they ought not to be tempted with exposure to even the most benign of liturgical texts.

Instead of profiting from understanding the priest's prayers, Harding claims that the congregation is led only to dangerous imaginings that have no efficacy for their devotional lives: "as the vulgar service pulleth their minds from private devotion to hear and not to pray, to little benefit of knowledge, for the obscurity of it; so the Latin giveth them no such motion." Rather than have their minds pulled away from devotion, the people are able to focus on their own prayers, "while the priest prayeth for all and in the person of all."[6] This distinction between hearing and praying lies at the very heart of the Catholics' argument: the English-language service promotes the worshippers' ability to listen, while the Latin service promotes their ability to "occupy themselves" in private worship. Moreover, because the priest petitions God "in the person of all" regardless of the language he uses, the Latin prayers represent the collective voice of the congregation just as powerfully as a vernacular liturgy. In short, Harding concludes, there is no benefit whatsoever to connecting the priest's and the laity's devotions.

If English Catholics insist that the public service ideally provides an occasion for the laity's private devotion, English Protestants defend precisely the opposite arrangement. For these sixteenth-century reformers, the danger of the laity's "lewd and perverse imaginings," a danger they do not deny, can be contained only by controlling the worshippers' attention and supplying their prayers. In this Protestant formulation, the church liturgy becomes the best mechanism to subsume personal and idiosyncratic worship within a collective devotional performance. Thus Cranmer mocks the Latin liturgy as "more like a game and a fond play to be laughed at of all men, to hear the priest speak aloud to the people in Latin, and the people listen with their ears to hear; and some walking up and down in the church, some saying other prayers in Latin, and none understandeth other."[7] This vision of mutual incomprehension and devotional mayhem—"more like a game and a fond play" than a religious service—fuels Cranmer's overwhelming desire to render the liturgy comprehensible to all.

As Jewel explains in his response to Harding, the liturgy was not meant to be one of the Christian "mysteries"—such as the Trinity, or the Eucharist, or aspects of creation—whose meaning God never intended his simple creatures to unravel. On the contrary: far from representing privileged utterances meant for a divine audience alone, the priest's prayers were specifically designed to be understood by the congregation. In one of many citations during this period of John Chrysostom's descriptions of public prayer, Jewel refers Harding to the fourth-century bishop's unambiguous declaration: "Unless the unlearned understand what thou prayest, he is not edified, neither can he give consent unto thy prayer; thou throwest thy words into the wind, and speaketh in vain." With this negative image of the Latin service, Jewel succinctly concludes: "And therefore the very substance of the public prayer resteth in the understanding of the hearer."[8]

Debates over whether the laity ought to understand the public service surround the Book of Common Prayer (1549), which represented the first vernacular liturgy used in the Church of England. Although the Prayer Book was not published until well into the period we associate with the English Reformation, it had been planned for more than a decade. As early as 1536, Cranmer had met at Lambeth, his London residence, with German reformers to develop a uniform Latin liturgy for distribution to churches throughout England. This book was designed to replace the many diverse service books that created, in Cranmer's eyes, "a confusion of tongues almost worse than Babel."[9] In the years that followed, Cranmer became increasingly focused on producing a vernacular prayer book to replace this Latin text so that public worship could be more instructive and edifying for the people. According to his recent biographer, Diarmaid MacCulloch, in 1539 Cranmer was already preoccupied with identifying the most effective way to include the laity in morning and evening prayer, and had expressed concern that the services should be kept to a shorter length so that the people were not "wearied by lengthy reading, [and] should not attend keenly enough."[10]

Notwithstanding the inevitable shifts in devotional climate under the tempestuous reign of Henry VIII, over the course of the 1540s Cranmer painstakingly compiled the vernacular texts that would constitute the Book of Common Prayer. Like the Latin liturgy that he had assembled in the 1530s, the Prayer Book was designed in part to create an entirely uniform model for public worship in the English church, as the preface to its first edition describes:

> Where heretofore, there hath been great diversity in saying and singing in churches within this realm: some following Salisbury use, some Hereford use, some the use of Bangor, some of York, and some of Lincoln: Now from henceforth, all the whole realm shall have but one use.

Cranmer was generally careful to retain what he could from Catholic rites in order to maintain some continuity between the two liturgical practices. Based largely on a combination of the pre-Reformation Sarum Rite, which was the most common "use" in England, and the Reformed German liturgies that Cranmer so deeply admired, the Prayer Book that was issued in 1549 tempered its innovative changes to public worship by incorporating traditional forms and prayers.[11] Although in this respect the Prayer Book was liturgically conservative, its alterations to the ways in which prayers were performed represented a radical transformation of the language of public worship.

Despite the prominence of the liturgical reforms that the Prayer Book introduced, their impact on early modern religious culture has often been underestimated. Religious scholars have considered the *theological* implications of the changes made to the blessing of the Eucharist in the Order for Holy Communion, and yet they have too often paid scant attention to the changes in *devotional* practice introduced by this service and those of morning and evening prayer.[12] When historians have acknowledged the extent to which the Prayer Book sought to standardize the devotional voice of both the laity and clergy, they have frequently represented this commitment to uniformity in terms of the religious establishment's political, and not devotional, motivations.[13] Those sympathetic to "traditional religion" have regarded common prayer as a superficial practice that had no real meaning for most English worshippers. By arguing that the English Reformation effectively eliminated devotional community by abolishing the crucial structures of medieval parish life—Corpus Christi guilds and plays;

penitential fraternities; saints' festivals and pageants—these scholars tend to discount, if not overlook, the competing model of community that the Protestants sought to generate through the church service itself.[14]

As this chapter seeks to establish, the invention of common prayer was not strictly part of a political strategy for creating obedient subjects; nor did it radically deplete the rich communal layers of the laity's devotional life. Instead, the new conditions of public worship—the wide availability of the Prayer Book as a material text; the audibility of the priest's words to all listeners; the emphasis upon the laity's comprehension of and engagement with the service—reconceived the relations between the language of personal and liturgical prayer, and between individual and collective devotion. What emerges from the texts and instructions of the Book of Common Prayer is not the triumphant celebration of religious interiority that we so often associate with the Reformation—as I have already briefly observed, this commitment to individualized worship would more accurately characterize the Catholic Church, not the Protestant. Instead, behind the introduction of a liturgy emphasizing the worshippers' active participation and consent lies the establishment's overarching desire to shape personal faith through public and standardized forms.

LAY FOLKS' DEVOTION

In order to create uniformity between lay and clerical prayer, the English reformers faced the daunting task of transforming the texts and practices that had structured medieval public worship. In the centuries preceding the Reformation, the church conceived of its daily services as rites primarily intended for the clergy, with the exception of Sundays and holy days, when the congregation was expected to attend. Thomas More, hardly an average churchgoer, comically speaks on behalf of the laity in asserting that "[s]ome of us lay men think it a pain once in a week to rise so soon from sleep, and some to tarry so long fasting, as on the Sunday to come and hear out their matins (Morning Prayer)." And yet, More consoles his readers, this weekly act of attending services was nothing compared with the monastic life that he knew firsthand from the Charterhouse: "[I]s not the matins in every parish . . . so early begun, nor fully so long in doing, as it is in the Charterhouse, ye know well."[15]

Although, as More acknowledges, the parish churches did not adhere to so rigorous a schedule of services as the monastic houses, they certainly did require a sizable array of texts to perform their daily "offices," the church's term for the services that included reciting set prayers, reading from Scripture, and offering thanksgiving and praise. The multiple books for these offices were reduced in the eleventh century to the two-volume Breviary, which simplified daily services by incorporating the previously separate Psalter, Antiphoner, Book of Collects, and Homilies. The Breviary did not include the liturgy for the Mass, which was provided in the Missal; occasional services, such as Baptism or Matrimony, which formed the Manual; special prayers and hymns to be sung during processions, which constituted the Processional; and so forth. In a world in which books were much scarcer than in the post-Gutenberg era, this level of demand weighed heavily upon parishioners, who were responsible for funding their church's supply of texts.[16] Cranmer's decision both to reduce the number of daily offices from eight to two (matins and evensong) and to include the Order for Holy Communion (formerly known as the Mass) along with other occasional services in the single Book of Common Prayer effected a fundamental reformation of these material demands. It is in response to the financial burden once imposed upon English parishes that the preface to the 1549 Prayer Book stipulates that "the curates shall need none other books for their public service, but this book, and the Bible: by the means whereof, the people shall not be at so great charge for books, as in time past they have been."[17]

In marked contrast, as we shall see, to the availability of the Book of Common Prayer to sixteenth-century Protestants, it was highly unlikely for a medieval worshipper to own any of the service books used by the clergy. Even literate worshippers who could afford books would not have had access to the church's official texts. Instead, they purchased Books of Hours or Primers, personal devotional manuals encompassing nearly all of their liturgical and domestic needs. A typical Primer included a selection of daily and occasional prayers; contents ranged from the Penitential Psalms and the Hours of the Virgin Mary to special petitions to be recited upon entering the church or going to bed. Even before the advent of printing, Primers were produced in a wide variety of styles that depended largely on the nature of illustrations. According to Eamon Duffy, whatever its size or quality, by the early sixteenth century a Primer was as likely to be seen in the hands of a worshipper as a string of Rosary beads.[18]

Because the Primer played so important a role among lay worshippers who were on the whole unlearned in Latin, we might reasonably assume that its prayers were generally supplied in the vernacular. However, even in the fourteenth and early fifteenth centuries, when English-language Primers were available, Latin texts remained more prevalent.[19] In the century or so preceding the Reformation, the already scarce vernacular Primers seem to have disappeared. Due largely to the threat posed by John Wycliffe and the Lollards, whose program to reform the Catholic Church included using English as the language of Scripture and worship in order to promote the laity's understanding, the ecclesiastical authorities began to associate vernacular texts with sectarian danger.

By the early fifteenth century, the ownership of religious books in English could be treated as incriminating evidence in cases of heresy, which were often punishable by death. [20] The sixteenth-century Protestant martyrologist John Foxe recounts the story of Thomas Harding, an early Lutheran altogether dissimilar to his Catholic namesake, who was burned at the stake for having relapsed to Lollardy after abjuring his heretical beliefs:

> At last the said Harding, in the year abovesaid [1532], about the Easter holidays, when the other people went to the church to commit their wonted idolatry, took his way into the woods, there solitarily to worship the true living God, in spirit and in truth; where, as he was occupied in a book of English prayers, leaning or sitting upon a stile by the wood's side, it chanced that one did espy him where he was, and came in great haste to the officers of the town, declaring, that he had seen Harding in the woods looking on a book: whereupon immediately a rude rabble of them, like mad men, ran desperately to his house to search for books, and in searching went so nigh, that under the boards of his floor they found certain English books of holy Scripture. Hereupon this godly father with his books, was brought before John Longland, bishop of Lincoln . . . [who] sent him to the bishop's prison, called Little-ease, where he did lie with hunger and pain enough for a certain space, till at length the bishop, sitting in his tribunal-seat like a potentate, condemned him for relapse to be burned to ashes. [21]

Harding's death cannot in fact be blamed on his possessing vernacular translations of Scripture. And yet, despite the sensational nature of Foxe's description —the "rude rabble" of Catholic men searching "desperately" for books—this passage accurately conveys the anxiety in the pre-Reformation church over the unauthorized spreading of the English word.

The one notable exception both to the predominance of Latin as the language of Primers, and to the restrictions imposed upon the circulation of English devotional books, was the vernacular guide to the Mass. The most popular of these texts has come to be known as *The Lay folks' Mass Book*, for which we have six remaining versions composed for different dialects and rites throughout England. [22] Unlike the average Primers, which included Latin rites from the liturgy in addition to private meditations and prayers, *The Lay folks' Mass Book* provided a step-by-step English manual of instruction and prayer for the laity to follow during the priest's Mass. Here the tolerance of the vernacular might be explained by the imperative to separate the language of the priest in this holiest of services from either the ears or the mouths of the congregation. With a few exceptions that include the Lord's Prayer and the Gloria in Excelsis, the prayers in *The Lay folks' Mass Book* are not translations from the clergy's Missal, but instead represent separate if often compatible texts for occupying the worshipper's attention.

One of the emblematic moments of separation between the laity and the congregation surfaces in relation to the priest's "secret prayers," called the Secreta.[23] While the priest recites the Secreta silently, *The Lay folks' Mass Book* instructs the congregation:

> When the priest goes to his book,
> his private prayers for to look,
> kneel thou down and say then this,
> That next in black written is:
> it will thy prayer much amend,
> If thou will hold up both thy hands,
> to God with good devotion,
> when thou say this orison,
> *God receive thy service.*[24]

This final line of the laity's prayer—"God receive thy service"—is meant to express the gist of the Secreta, in which the priest asks God to accept the offertory gifts of bread and wine. The priest indicates that the Secreta has ended by saying aloud, "per omnia secula saeculorum," a signal to the congregation that is repeated after the silence of the Canon, the prayer (or series of short prayers) of consecration. According to the fifteenth-century canonist Lyndwood, the silence of the Canon was intended to allow the laity to remain in private devotion.[25]

During the prayers of consecration, the laity is kept occupied with its own prayers—repetitions of the Pater Noster—until the priest indicates he has concluded:

> Look pater-noster thou be praying,
> Until thou hear the priest be saying:
> *per omnia secula* all on high,
> then I would thou stood upright,
> for he will say with high steven* [with a loud voice]
> pater-noster to God of heaven;
> harken him with good will . . .
> when this is done, say privately
> other prayer none thereby.
> pater-noster first in latin,
> and then in english as here is written.[26]

The priest's utterance of the Lord's Prayer, which is said aloud ("with high steven") to the standing congregation, represents one of the few moments in the service in which the congregation is told to pay strict attention and desist from its own prayers. This moment is followed by a resumption of private prayer that echoes the priest's words by repeating the Pater Noster in English as well as in Latin.[27] During the priest's post-Communion prayer the laity is similarly directed first to recite its own "prayer to Christ for protection in all dangers," and then once again to resume repetitions of the Lord's Prayer:

> When this is said, kneel down soon,
> say pater-noster 'til mass be done,
> for the mass is not sest,* [over]
> until time of ite, misa est.
> then when thou hear say ite,
> or benedicamus, if it be,
> then is the mass all done.[28]

This division in prayer between the priest and the congregation as well as among the worshippers ought not to suggest, however, that the service was devoid of shared devotional experiences. Although the Mass did not include congregational acts of prayer, it did promote a visual instance of totalizing continuity: the elevation of the Host. Immediately after the sacring, the priest would raise the Host above his head for the worshippers to see, a moment that indisputably represented the climactic lay experience of the Mass. This crucial instance of congregational unity came on the heels of private absorption in prayer: immediately before the sacring a bell was rung in order to warn the congregation to end its devotions and focus all attention on the imminent consecration and elevation.

So intent was the laity on witnessing the Host as frequently as possible that Masses celebrated within a single church were staggered so as not to occur simultaneously; bells were then rung to notify eager worshippers to come quickly to a chapel where the Host was about to be raised.[29] During the brief return to Catholic practice under Mary I, the bishop of London, Edmund Bonner, nervously inquired into the possible residue of Protestants in the church, asking his clergy "whether there be any, that at the sacring time, which do hang down their heads, hide them selves behind pillars, turn away their faces, or do depart out of the church at that time."[30] In a time of deepest religious uncertainty, one of the definitive distinctions between Catholic and Protestant worshippers was the Catholic practice of looking up.

HEARING PRAYER

At the heart of the liturgical changes introduced during the Reformation was the shift of emphasis from a visual to an auditory register. In place of the Latin Mass, whose crucial moment of collective experience was the sight of the elevation of the Host, the Reformed English service was designed specifically to be heard. The Protestants' decision to eliminate the raising of the Host reflected a systematic effort to stress the ears and not the eyes as the vehicle for the laity's interaction with the priest; as Cranmer remarks in his preface to the 1544 English Litany, a processional service of intercession that was the first part of the vernacular liturgy to be published, the emphasis should fall on what "enters in at their ears."[31] This position resonates throughout the writings of midsixteenth-century reformers: the German reformer Martin Bucer recommends in De Regno Christi (1550), a book of instruction on building a commonwealth that he wrote for Edward VI, that the priest must speak "with greatest devotion and solemnity from a place where everything can be heard by everyone present"; Edmund Hooper, bishop of Gloucester, explains in 1551 that "it is not sufficient to speak or read in the English, or mother-tongue, but that there be due and distinct pronunciation, whereby all the people may have true knowledge"; and Thomas Bentham, bishop of Coventry and Lichfield, orders his clergy in 1565 "that you do say your Divine Service on the Holy days distinctly with an audible voice," concluding with the instruction that they must neither "mumble nor tumble all things without devotion, as you did at such time you had the service in the Latin tongue."[32]

As we have already observed, the Protestants wanted the congregation not only to hear, but also, more crucially, to understand the prayers of the priest. In the preface to the Prayer Book, Cranmer emphasizes the necessity of comprehension as the basis for liturgical practice:

> Whereas St. Paul would have such language spoken to the people in the church as they might understand and have profit by hearing the same, the service in this church of England (these many years) hath been read in Latin to the people, which they understood not, so that they have heard with their ears only: and their hearts, spirit and mind have not been edified thereby. (1:34)

Unlike the Latin service, which, Cranmer contends, at best fills the worshipper's ears, but fails to penetrate within, the English liturgy was designed to connect the faculty of hearing to its cognitive and spiritual counterparts.

This emphasis on the laity's comprehension did not correspond, however, to a wide-scale distribution of Prayer Books in the church. Our contemporary assumption that each pew held multiple copies of the liturgy is quickly dismissed by sixteenth-century records confirming the small quantity of Prayer Books actually purchased by individual parishes. The parish of Stratton, Cornwall, for example, lists the purchase of "iii new books noted for Matins and Evensong in English" in 1549, and a single "communion book" in 1553, presumably a reference to the newly revised Prayer Book issued in 1552.[33] Edmund Grindal, the archbishop of York, likewise demands in 1571:

> That the churchwardens in every parish shall, at the costs and charges of the parish, provide (if the same be not already provided) all things necessary and requisite for common prayer and administration of the sacraments, on this side the

20th day of _____ next ensuing, specially the book of Common Prayer, with the new calendar, and a Psalter to the same, the English Bible in the largest volume, the two tomes of the Homilies.[34]

Because the Reformed church did not supply anyone but the clergy with its liturgy, only those worshippers who brought their own Prayer Books could read along with the minister. The wide range in size, print, and physical quality of the Books of Common Prayer surviving from the sixteenth century gives some indication of the multiple markets that existed for this text: a folio-size book designed for the clergy strikingly contrasts with a small (duodecimo) volume meant for individual use. In an effort to facilitate the churchgoers' ability to purchase their own Prayer Books, Edward VI issued a royal decree capping its maximum price:

> The King's Majesty . . . straightly chargeth and commandeth, that no manner of person do sell this present book unbound, above the price of ii. shillings and ii. pence the piece. And the same bound in paste or in boards, not above the price of three shillings and viii. pence the piece.[35]

Assuming the average skilled worker's weekly wage was approximately five shillings, an unbound Prayer Book would cost slightly less than half of these earnings, or the equivalent of two decent seats at the Blackfriars theater in the 1590s.[36]

And yet, although Prayer Books were neither prohibitively expensive nor rare in the book market of sixteenth-century London, there was no expectation whatsoever that parishioners would purchase their own texts. Indeed, for Cranmer, the ability to read did not necessarily enhance the experience of the liturgy. He explains his opinion in the preface to his 1544 Litany:

> As these holy prayers and suffrages following are set forth of most godly zeal for edifying, and stirring of devotion of all true faithful christian hearts: so is it thought convenient in this common prayer of procession to have it set forth and used in the vulgar tongue, for stirring the people to more devotion: and it shall be every christian man's part reverently to use the same.

For those who have books and can read them without disturbing their fellow worshippers, Cranmer recommends that they do so; for those who cannot read, he asks that they "quietly and attentively give audience in time of the said prayers, having their minds erect to almighty God, and devoutly praying in their hearts, the same petitions which do enter in at their ears." The result, he concludes, ought to be that "with one sound of the heart and one accord, God may be glorified in his church."[37]

In this account of the vernacular as the superior vehicle for "stirring the people to more devotion"—a phrase that is used repeatedly in justifications for creating the Common Prayer Book four years later—Cranmer differentiates between those who "have books and can read them," and those who "can not read"; and yet, neither literacy nor the possession of books was considered essential for the spiritual task of aligning the spirit and the tongue in a common "accord." Unlike the pre-Reformation service, which allowed for a wide variety of prayers to be spoken or read simultaneously during the church service, the practice of common prayer depended upon complete uniformity: there should be no division between the devotional utterances of the illiterate or bookless and the prayers of the learned, between that which the worshippers feel in their hearts and that which is said out loud.

If the Protestant establishment did not require Prayer Books to be brought to services, it certainly did not tolerate Catholic Primers or devotional guides either inside or outside the church. The reformers' alterations to liturgical practice were accompanied by an absolute intolerance of any remaining service books from pre-Reformation practice. Immediately following the wide-scale distribution of the Prayer Book in 1549, Edward VI issued *An act for the abolishing and putting away of divers books and images*, demanding that all prior service books used by the clergy be surrendered to church authorities:

> [We] straightly . . . command and charge you, that immediately upon the receipt hereof, you do command the dean and prebendaries of the cathedral church, the parson, vicar or curate and church wardens of every parish, within your diocese, to bring and deliver unto you or your deputy—all antiphoners, missals, grails, processionals, manuals, legends, pies, portasses, journals, and ordinals, after the use of Sarum, Lincoln, York, or any other private use, and all other books of service, the keeping whereof should be a let to the usage of the said book of common prayers, and that you take the same books into your hands—and them so deface and abolish that they never after may serve either to any such use, as they were provided for, or be at any time a let to that godly and uniform order. [38]

The only exception to King Edward's injunction to destroy all books, with a fee of forty pounds if neglected, pertained to the Primer of Henry VIII, which was allowed to remain so long as "the sentences of invocation of prayer to saints [were] blotted or clearly put out of the same." [39] The parish priest is now cast as amateur censor, ferreting out all materials deemed offensive to the Protestant regime. Although this habit of "blotting" Catholic traces was officially prescribed only for Henry's Primer, many other vernacular manuals from the 1530s show signs of similar editorial work. A Salisbury Primer, for example, of domestic (octavo) size that was printed in Paris in 1532 has xs marked through its prayers to saints as well as all references to purgatory and the pope.

Both the urgency and irreversibility of Edward's ruling to "deface and abolish" all former liturgical texts reflect the reformers' deep—and, given Queen Mary's imminent rule, well-founded—anxiety over the residual use, and the future return, of the outlawed Catholic rites. In the lists of specific inquiries issued for the biennial or triennial inspection of dioceses known as "visitation articles," bishops repeatedly inquire into the status of forbidden texts.[40] For example, Cranmer instructs the clergy of Canterbury in 1550 to discover "where, when, and to whom the books of the Latin service were delivered, and how many, and whether any of them were sold, and by whom, or doth remain still in the hands and custody of any of this church"; and Hooper inquires in 1551 "whether any man do occupy any such primers or books of prayers in Latin as be forbidden by the laws of the realm."[41] As late as 1570, eleven years after the end of Mary's Catholic regime, the problem that Hooper had anticipated seems stubbornly to persist: in the records of ecclesiastical proceedings in the courts of Durham, a case is brought against Arthur Chapman, a blacksmith, for "reading of an English book, or primer, while as the priest was saying of his service, not minding what the priest read, but tending his own book and prayer."[42] What once counted as exemplary behavior in the context of the Catholic service—reading one's own prayer book in church—now constitutes a criminal act.

The church reacted strongly to seemingly minor infractions like Chapman's because it believed that the efficacy of the public service for the parishioners depended entirely upon engaging their complete attention; only when the prayers of the priest were both heard and understood could he legitimately speak on the congregation's behalf. This position was fueled by an outright dismissal of the Catholic principle of *ex opere operato,* which held that the rites and sacraments of the church worked independently of the dispositions of the persons involved. As Thomas Aquinas had influentially argued in relation to the Eucharist, so long as the Host was properly blessed and administered, its sacramental status was invulnerable to the specific condition of the communicant. From Cranmer's perspective, which was heavily influenced by Luther, the Catholic Church had mistakenly extended this already flawed account of *ex opere operato* sacramentalism onto the domain of public prayer: by imagining that the effectiveness of the priest's petitions was determined only by his strict performance of the liturgical texts and not also by the worshipper's comprehension and participation, the Catholic Church eliminated the laity's essential role in the service.

For English Protestants, the proper relationship between laity and clergy depends upon an explicit delegation of devotional voice from one body to the other; the efficacy of priest's prayers could be measured only by the extent to which the worshippers felt adequately represented. Hence in 1549, when a group of rebels in Devon rejected the new English liturgy on the grounds that they "will have the mass in Latin, as was before, and celebrated by the priest, without any man or woman communicating with him," Cranmer explains that because everything conducted during the public service should be done on be-half of the entire congregation as well as the priest, "it is with reason, that the priest should speak for you, and in your name, and you answer him again in your own person." And yet, he points out, "you understand never a word, nei-ther what he [the priest] saith, nor what you say yourselves." Incensed by this arrangement of total incomprehension, Cranmer exclaims:

> Will you neither understand what he saith, nor let your hearts understand what your own tongues answer? Then must you needs confess yourselves to be such people as Christ spoke of, when he said, "These people honour me with their lips, but their hearts be far from me." Had you rather be like pies or parrots, that be taught to speak, and yet understand not one word what they say, than be true christian men, that pray unto God in heart and in faith?

Having provided the choice between behaving like "pies and parrots" or true Christian men, Cranmer shifts to a secular analogy:

> If you were before the king's highness, and should choose one to speak for you all, I am sure you would not choose one that should speak Greek or Hebrew, French or Italian; no, nor one that should speak Latin neither. . . . But if reason will not persuade you, I will prove what God's word will do unto you. St. Paul, in the first epistle to the Corinthians, saith, that whosoever shall speak to the people in the church to their edification, must speak such language as the people may understand; or else he willeth him to hold his peace, and speak softly to himself and to God.[43]

At the heart of this passage lies a question central to political as well as reli-gious representation: whom do you allow to "speak for you, and in your name," and under what conditions? Cranmer proposes that an authentic delegation of voice depends upon understanding the words that are delegated: if the congre-gation cannot comprehend the prayers of the priest, these prayers can have little efficacy in representing their petitions, confessions, or thanksgivings to God. The analogy from the world of the royal court serves to demystify devotional representation, transforming it from the mysteries of *ex opere operato* into a willed and rational set of decisions: to "answer . . . in your own person" is not to assent to whatever the priest may or may not have said, but instead to affirm that your personal voice has been justly represented.

Six years after the Devon rebellion, in a very different political climate, Cran-mer offers a nearly identical justification of the vernacular liturgy to Queen Mary. Invoking St. Paul's declaration that a priest who speaks in a language that the congregation cannot understand "may profit himself, but profiteth not the people," Cranmer argues that the verse applies not only to preaching, as many have claimed, but also to public prayer:

For he speaketh by name expressly of praying, singing, lauding, and thanking of God, and of all other things which the priests say in the churches, whereunto the people say Amen . . . *that then all the people, understanding what the priests say, might give their minds and voices with them, and say Amen, that is to say, allow what the priests say*. . . . But the aforesaid things cannot be done when the priests speak to the people in a language not known; and so they (or their clerk in their name) say Amen, but they cannot tell whereunto. Whereas St. Paul saith, "How can the people say Amen to thy well saying, when they understand not what thou sayest?"[44]

Only months before his execution as an enemy of the Catholic regime, Cranmer struggles in this letter to defend the necessity of understanding the priest by turning to the most universal and uncontentious act of prayer: saying "amen." Even the simple task of responding with an amen requires a prior act of comprehension in order to fulfill its essential function in the liturgy; without this confirmation from the laity, Cranmer insists, the clergy's petitions remain unsanctioned. At its very core, the petitions of the Common Prayer Book represent Cranmer's attempt to expand the role of the congregation from one of intoning passive if comprehending amens to one of active participation.[45]

GENERAL CONFESSION

Despite the complaints of non-conformists in the 1570s that the Book of Common Prayer was nothing more than a translation into English of the papist service, the new liturgy consistently reconceived petitions once reserved for the clergy into common acts of prayer. Not all of these changes were introduced in the 1549 edition: due in part to the influence of Swiss and German reformers who came to England in the early 1550s, and in part to the lessening hold of those more conservative Protestants who had wielded power under Henry VIII, the evangelical spirit was vastly strengthened in the years between 1549 and 1552, when the second edition of the Common Prayer Book was published. Comparison of the 1552 text with its 1549 predecessor reveals Cranmer's rapidly evolving commitment both to dismantling the divisions between clerical and lay worship, and to creating an increasingly collective model of public prayer. Thus the 1549 Prayer Book tentatively begins what the 1552 edition more fully achieves: the transformation of the liturgy from one based on private reading and silent prayers to a practice built upon shared or responsive texts read aloud by minister and congregation.

One of the clearest differences between the devotional language of the two successive Prayer Books lies in the use of the first-person pronoun I. Whereas the earlier text sustains the distinction between singular and plural speakers, the 1552 version more frequently adopts the collective we. The 1549 series of versicles and responses in morning prayer, for example, employs the first-person-singular form for both the priest and the congregation:

> [Priest] O Lord, open thou my lips
> [Answer] And my mouth shall show forth thy praise
> [Priest] O God, make speed to save me.
> [Answer] O Lord, make haste to help me.

In the revised 1552 text, these utterances are transformed into a series of collective petitions:

> [Priest] O Lord, open thou our lips
> [Answer] And our mouth shall show forth thy praise
> [Priest] O God, make speed to save us.
> [Answer] O Lord, make haste to help us.[46]

The replacement of "my" with "our" and "me" with "us" suggests a subtle but important difference in the relationship between individual and corporate speech: although the 1549 congregation would have been speaking out loud, using the same words at the same time, the voice of each worshipper had previously represented only itself.

The shift in pronouns that we find in the 1552 text reflects a more pervasive revision: prayers once read by the priest alone are now presented as congregational utterances. Whereas the 1549 service directs only the minister to "say the Creed and the Lord's Prayer in English, with a loud voice," the 1552 version of morning prayer instructs: "Then shall be said the Creed, by the minister and the people, standing." This is followed by the rubric: "the minister, clerks and people, shall say the Lord's Prayer in English, with a loud voice" (1:145–47). In the first text, the "loud voice" of the minister is meant to reach the silent and attentive congregation, which is presumably hearing many of these translations for the first time. By 1552, the focus has turned to engaging the congregation in reciting the prayers themselves.

These types of changes to the daily offices are extended as well to the Order of Holy Communion, which, as we have seen, was structured in the pre-Reformation liturgy around separating the priest's and the laity's utterances. In the Prayer Book's first edition, the Communion service begins with several prayers of the priest (the Lord's Prayer, a Collect, and a Psalm), and then either the priest or the clerics say what was formerly known as the Kyrie Eleison ("Lord have mercy upon us"). These prayers are followed by a brief exchange between the priest and the clerics, before the priest addresses the congregation with the blessing "the Lord be with you," to which the people answer, "And with thy spirit." Apart from the Collect and Psalm recitation, which are not part of the Catholic Mass at this point of the service, this series of vernacular petitions and exchanges is more or less identical with its Latin, pre-Reformation counterpart.

The 1552 text, by contrast, introduces an entirely new rubric following the minister's recitation of the daily Collect: "Then shall the Priest rehearse distinctly all the x. Commandments: and the people kneeling, shall after every Commandment ask God's mercy for their transgression of the same" (2:641). This set of responsive readings between the "Minister" and the "People" rewrites the Kyrie Eleison: in place of the former instruction for "the Priest to say, or else the Clerks to sing 'Lord have mercy upon us,'" the congregation incorporates these words in its answer to each of the Ten Commandments: "Lord have mercy upon us, and incline our hearts to keep this law" (2:641–45). What had been spoken by the clergy has become the domain of common prayer.

The most dramatic instance of the liturgical transition from a private and individual to a public and collective emphasis lies in the practice of confession. As has long been maintained, one of the most significant consequences of the Reformation was the elimination of mandatory confession to the priest before the parishioner could take Holy Communion, a rite first instituted by the Fourth Lateran Council in 1215. For centuries, Catholics had performed this annual rite, in which individuals made a compulsory "complete confession" and received absolution from the priest, thereby gaining the right to receive the Eucharist. For Luther, the ecclesiastical abuses stemming from the priest's power of granting absolution—not to mention his theological disagreement with the efficacy of a "complete confession"—were more than sufficient grounds for abolishing the entire practice as part of the church's regular liturgy. Luther was not against the unburdening of the conscience per se, but did take issue with instituting this practice as a sacramental act. In the Reformed Church of England, private confession was less violently condemned than it had been in Germany, but underwent a series of gradual adjustments over the course of the 1530s and 1540s until it had been more or less incorporated into part of the collective liturgy. By the time the second edition of the Prayer Book was published in 1552, Cranmer had fully transformed the practice of pre-Communion confession from a personal exchange between priest and penitent to a standardized utterance performed by the entire congregation.

The first important revision of the confessional tradition in England emerged in 1536 from Cranmer's meeting at Lambeth with German reformers, after which Cranmer reduced the status of confession from something "indispensable" (*summe necessaria*) to something "very appropriate" (*commodissima*).[47] In practical terms, confession became an option rather than an obligation, something that worshippers could choose to perform based on individual need. Hence Hugh Latimer, the prominent Edwardian preacher and eventual Marian martyr, explains in a 1552 sermon:

Here our papists make ado with their auricular confession, proving the same by this place. For they say Christ sent this man unto the priest to fetch there his absolution; and therefore we must go also unto the priest, and, after confession, receive of him absolution of our sins. But yet we must take heed, say they, that we forget nothing: for all those sins that are forgotten, may not be forgiven. And so they bind the consciences of men, persuading them that when their sins were all numbered and confessed, it was well. And hereby they took clean away the passion of Christ. For they made this numbering of sins to be a merit; and so they came to all the secrets that were in men's hearts: so that emperor nor king could say or do, nor think any thing in his heart, but they knew it.[48]

In this reiteration of Luther's initial complaint, Latimer charges that the logic behind the medieval practice of the "numbering of sins"—that penitents could receive the Eucharist only by articulating fully every aspect of their sinfulness—was deeply incompatible with the Protestant replacement of works with faith, merit with grace. As Luther had argued before, the mere notion that anyone could even know all of his or her sins, with or without the priest's help, assumed a level of insight and scrutability that, according to Latimer, belonged solely to God.[49]

And yet, although Latimer expresses his utmost contempt for the mandatory practice of a complete confession, he retains Luther's belief in the usefulness of confessing one's sins in private conversation without the sacramental overtones of the Catholic rite. "But to speak of right and true confession," he concludes, "I would to God it were kept in England; for it is a good thing. And those which find themselves grieved in conscience might go to a learned man, and there fetch of him comfort of the word of God, and so to come to a quiet conscience."[50] The priest endowed with heavenly powers gets replaced with the "learned man," an early modern therapist meant to comfort, not to absolve. In this resistance to eliminating confession altogether, Latimer's account reflects Cranmer's general strategy in revising confessional practice: he seeks to accommodate the personal impulse to unburden one's grief at the same time that he distances this act of unburdening from that of receiving Communion.

The first vernacular Order for Holy Communion was published in 1548, one year before the Book of Common Prayer. In this prelude to the Prayer Book service, Cranmer begins to explore the ways in which confession could be used as a congregational, not an individual, practice. Whereas in many of the pre-Reformation Missals the priest was instructed to remind his parishioners to perform their annual confession several days in advance of taking Communion, Cranmer adjusts this instruction in 1548 so that it serves only the most "troubled and grieved" of the group. Anyone having particular needs is welcome, he insists, to speak with him or "some other discreet and learned priest," so that the penitent might "open his sin and grief secretly, that he may receive such ghostly counsel, advice, and comfort that his conscience may be relieved." However, for those who do not sorely need special comfort or counsel, Cranmer hopes that they will be "satisfied" with the General Confession to the Church, and also admonishes that they refrain from judging others who choose to perform the "auricular and secret confession . . . for the quietness of their own consciences."[51]

In contrast with the Catholic confessional mandate, which was imposed indiscriminately upon the entire body of worshippers, this 1548 text envisions the congregation as containing two kinds of worshippers: on the one hand, those with private burdens, who are encouraged to confess their sins "secretly"; and on the other, those who can manage with a General Confession. The differentiating characteristic between the two categories turns on the condition of the inner self: only those who feel the heaviness of their consciences, and desire on their own initiative to relieve their burdens, are recommended to auricular confession. The sacramental status of confession in the Catholic Church, which Luther so forcefully opposed, has entirely disappeared. The passage speaks of "satisfaction" not in the doctrinal sense of absolution, but in the psychic sense of achieving personal comfort.[52]

Although the 1548 text already moves significantly away from its previous depiction of auricular confession as the precondition for receiving the Eucharist, it still accommodates the private needs of the individual worshipper. This flexibility is weakened in the Book of Common Prayer published the following year, which provides for private confession only under very restricted conditions of personal neglect or deviancy. The 1549 Prayer Book instructs the priest to address those worshippers who are "negligent to come to the Communion . . . to dispose themselves to the receiving of the Holy Communion more diligently, saying these or like words unto them," and then reprints the aforementioned passage from 1548, urging those with "troubled and grieved" consciences to confess individually to the priest.

Apart from this provision for certain resistant communicants, who are still allowed a private confession, the 1549 text stipulates a new set of conditions as a prerequisite for taking Communion:

> And if any of those be an open and notorious evil liver, so that the congregation by him is offended, or have done any wrong to his neighbours, by word or deed: The Curate shall call him, and advertise him, in any ways not to presume to the lord's table, until he have openly declared himself to have truly repented, and amended his former naughty life: that the congregation may thereby be satisfied, which before were offended: and that he have recompensed the parties, whom he hath done wrong unto, or at the least be in full purpose so to do, as soon as he conveniently may. (2:638)

Gone is all attention to the relationship between the individual and his conscience: the focus falls instead on the harmony of social relations. What had been a personal, confidential confession from the worshipper to the priest becomes a public admission made before the entire congregation. In this case, the "satisfaction" of the collective group, not the "quietness" of the inner self, renders the aspiring communicant worthy of admission.

The revised service of 1552 does not alter this passage from the 1549 Prayer Book, which remains at the very opening of the Communion service. It does, however, further distance itself from the 1548 Mass by effacing all mention in the priest's pre-Communion "exhortation" of the possibility for a private or "secret" act of confession. In place of the injunction to "let him come to me, or to some other discreet and learned priest . . . *and confess and open his sin and grief secretly*," we find the simplified "let him come to me, or some other discreet and learned minister of God's word, *and open his grief*"; instead of the reference to an "auricular and secret confession to the Priest," the new rubric ends simply by assuring the suffering worshipper that his conscience "may be relieved, and that by the ministry of God's word he may receive comfort and the benefit of absolution" (2:673; emphases mine).

No longer a practice that requires an individualized act of auricular confession, the Sacrament of Holy Communion is now preceded by a General Confession that becomes the crucial utterance of pre-Eucharistic piety:

> Almighty God, father of our Lord Jesus Christ, Maker of all things, Judge of all men, we acknowledge and bewail our manifold sins and wickedness . . . we do earnestly repent, and be heartily sorry for these our misdoings: the remembrance of them is grievous unto us, the burden of them is intolerable: have mercy upon us, have mercy upon us, most merciful Father. (2:681)

Individual identities are temporarily suspended in the face of this collective voice that does not differentiate among its speakers. As a further sign of Cranmer's intentions of creating a profoundly common text, we find the startling order in both the 1549 and 1552 Prayer Books that the General Confession be pronounced "in the name of all those that are minded to receive the Holy Communion, either by one of them, or else by one of the ministers, or by the Priest himself." All distinctions among the various kinds of communicants are with a single stroke collapsed; within this confessional utterance, even the priest becomes interchangeable with the lay worshipper.[53] This premise of interchangeability may have been egregiously misapplied to the act of taking Communion itself: according to the reports of a Venetian ambassador in 1551, families in London were appointing one member of the household, often a servant, to attend Communion as a representative for the whole; and Hooper's visitation articles of the same year command that "no man ought to receive the communion of the body and blood of our Lord for another, neither yet one for many, but every man for himself."[54]

Although initially limited to the Holy Communion service, the General Confession emerges for the first time as part of morning and evening prayer in the 1552 Prayer Book. In a rubric entirely absent from the 1549 matins and evensong services, the priest is instructed to begin:

> Dearly beloved brethren, the scripture moveth us in sundry places, to acknowledge and confess our manifold sins and wickedness, and that we should not dissemble nor cloak them before the face of almighty God our heavenly father, but confess them with an humble, lowly, penitent, and obedient heart, to the end that we may obtain forgiveness of the same by his infinite goodness & mercy. And although we ought at all times, humbly to acknowledge our sins before God: yet ought we most chiefly so to do, when we assemble and meet together. . . . Wherefore I pray and beseech you, as many as be here present, to accompany me with a pure heart & humble voice, unto the throne of the heavenly grace, saying after me . . . (1:131)

The General Confession that follows is meant to be said by the entire congregation in unison:

> Almighty and most merciful father, we have erred and strayed from thy ways, like lost sheep. We have followed too much the devices and desires of our own hearts. We have offended against thy holy laws. We have left undone those things which we ought to have done, and we have done those things which we ought not to have done: and there is no health in us: but thou, O Lord, have mercy upon us miserable offenders. Spare thou them, O God, which confess their faults. Restore thou them that be penitent, according to thy promises declared unto mankind, in Christ Iesu our Lord. And grant, O most merciful father, for his sake, that we may hereafter live a godly, righteous, and sober life, to the glory of thy holy name. Amen. (1:131)

Despite the prominence of its collective *we*, this petition was not meant exclusively as a means to facilitate communal penance during morning and evening prayer. Instead, it represented a more pervasive commitment to reforming confession in private as well as in public worship. Evidence for this shift into the personal and domestic sphere surfaces in the official Primer published under Edward VI in 1553. Whereas the Catholic Primers were largely oriented toward providing lay worshippers with devotional texts for use either at home or during public liturgical services, this Protestant version sought to transform the public liturgy into a complete text for domestic use; instead of the church supplying a space for private worship, the home was now imagined as an additional site for common prayer.

Nowhere is this re-imagining of the "private" sphere more apparent than in the Edwardian Primer's rubric for personal confession. In the "Order of Private Prayer for Morning and Evening Service," the Primer's equivalent of the church's daily offices, the text instructs the worshipper: "At the beginning of morning and evening private prayer, thou shalt daily read, meditate, weigh and deeply consider one of these sentences of holy scripture that follow. And then from the bottom of thine heart add the confession of thy sins and the prayer following."[55] This rubric may initially sound as if the church is instructing the worshipper to perform his or her own confession, to abandon the paradigms that have been provided in favor of a personal and intimate utterance. And yet, this is decidedly not the case: after a series of "sentences of holy scripture" identical with those used in the public service, the text provides its "confession of sins," which is nothing other than an individualized version of the General Confession from morning and evening prayer. In place of the text that begins "we have erred and strayed from thy ways, like lost sheep; we have followed too much the devices and desires of our own hearts," we find "I have erred and strayed from thy ways, like a lost sheep; I have followed too much the devices and desires of mine own heart."[56] What is designated as a personal utterance—"from the bottom of thine heart add the confession of thy sins"—turns out to involve a prescribed set of words that do not necessarily reflect or accommodate the specific conditions of the speaker. The devotional I that the Primer puts forth is no more nor less than a singular version of the liturgical we.[57]

This single example from the Primer in many respects embodies the culmination of Cranmer's liturgical aim: to restructure corporate worship so that it is entirely compatible with as well as conducive to the practice of personal devotion. Just as the priest conducting the 1552 morning prayer service declares that we are most likely "to acknowledge our sins before God . . . when we assemble and meet together," so too does the 1553 Primer seem to build upon the assumption that we can best unburden our consciences, even in the privacy of our own homes, in words that have been prescribed by the public liturgy. The church's project of common prayer, as we shall repeatedly see, extended far beyond the solicitation of outward conformity from its subjects.

CHAPTER TWO

Reading Prayer

SPONTANEITY AND CONFORMITY

O ne hundred years after the production of the Book of Common Prayer, at
the turning point of the English civil war and immediately following the
execution of the king, John Milton decries the use of set forms of prayer as an
assault upon devotional freedom:

> This is evident, that they who use no set forms of prayer, have words from their affec-
> tions; while others are to seek affections fit and proportionable to a certain doss of
> prepar'd words. . . . [So] to imprison and confine by force, into a Pinfold of set
> words, those two most unimprisonable things, our Prayer and that Divine Spirit of
> utterance that moves them, is a tyranny that would have longer hands than those
> Giants who threatn'd bondage to Heav'n.[1]

The accusations of political tyranny and bondage that characterize Milton's account of Charles I throughout most of *Eikonoklastes* are here transformed into a
comparable set of devotional charges: for Milton, the practice of common
prayer, like the rule of an unlawful monarch, violently restricts the individual's
capacity to express the inward self.

By substituting the texts of the Prayer Book for those devotional utterances
generated spontaneously, the church severs the ideal relationship between the
worshipper's "words" and "affections," a relationship, Milton contends, that reflects not only the personal but also the "Divine Spirit" of prayer:

> As he left our affections to be guided by his sanctifying spirit, so did he likewise
> our words to be put into use without our premeditation; not only those cautious
> words to be us'd before Gentiles and Tyrants, but much more those filial words, of
> which we have so frequent use in our access with freedom of speech to the
> Throne of Grace. Which to lay aside for other outward dictates of men, were to
> injure him and his perfect Gift, who is the spirit, and the giver of our ability to
> pray; as if his ministration were incomplete, and that to whom he gave affections,
> he did not also afford utterance to make his Gift of prayer a perfect Gift, to them
> especially whose office in the Church is to pray publicly.[2]

For Milton, the "perfect Gift" of God lies in the unpremeditated devotional voice, the "freedom of speech" that each individual ought by right to possess. To worship according to the "outward dictates of men" instead of the inward "sanctifying spirit" means to prefer humanly authored texts to divine ordination—to commit the act of idolatry.

In his final reference to persons most afflicted by the cruel punishment of liturgical forms as those "especially whose office in the Church is to pray publicly," Milton invokes one of the crucial issues that had plagued the Church of England since the 1570s: whether ministers should have the liberty to pray according to their own will, or be restricted to the texts of the Prayer Book. Milton's impassioned plea for liturgical freedom clearly rehearses the terms of the first Protestant attacks upon the Book of Common Prayer in the late sixteenth century; although these Elizabethan dissenters often adopt a sectarian rhetoric that buries more serious devotional concerns, they share with Milton the profound desire to liberate the minister's voice from the perceived limitations of the Prayer Book.

In the decades following the initial production and distribution of the Common Prayer Book, English Protestants became increasingly divided over their legacy, which advocated unequivocally the recitation of standardized prayers instead of original prayer and preaching. No longer did the questions surrounding liturgical practice turn on the use of English versus Latin, or the worshipper's private versus public prayer during the church service—these issues had been adequately addressed, if not entirely settled, by the time Elizabeth I ascended the throne. In their place came a new series of challenges to public devotion, challenges that arose from within Protestant, not Catholic circles, and focused attention on a feature of the English service whose efficacy Thomas Cranmer seems to have taken for granted: the minister's reliance upon reading aloud as the crucial vehicle for edifying the congregation.

At the heart of Elizabethan debates over the use of the Prayer Book lie disparate views on the relationship between the formalized reading of prayers and the cultivation of personal faith. What to the establishment represented a successful mechanism for edifying large numbers of people was to the nonconformists a spiritually deadening imposition upon minister and congregation alike. As the pamphlet wars waged against the church during the 1570s and 1580s make abundantly clear, the church's early Puritan opposition sought to replace the Prayer Book with an order of service that privileged original prayers and sermons over readings from liturgical texts.

This attack upon the artificial and restrictive nature of common prayer fuels the defense of the Prayer Book launched by Richard Hooker, whose *Lawes of Ecclesiastical Politie* represents the most thorough and complex account of the establishment's practice that the church had yet to offer. In response to the opposition's calls to release the minister's spiritual powers of original prayer, Hooker does not simply defend the importance of liturgical uniformity for the state, nor does he argue exclusively for the necessity of edifying the people through standardized texts. Instead, his justification of the Prayer Book relies upon a re-imagining of liturgical freedom as a dangerous threat to the worshipper's spiritual welfare. For Hooker, as for many of his fellow churchmen, the efficacy of common prayer lies precisely in its capacity to compensate for the natural deficiencies of spontaneous and private devotion.

SAYING "AMEN"

In their 1572 pamphlet, *An Admonition to the Parliament,* two London clergymen, John Field and Thomas Wilcox, attack the Book of Common Prayer as an "unperfect book, culled and picked out of that popish dunghill, the Mass book full of all abominations."[3] Cranmer's efforts to transform the Catholic liturgy into a Protestant practice of prayer are now turned on their head; far from viewing the Prayer Book as a devotional liberation, these disgruntled non-conformists charge that the liturgy actually perpetuates the idolatry of the papists. Field and Wilcox focus their rage in particular upon the church's requirement that all ministers, regardless of learning and talent, use the Prayer Book and the volume of official Homilies to perform the public service. "By the word of God," they bitterly exclaim, "it is an office of preaching, they make it an office of reading." Although the church's ministers are enjoined by Christ to "feed God's lambs," many are admitted to the ministry who can do no more than read from prescribed liturgical texts:

> And this is not the feeding that Christ spoke of, the scriptures are plain. Reading is not feeding, but it is as evil as playing upon a stage, and worse too. For players yet learn their parts without book, and these, many of them can scarcely read within book.[4]

This passage turns on a subtle yet crucial discrimination between the acts of reading and preaching: to read from the Prayer Book or Homilies means neither to edify the congregation nor to pray from the heart, but instead represents a fraudulent performance likened to theatrical playing.[5] The "feeding" that the minister ought to provide cannot be achieved, the authors contend, so long as he is constrained by a scripted and artificial role. These opponents of the liturgy repeatedly hurl the Pauline verse—"I will pray with the Spirit, and will pray with the understanding also"—against the established church as evidence of its perfidy in preferring a human text to the divine spirit as the generative source of prayer.[6] As Thomas Cartwright, the author of *A Second Admonition to the Parliament,* and subsequently the leading spokesman for the non-conformists' position, concludes: "the [prayer] book is such a piece of work as it is strange we will use it; besides I cannot count it praying, as they use it commonly, but only reading or saying of prayers, even as a child that learneth to read, if his lesson be a prayer, he readeth a prayer, he does not pray."[7] Cartwright's distinction between reading and praying extends from the practice of the minister to that of the congregation, whose participation in the service is now likened to a child's rote recitation of a text. According to Cartwright, the act of reading prayers aloud does not necessarily produce or even reflect a sincere experience of those prayers, but instead sustains an undesirable gap between the individual's outward performance and inward state of mind. In the realm of public devotion, reading cultivates at best passivity, at worst hypocrisy.

By encouraging a mechanical and even theatrical performance of the service, the Prayer Book fails in its central aim of edifying the congregation; as Field and Wilcox declare, "in all their order of service, there is no edification, according to the rule of the Apostle, but confusion." The Admonitioners scornfully compare the antiphonal recitation of the Psalms to an exchange of volleys in a game of tennis: "they toss the Psalms in most places like tennis balls. The people some standing, some walking, some talking, some reading, some praying by themselves, attend not to the minister."[8] Here Cranmer's critique of the pre-Reformation liturgy is directed against the Reformed liturgy itself: as we saw in chapter 1, Cranmer scornfully characterized the Catholic service as "more like a game and a fond play to be laughed at of all men . . . some walking up and down in the church, some saying other prayers in Latin, and none understandeth other."[9] By criticizing the Protestant service for its level of "confusion," Field and Wilcox hit a sensitive nerve in the establishment's defense of its own practices: whereas the Catholic liturgy did not demand the laity's full attention, the reformers understood the efficacy of the public service to depend upon the worshippers' active engagement in liturgical readings.

Although the established church certainly could not control the worshippers' internal focus on the service, it actively sought to combat visible manifestation of distraction. We may recall, for instance, the case of the blacksmith Arthur Chapman, who was prosecuted in 1570 for reading his own English-language Primer while the minister performed the service.[10] Cartwright mocks a similar episode in the Second Admonition, where he describes a worshipper who "hath so little feeling of the common prayer that he bringeth a book of his own: and though he sit when they sit, stand when they stand and kneel when they kneel, he may pause sometime also, but most of all he intendeth his own book."[11] The difference here between "intending" and reading gets at the core of the Admonitioners' complaints: sixteenth-century uses for the verb "to intend" suggest a serious, internal process—the Oxford English Dictionary lists, among other definitions, "to turn one's thoughts to, fix the mind on . . . occupy oneself with"[12]—while "to read" could describe an experience entirely void of absorption.

Whereas the established churchmen would no doubt attribute these instances of private reading during the public liturgy to lingering habits of Catholic worship, Cartwright squarely lays the blame upon the Book of Common Prayer, and in particular its inclusion of responsive readings between the minister and the congregation. Although these texts were designed to involve the laity in the service, Cartwright claims that they are largely responsible for the average parishioner's inattentiveness to the minister's prayers: "All the people are appointed in diverse places to say after the Minister, whereby not only the time is unprofitably wasted, and a confused voice of the people, one speaking after another, caused, but an opinion bred in their heads, that those only be their prayers which they say and pronounce with their own mouths."[13] According to Cartwright, because the worshippers feel responsible only for those petitions that they themselves speak, they are much more likely to detach themselves from the rest of the service. And yet, he continues, this occasional participation not only obstructs the purpose of edification, but also violates the ordained purpose of the minister:

> For God hath ordained the minister to this end, that as in public meetings, he only is the mouth of the Lord from him to the people, even so he ought to be only the mouth of the people from them unto the Lord, and that all the people should attend to that which is said by the minister, and in the end both declare their consent to that which is said, and their hope that it should so be and come to pass which is prayed, by the word Amen.[14]

These passages raise one of the crucial questions surrounding the performance of public prayer: how are the worshippers to determine when they must pray on their own behalf, and when the minister's prayers represent them? Or, to put it more specifically in Cartwright's terms, how can the congregation be expected to understand both its vocal participation and its quiet listening as equivalent acts of devotion? By insisting that the minister ought to serve as "the mouth of the people," Cartwright advocates a model of ministerial intercession that Cranmer and his fellow liturgists had repeatedly sought to avoid. As we will recall, the Prayer Book's intermingling of collective and responsive prayers with those uttered only by the priest, as well as instructions that a petition be uttered "either by one of [the communicants], or else by one of the ministers, or by the Priest himself," were designed to avoid the delegation of devotional voice to any single speaker.[15] Cartwright's desire to reduce the congregation's participation to the utterance of "Amen" peculiarly echoes aspects of pre-Reformation practice: although the congregation would understand the minister's words and accordingly offer a different kind of "consent" from the uncomprehending response of the Catholic laity to the priest's Latin prayers, the liturgy that Cartwright envisions shares with its Catholic predecessor a nearly complete silencing of the worshipper's voice.

This drastic reduction of the congregation's role provoked an unusually lively response from Cartwright's normally phlegmatic opponent, John Whitgift, bishop of London, whose *Answere to a certen Libel intituled, An admonition to the Parliament* (1572) and the subsequent *Defense of the answere* (1574) represent the church's first formal rebuttals of the Admonitioners' platform. After citing Cartwright's passage in full, Whitgift declares that he can hardly believe what Cartwright proposes: namely, that the people should never join with the minister in reciting public prayers, outside of the mere utterance of "Amen." According to Whitgift, Cartwright's position mistakenly collapses two separate aspects of ministerial representation; although it is true that the minister speaks on behalf of God to the people, it by no means logically follows that he represents the congregation's mouthpiece to the Lord. Moreover, although Scripture does instruct the people to show their consent by saying "Amen," there is no precedent for restricting their participation to this single word: "besides the weakness of your conclusion," Whitgift exclaims, "the practice of the Church of God will sufficiently confute you."[16]

Whitgift supports his position with extensive scriptural and patristic citations, all of which point to the importance of the congregation's vocal as well as spiritual contribution to the public liturgy:

> Chrysostom going about to prove that in some respect there is no difference betwixt the priest and people, useth this for an example, that in public prayer they sometime join together. . . . Basil likeneth the sound of men, women, and children praying in the Church, to the roaring of the waves against the sea banks. This might you have seen also even in that place of Justin Martyr which you quote: for there describing the liturgy, he saith, that after the exhortation or sermon, *Omnes surgimus et comprecamur*, we do all rise and pray together.[17]

Although Whitgift does not pursue its significance, the position that Chrysostom articulates—"in some respect there is no difference betwixt the priest and people"—directly confronts one of the central paradoxes of early Puritan proposals for reform. As we have already had occasion to observe, Elizabethan nonconformists shared with the Catholic Church an interest in sustaining the difference between the utterances of the priest and the congregation, a difference that the English reformers had sought to dismantle. However, whereas the Catholics emphasized the priest's unique role in relation to administering the sacraments, these Protestants focused their attention on the minister's chosen status as preacher. In the decade or so following the publication of *An Admonition to the Parliament*, English non-conformists sought above all else to elevate the sermon to the central act of public worship.

Whitgift and his fellow churchmen were not opposed to the preaching of sermons per se. In *The Defense of the answere to the Admonition*, Whitgift asserts that both praying and preaching are suitable means to edify the congregation, and prepare them for Communion. "Besides this," he acknowledges, "he that is weak in faith, corrupt in judgment, ignorant in the right use of the Sacrament, may be admitted to prayer, and to the hearing of the word, that he may be instructed, for *fides ex auditu*, faith cometh by hearing."[18] And yet, at the same time that his invocation of St. Paul's declaration "faith cometh by hearing" may seem to affirm the power of sermons, Whitgift assimilates sermons to the "hearing of the word," a position that the non-conformists specifically contest.

The accusation that the church was caught up in "bare reading" applied both to the minister's dependence upon the Book of Common Prayer and to the mandatory use of the Book of Homilies, a collection of sermons published by Cranmer in 1547 in order to standardize preaching, just as the Prayer Book two years later would standardize prayer. Hence the Preface to the Homilies' first edition stipulates that "to put away all contention which hath heretofore risen through diversity of preaching . . . [and so] that all curates, of what learning soever they be, may have some godly and fruitful lessons in a readiness to read and declare unto their parishioners," the king commands the homilies to be read every Sunday at high Mass, "when the people be most gathered together."[19] When the whole book of twelve homilies has been read, the law stipulates that the parish should begin the volume again, reading and rereading the same texts throughout the year.

Cranmer's provision against "diversity of preaching" is strengthened in the newly revised preface to the Homilies issued upon Elizabeth's accession to the throne. It not only addresses the possible contentiousness of original sermons, but also acknowledges the problem of ignorance that the Homilies are meant to combat:

> Considering how necessary it is that the Word of God . . . should at all convenient times be preached unto the people . . . and also to avoid the manifold enormities which heretofore by false doctrine have crept into the church of God, and how that all they which are appointed ministers have not the gift of preaching sufficiently to instruct the people which is committed unto them, whereof great inconveniences might arise and ignorance still be maintained, if some honest remedy be not speedily found and provided.[20]

The abundance of "false doctrine" conspires with the paucity of talent to create a church in which too few ministers can be trusted with the freedom that the pulpit potentially offers. According to Elizabeth's Royal Injunctions of the same year, the priest was expected to read from the Book of Homilies every Sunday, except when a licensed preacher may be present to deliver his own sermon, an occasion that is to be arranged in every parish at least four times annually.[21] The

1559 preface attributes this highly infrequent performance of sermons to the scarcity of ministers with the "gift of preaching," but the problem was in fact of a more mundane and practical nature: too few ministers were able to obtain a license to preach, which typically required the possession of an advanced university degree. Only a small number of the beneficed clergy in even the most educated dioceses seem to have had Master of Arts degrees: according to a modern study, 19 percent of the clergy in Worcester, and 38 percent in Oxford, had any degrees at all.[22] The result of this system was that in the poorer and more rural dioceses the minimal quarterly sermon became very difficult to arrange.

Although they certainly lamented the state of affairs that had befallen their clergy, the religious establishment explained the lack of licensed preachers as one of the inevitable challenges in running a national church. As Whitgift conceded in 1584, fewer than 10 percent of England's parishes could produce an income capable of attracting a minister with the requisite academic credentials.[23] In his *Admonition to the people of England*, Thomas Cooper, the bishop of Winchester, confirms that there are many parishes whose resources "are so small that no man sufficiently learned will content himself with them." "To place able men in them," Cooper declares, "is impossible: For neither sufficient number of learned men can be had, nor, if there could, would they be contented to be to such places appointed."[24]

Cooper's text is a defensive response to a series of anonymous tracts against church government published in the late 1580s under the name "Martin Marprelate." Far more radical and scurrilous than the more sober *Admonitions* of the previous decade, these illegally printed pamphlets cast as their target the corruptions of English bishops, who, Martin claims, are nothing but "swine, dumb dogs . . . lewd drunkards, cormorants, rascals" who "would have the people content themselves with bare reading only, and hold that they may be saved thereby ordinarily."[25] Cooper replies to these charges with pleas for moderation: there are many parishes, he admits, in which the ministers cannot preach, but at least they can read from the Prayer Book, administer the sacraments, and keep the congregation from "a heathenish forgetfulness of God." Although he claims to agree with Martin's general call for a more learned ministry, he begs Martin to "tolerate some of the meaner sort of Ministers, having careful consideration, so much as diligence can do, that the same may be of life and behavior, honest, and godly, and such at the least, as may be able to instruct the parish in the Catechism."[26]

This call for tolerance "of the meaner sort of Ministers" reveals the crucial disjunction between the conformist and non-conformist views. For Cooper, the primary responsibility of the minister is the performance of liturgical duties that thankfully do not require any unusual skills. For the non-conformists, by contrast, the status of the sacraments, the common prayers, and the catechism had precipitously fallen as preaching became the single most significant means of Protestant instruction and faith. One of the most palpable manifestations of this trend lies in the rise of "prophesyings," or meetings of local ministers, visiting preachers, and members of the community, in which the less learned clergy gave trial sermons, received criticism and advice, and sought a general education from the more experienced preachers that were present.[27] As early as 1575, Edmund Grindal, the archbishop of York and soon to be archbishop of Canterbury, had stated to Queen Elizabeth that "public and continual preaching" was "the ordinary mean and instrument of the salvation of mankind." Grindal's support for the prophesyings eventually cost him his job: in 1577, the queen suspended him for refusing to put an end to these unorthodox events, which she regarded as a dangerous forum for nonconformity.[28]

Despite the queen's replacement of Grindal with the conservative Whitgift, the threat that the prophesyings posed did not abate. By the time Cooper defended the church against Martin Marprelate, he found himself battling against the position that preaching was not simply the "ordinary" but the only path to salvation. The Welshman John Penry, one of the probable authors of the Marprelate tracts, protested to Parliament over the lack of preaching in the vernacular in Wales, where English sermons, he claimed, were endangering the devotional welfare of a largely non-English-speaking population.[29] Martin recounts with obvious relish Penry's provocative testimony before Cooper and John Aylmer, bishop of London:

> John London [Bishop Aylmer] demanded whether preaching was the only means to salvation? Penry answered that it was the only ordinary means although the Lord was not so tied unto it but that he could extraordinarily use other means. . . . This point being a long time canvassed at the length his worship of Winchester [Cooper] rose up and mildly after his manner broke forth into these words. I assure you my Lords it is an execrable heresy: An heresy (quoth John Penry) I thank God that ever I knew that heresy: It is such an heresy that I will by the grace of God sooner leave my life then I will leave it.[30]

Cooper's "mild" explosion of disapproval in response to Penry's assertions comes as no surprise. As Martin argues in a later tract, the churchmen had no choice but to regard Penry's position as heretical; "otherwise," Martin concludes, "your case is damnable that causes the people to content themselves with reading and hold that they may ordinarily be saved thereby."[31] The anonymous author of "The lamentable Complaint of the Commonaltie" included in a volume of non-conformist tracts published by the Marprelate printer Robert Waldegrave puts the case even more vividly, lambasting the bishops not only as "dumb idols which oppress us," but as violent murders: "for who is appointed to murder God's people but they?"[32]

This outpouring of incendiary rhetoric in the late 1580s was both the occasion for and the response to the church's harsh persecution of its opponents. Already in the early 1570s John Field and Thomas Wilcox had landed themselves in jail for their *Admonition to the Parliament;* by the 1580s, prominent figures such as Cartwright along with more extreme sectarians were repeatedly brought to trial, imprisoned, and, in many cases, including Penry's, sentenced to death.[33] And yet, although the state's efforts to contain those non-conformists whom, as Martin puts it, the church "falsely called puritans" have been well recorded, historians have largely overlooked the specifically liturgical terms of the challenge that these non-conformists posed.[34]

At the same time the Marprelate tracts were circulating illegally throughout London, their printer, Waldegrave, was also involved in publishing a new liturgy designed to replace the Common Prayer Book. Entitled *A booke of the forme of common prayers, administration of the Sacraments, &c. agreeable to Gods worde, and the use of the reformed Churches,* this service book was closely based upon the more radical Protestant liturgy used by congregations in Geneva. First issued in 1584, and then again in 1586 and 1587, it sought to strip the public service of almost all mandatory forms in order to provide the maximum level of freedom to the minister. The service was accordingly organized around the central act of preaching, with occasional prayers flanking the sermon.

Although individual rites and sacraments are described in detail, the new liturgy avoids providing specific prayers for the minister. Instead, it confines itself to *examples* of appropriate prayers intended for the rare instance when the minister cannot spontaneously conceive his own. "The confession of our sins before the sermon," for example, is preceded by the following rubric: "When the Congregation is assembled at the hour appointed, the Minister useth this confession, or like in effect, exhorting the people diligently to examine them selves, following in their hearts the tenor of his words." In a similar vein, at the end of the "Public exercises in the Assemblies," the text adds:

> It shall not be necessary for the Pastor daily to repeat all these things before mentioned, but beginning with some like confession, to proceed to the Sermon, which ended, he either is to use the prayer for all estates before mentioned, or else to pray, as the Spirit of God shall move his heart, framing the same according to the time and manner which he hath entreated of.[35]

The prescriptions both for the people to "[follow] in their hearts," but presumably not with their tongues, and for the minister to pray "as the Spirit of God shall move [him]" rather than with set forms, provoked reactions of mingled astonishment and rage on the part of the ecclesiastical establishment. In 1586 Whitgift, now archbishop of Canterbury, rebuked the non-conformists for misconceiving the purpose of a public liturgy, which, in his account, was meant to ensure that the often illiterate congregation would hear a regular set of texts. "Shall we [not] have a Book of Common Prayer to be usually read and ob-

served in our churches," Whitgift argues, "so as the common people who cannot read, by often hearing one form of prayer, may learn the same, to their great
comforts elsewhere?"[36] According to Whitgift, the laity's repeated exposure to
the identical prayers not only ensured their edification, but also created a level of
comfort for the bookless worshipper, who was imprinted, as it were, with liturgical forms that could be retrieved "elsewhere," in moments of devotional need.
As Judith Maltby has recently shown, Whitgift's concerns about the minister's
deviation from the liturgy were in fact confirmed by the complaints of discon-
tented parishioners, who frequently filed suits against non-conformist clergymen who refused to follow the Prayer Book's texts.[37] Instead of cultivating a
similar set of tools for the parishioner's use, the non-conformists' liturgy promotes the minister's freedom at the expense of edification:

> There is a form of service set down to be used before and after the sermon: which
> is indeed the whole service: and yet in the rubric after the same it is thus written,
> It shall not be necessary for the Minister daily, &c. And in the chapter of Baptism, because
> he prayeth in this manner, or such like. And in the chapter of the Lord's Supper, the Min-
> ister giveth thanks in these words following, or the like in effect.[38]

Although the non-conformists pretend to provide a material text, Whitgift
claims there is "no matter" in this book at all: the standardized pages of the
Prayer Book are replaced by the fleeting words of the minister.

In the face of the continued threat posed by the Marprelate tracts, and in the
wake of the third publication of the alternative prayer book, Whitgift's eventual
successor as archbishop of Canterbury, Richard Bancroft, delivered a public sermon in defense of the established church at the outdoor pulpit of St. Paul's Cross
in 1589. The text of the sermon—"Dearly beloved, believe not every spirit, but
try the spirits whether they be of God: For many false prophets are gone out into
the world"[39]—was aimed specifically at those "private men" who had "in a
corner framed a book of the form of common prayer."[40] Bancroft attacks the
non-conformists not only for producing this book but for revising it so frequently; he insists that the purpose of issuing new versions in 1584, 1586, and
1587 is not to improve the former text, but instead to confuse and destabilize the
congregation. "A simple man would conceive thereby that their purpose is, we
should have a prescribed and set form of public prayer to be used from time to
time in our several congregations, so as poor men by often hearing of them
might the better know and understand them." And yet, Bancroft contests, "they
have no such intent: for you must imagine, though (as the serpent before mentioned) they have many implications and turnings, yet they have always means
and ways to shift for themselves."[41]

For Bancroft, as for Whitgift before him, the effectiveness of the church
liturgy lies in its capacity to be anticipated and absorbed by the worshipper.[42]
Far from supplying a purely external set of prayers that are superficially per-

formed, the Prayer Book creates a devotional practice in which the worshippers' "hearts might fully concur with [the minister] in every particular sentence." Only this state of inward as well as outward "concurrence" engenders the sincere and comprehending utterance of "Amen," an utterance that cannot be comparably made if the minister is encouraged "either [to] pray as there it is set down, or else as the spirit of God shall move his heart, to that effect, framing himself according to the time and occasion."[43] Bancroft considers the nonconformists' nonregulated and unpredictable model of prayer manipulative in that the worshippers offer their amens without necessarily understanding the full meaning of the minister's words:

> So as you see your selves in this point left to the minister's discretion. If he conceiving a prayer upon the sudden, shall after say it was to the same purpose that is prescribed in the book, you may not control him. And how by such kind of prayers you are like to be edified, and in what danger you are thereby left, he is of simple judgment that cannot discern it. . . . For sometimes they will so wander either by error or malice, in framing their prayers answerable to their affections (which are oftentimes maliciously bent against any thing or matter wherewith they are displeased); that no true christian, if he had time to consider of their meaning, ought in charity when they have done, to say, Amen.[44]

The problem that Bancroft identifies lies in the nature of consent, a problem which, as we have seen, Cranmer discussed forty years earlier in relation to the Catholic liturgy. As Cranmer explained in one of his final letters to Queen Mary, the church must have a vernacular service so that "all the people, understanding what the priests say, might give their minds and voices with them, and say 'Amen,' that is to say, allow what the priests say." And yet, Bancroft's account of the exchange between minister and congregation is substantially more complex: his concern is not simply that the worshippers will be left unedified, but that they will be duped into agreeing to malicious or heretical petitions, so that "no true christian, if he had time to consider of their meaning, ought in charity . . . to say, Amen." The "danger" that he describes turns on the apparent irreversibility of saying "amen," as if the minister's prayers will automatically be sealed and sent to heaven regardless of the congregation's comprehension or assent. If "amen" implicitly functions as a kind of Protestant magic, a liturgical speech act whose efficacy in reaching God seems relatively invulnerable to the worshipper's internal disposition, its utterance needs to be guarded with the utmost care.[45]

HOOKER'S "EARWITNESSES"

Bancroft's sermon at St. Paul's must have met with a sympathetic response from Richard Hooker, whose *Lawes of Ecclesiastical Politie*, composed over the course of the 1590s, has widely been credited with paving the *via media* of the English church, and even with the creation of Anglicanism.[46] Hooker's extensive defense of common prayer in book 5 of the *Lawes* has similarly been praised for revealing the crucial role of the liturgy in maintaining "the health and survival of the commonwealth."[47] And yet, what is striking about Hooker's work is less his secular project of defending the national church than his interest in uncovering the devotional advantages that emerge from common prayer. Although Hooker may be keenly interested in cementing religious uniformity through forms of public devotion, he seems equally engaged with, and perhaps more creative about, the ways that the Prayer Book compensates for affective inclinations and weaknesses. In order to represent as devotional benefits what the nonconformists regard as the Prayer Book's primary defects—its dependence upon reading instead of original prayer or preaching and its formulaic utterances in place of personally inspired speech—Hooker conceives of common prayer as a mechanism that successfully molds the naturally flawed impulses of the worshipper, whose faith can only be stimulated through regulated external forms. What Cranmer, Whitgift, and Bancroft envision primarily as a project of edification becomes for Hooker a means to provide the congregation with an otherwise unattainable spiritual and psychic relief.

Near the beginning of book 5 of the *Lawes,* under a section entitled "the rule of men's private spirits not safe in these cases to be followed," Hooker explores one of the crucial weaknesses in the non-conformists' model for public worship: that the personal gifts of the minister should determine the people's communal devotion. According to Hooker, the minister legitimately represents his worshippers only to the extent that his voice accurately represents the collective will of the corporate church; by encouraging the minister to follow his inward spirit and not a prescribed text, the non-conformists unleash "the manifold confusions . . . where every man's private Spirit and gift (as they term it) is the only Bishop that ordaineth him to this ministry."[48] Hooker argues that the public sphere of worship cannot sustain the imposition of individual liberty upon the collective body:

> If it should be free for men to reprove, to disgrade, to reject at their own liberty what they see done and practiced according to order set down . . . [if] the Church did give every man license to follow what [he] himself imagineth that *God's spirit doth reveal* unto him, or what he supposeth that God is likely to have revealed to some special person whose virtues deserve to be highly esteemed, what other effect could hereupon ensue, but the utter confusion of his Church under pretense of being taught, led, and guided by his spirit. (2:46)

In order for the congregation to be "taught, led, and guided," it must not rely upon "some special person" whose claims to God's spirit are impossible to discern. Unlike Milton, who argues in Eikonoklastes that God delivers "his Gift of prayer . . . to them especially whose office in the Church is to pray publicly," Hooker contends that if personal gifts and not liturgical forms are allowed to determine the public service, there will be nothing but "utter confusion."

Thus Hooker identifies what he regards as a contradiction in the enemies' logic: although the non-conformists repeatedly affirm their interest in promoting the public sphere of worship, they refuse to relinquish their commitment to the essentially personal choices of the minister in determining the liturgical service. This preference for an original over a prescribed model of devotion explains why "they utterly deny that the reading either of scriptures or homilies and sermons can ever by the ordinary grace of God save any soul," a position that results in what Hooker terms an "accidental" and we might call a "performative" set of requirements. Hooker sarcastically imagines that even if the church were to possess a book of original sermons recorded verbatim from the apostles themselves, any one of which could "convert thousands of the hearers unto Christian faith," the non-conformists would still deny that these texts possessed any devotional efficacy:

> Whereupon it must of necessity follow the vigor and vital efficacy of sermons doth grow from certain accidents which are not in the [sermons] but in their maker; his virtue, his gesture, his countenance, his zeal, the motion of his body, and the inflection of his voice who first uttereth them as his own, is that which giveth them the form, the nature, the very essence of instruments available to eternal life." (2:107–8)

By attacking the notion that the minister's physical gestures or characteristics should play so prominent a role in stirring the congregation's faith, Hooker asserts the preeminence of the written word as the most reliable instrument for salvation. His detailed list of the potential variables in the minister—"his virtue, his gesture, his countenance," and so on—conjures up the multiple contingencies that threaten the non-conformists' service. Because the Prayer Book, by contrast, does not depend for its proper usage upon any human characteristics outside of a general competence in reading and speaking aloud, it represents a much more reliable means for the church to sustain and edify its members.

Hence in response to the argument that "sermons be the only ordinary way of teaching whereby men are brought to the saving knowledge of God's truth," Hooker asks his readers whether it is possible that God's grace is likely to be left to the "private discretion" of each minister, or whether it can better be found in the public reading of Scripture (2:83). Why, he asks, should we entrust our faith to individually authored sermons instead of the Holy Word that the "whole Church hath solemnly appointed to be read for the people's good?" (2:101) By depicting the use of sermons to distribute God's word as an act of scriptural hoarding, Hooker aims to reverse the "papist" label directed against the church for its seemingly Catholic practices: whereas the established churchmen embody the Protestant spirit by spreading God's word through the reading of Scripture aloud, the non-conformists duplicate Catholic habits by subjecting the congregation to the whims of the minister.

Unlike the Catholic residues in the non-conformists' practice, Hooker claims that the church's commitment to reading both maintains the Protestant commitments to *sola scriptura* and conforms to the traditions of the earliest Christian congregations. He contends that "open reading" was first required by Paul as a means to ensure that whatever the church had occasion to write would be read aloud to the people in order to foster their instruction:

> When the very having of the books of God was a matter of no small charge and difficulty, in as much as they could not be had otherwise than only in written copies, it was the necessity not of preaching things agreeable with the word, but of reading the word it self at large to the people, which caused Churches throughout the world to have public care that the sacred oracles of God being procured by common charge, might with great sedulousness be kept both entire and sincere. (2:88)

Hooker describes a world long before the advent of print, in which the cost of producing individual manuscripts made it highly unlikely that people possessed their own books. And yet, if we can safely assume that Hooker knew the limitations of both literacy and book ownership for late sixteenth-century as well as apostolic worshippers, this historically distanced account of the efficacy of reading the Word aloud would have had obvious contemporary resonances. In criticizing the non-conformists' reliance upon preaching over what they scornfully call "bare reading," Hooker pointedly if subtly indicts his opponents for their elitist indifference to the illiterate and bookless masses.

Hooker's interest in broadening the scope of public participation as well as his distrust of men's "private discretion" extend far beyond his polemical response to specific non-conformist proposals. Repeatedly throughout the *Lawes*, he demonstrates his overarching concern with forging an ecclesiastical polity in which sacrifices of personal voice are exacted in exchange for the collective good. In the preface to the first four books, published in 1593, Hooker declares that public welfare depends upon the "overruling" of private opinion and belief: "so that of peace and quietness there is not any way possible, unless the probable voice of every entire society or body politic overrule all private of like nature in the same body" (1:33–34). According to the sixteenth-century uses recorded in the *Oxford English Dictionary*, "probable" here conveys less a sense of likelihood than of something either provable, or, perhaps even more relevant to Hooker's passage, worthy of approbation;[49] the notion of a "probable voice" invokes a model of collective, visible will that would subsume whatever private dissension lurks beneath the surface. Given these connotations, Hooker's further declaration that "the public approbation given by the body of this whole Church unto those things which are established, make it but probable that they are good" suggests a definition of *goodness* that depends upon the appearance, if not the reality, of corporate affirmation. The private is not eliminated so much as pushed down for the benefit of creating "public consent."[50]

This commitment to the power of public consensus—one of the many instances we might cite of what Debora Shuger has identified as Hooker's "populist" strain—complicates at the same time that it justifies the familiar account of the Elizabethan settlement, which, as we have already noted, maintains the church's lack of interest in the worshippers' inward beliefs so long as they manifest outward signs of conformity.[51] On the one hand, although Hooker does at times acknowledge the separate claims of the private and public realms of worship, he seems almost entirely indifferent to what transpires outside the walls of the church. On the other hand, what separates Hooker from the stereotypical vision of the Elizabethan establishment, and what perhaps best characterizes his innovative approach to defending the church, lies in his absolute certainty that the liturgical practices of the public sphere are more devotionally effective than their private and spontaneous counterparts. I will return to what I mean by *devotional effectiveness,* but first I want to underscore the radicalness of Hooker's position within the English tradition that preceded him. For however committed Cranmer and his followers were to reformulating public worship—and their commitments were anything but trivial—Hooker represents the first English ecclesiastic to argue unequivocally for the general superiority of public over private prayer. Whereas Whitgift, for one, had delegated to the private sphere a range of "spiritual imperatives" that he simply could not imagine addressed within the public world, Hooker makes no such concessions.[52]

The wide range of benefits that Hooker assigns to public prayer shares a set of devotional, and, to our minds, psychological, advantages: in a striking departure from traditional justifications of collective prayer as a superior means to reach the ears of God, Hooker focuses instead on its efficacy in producing spiritual ease and heightening devotional affect among the members of the congregation. Evidence for this shift from a divine to a human register surfaces very clearly in Hooker's use of the Old Testament story of the Ninevites. In this episode from the Book of Jonah, God sends Jonah (via a short detour in the belly of a giant fish) to the city of Nineveh to warn the people of their imminent destruction because of their "evil ways." After Jonah delivers the dire message, the Ninevites repent their former wickedness, and join to pray for God's forgiveness; "they put on sackcloth from the greatest of them even to the least of them

. . . and cry mightily unto God."[53] Much to the dismay of Jonah, who thinks his errand has been futile, God hears the Ninevites' pleas and spares the city.

In a passage quoted by Hooker's early patron John Jewel from Chrysostom's third homily on prayer, Chrysostom points to this biblical story as evidence of God's preference for collective over individual prayer:

> If the prayer of a single person is so powerful, much more so is the prayer which is offered along with many other people. The sinewy strength of such a prayer and the confidence that God will hear it is far greater than you can have for the prayer you offer privately at home. . . . Listen to God himself when he says that he respects the throng of people which invokes him with affection. When he was defending his action in the case of the gourd plant against Jonah's complaint, he said: "You had pity on the gourd for which you suffered no distress nor did you rear it; shall I not spare Nineveh, the great city, in which dwell more than a hundred and twenty thousand persons?" He does not mention the large number without purpose. He does so in order that you may learn that any prayer which is offered with a unison of many voices has great power.[54]

For Chrysostom, the efficacy of common prayer is measured entirely in terms of the power that such prayer wields in relation to God; the "unison of many voices" generated by the Ninevites succeeds, to borrow George Herbert's phrase, as an "engine against th'almighty," a devotional tool or weapon that God cannot withstand.[55]

Hooker certainly does not dispute Chrysostom's conclusion about the strength that lies in collective, unified prayer; on the contrary, he himself asserts that "[t]he Prince and the people of Nineveh assembling them selves as a main army of supplicants, it was not in the power of God to withstand them."[56] However, this particular justification of common prayer does not prevail as the decisive or compelling one for Hooker, who quickly shifts his focus from the power of common prayer as a means to obtain God's attention to its power within the human community itself. After his brief mention of the Ninevites and a supporting passage from Tertullian confirming the efficacy of "being banded as it were together . . . to besiege God with our prayers," Hooker remarks:

> When we publicly make our prayers, it cannot be but that we do it with much more comfort than in private, for that the things we ask publicly are approved as needful and good in the judgment of all, we hear them sought for and desired with common consent. Again, thus much help and furtherance is more yielded, in that if so be our zeal and devotion to Godward be slack, the alacrity and fervor of others serveth as a present spur. (2:112)

In arguing that the collective zeal of the congregation serves as a "spur" for the individual worshipper, Hooker directly confronts the non-conformists' charges that common prayer produces only spiritual distraction and passivity among the congregation. For Hooker, common prayer serves as a combatant against the distraction and devotional lethargy that emerge from the difficulty of praying privately or individually without liturgical guides. In his 1586 work, "A Learned Discourse of Justification," Hooker discusses the difficulty of sustaining concentration during private devotion, and laments that while "we are never better affected unto God than when we pray, yet when we pray how are our affections many times distracted" (5:115). John Donne will offer a similar account of this phenomenon in a 1622 sermon preached to the Earl of Carlile:

> Where shall I find the Holy Ghost? I lock my door to my self, and I throw my self down in the presence of my God, I divest myself of all worldly thoughts, and I bend all my powers, and faculties upon God, as I think, and suddenly I find my self scattered, melted, fallen into vain thoughts, into no thoughts . . . *I believe in the Holy Ghost*, but do not find him, if I seek him only in private prayer; but *in Ecclesia*, when I go to meet him in the *Church*, when I seek him where he hath promised to be found . . . instantly the savor of this Myrrh is exalted, and multiplied to me; not a dew, but a shower is poured out upon me.[57]

The disjunction Donne describes between the state of distraction, of "scattered, melted, . . . vain thoughts," that characterizes his private prayer, and the ecstatic satisfaction of his public prayer—"not a dew, but a shower, is poured out upon me"—underscores the qualitative distinction between the two methods of devotional practice. For Donne, as we shall see in chapter 4, the public space of the church is the site for achieving selfhood, for maintaining personal wholeness, for realizing the individual "I" not in spite of, but precisely because of, a collective act of prayer.[58]

Just as Donne imagines his devotional self to be enabled only within the corporate sphere of the church, so too does Hooker envision the practice of common prayer as conferring a legitimacy upon the petitions that the congregation utters: "for that the things we ask publicly are approved as needful and good in the judgment of all, we hear them sought for and desired with common consent." According to this logic, public prayers are "needful and good" because the individual worshipper cannot pray for what the community would condemn; the echoing throughout the church represents a "common consent" that has been achieved only through the active suspension of potentially conflicting voices.

This act of suspension or suppression of the personal in favor of the common produces the high level of devotional comfort that Hooker imagines, as the worshippers feel reassured that their petitions have not strayed from the path of the church. Hooker is not the first sixteenth-century Protestant to describe this phenomenon. In his *Commentary on Jeremiah*, John Calvin observes: "There is hardly one in a hundred who is as steadfast as he ought to be when God alone is

witness. But shame renders us courageous and constrains us to be constant . . .
[thus] the vigor that is almost extinct in private is aroused in public."[59] Hooker
extends this mechanism of shame to a more explicit practice of mutual surveil-
lance:

> Could there be anything better than that we all at our first access unto God by
> prayer should acknowledge meekly our sin and that not only in heart but with
> tongue, all which are present being made earwitnesses even of every man's dis-
> tinct and deliberate assent unto each particular branch of a common indictment
> drawn against our selves?[60]

"All which are present being made earwitnesses": the source of devotional satisfaction that Hooker describes lies in this extraordinary notion of "earwitness-
ing," a neologism that invokes the simultaneous act of aurally affirming and
monitoring one's fellow worshippers. The individual's personal experience of
the liturgical utterance is heightened rather than diminished by the collective
performance, whereby "every man's distinct and deliberate assent" to the "common indictment" reverberates throughout the church. Cranmer's insistence that
the emphasis of the liturgy must fall on what "enters in at their ears," and Whitgift's reiteration of the Pauline verse "faith cometh by hearing," take an interest-
ing turn: the act of hearing is directed not toward the prayers or readings of the
minister, but toward the utterances of the worshippers themselves.

The stakes of this collective listening become clearer if we consider Hooker's
understanding of the welfare of the Christian *corporatio* as dependent upon the
active and uncompromised participation of each worshipping member. Thus
Hooker explains that the efficacy of public prayer is so much greater than prayer
in private, because the benefits of praying privately do not reach beyond the
individual self. But with public prayer, he insists,

> the whole church is much bettered by our good example, and consequently
> whereas secret neglect of our duty in this kind is but only our own hurt, one
> man's contempt of the common prayer of the Church of God may be and often-
> times is most hurtful unto many. (2:113)

The very familiar notion in this period of generating public examples, whereby
a congregation, theater audience, or group of citizens is "bettered" by observing an exemplary performance, slides into murkier terrain as Hooker anticipates
the damage that ensues from even a single worshipper's negative behavior
during the church service. Although the nature of this damage remains, not
surprisingly, unspecified, the lurking potential for contagion, for "one man's
contempt of the common prayer" to prove "hurtful unto many" reflects the culmination of the church's theological commitment to the necessity of engaging
the entire congregation in the service. It is this threat of collective vulnerability

that Herbert so cannily registers in his warning to the misbehaving parishioner in "The Church Porch": "Jest not at preachers language, or expression / How know'st thou, but thy sins made him miscarry?"[61]

What contains this danger for Hooker at least partially are the texts of the Prayer Book, which remain invulnerable to the performative aberrations of either the minister or the congregation. "But of all helps for due performance of this service," Hooker asserts, "the greatest is that very set and standing order it self, which framed with common advice hath both for matter and form prescribed whatsoever is herein publicly done."[62] By compensating for our natural deficiencies, the Prayer Book "helps that imbecility and weakness in us, by means whereof we are otherwise of our selves the less apt to perform unto God so heavenly a service, with such affection of heart, and disposition in the power of our souls as is requisite" (2:113). The devotional abilities that the Prayer Book enhances are by no means strictly external: instead, Hooker speaks of the internal realm, of the "affection of heart" and the "disposition . . . of our soul." In this respect, Hooker seems to extend Cranmer's hope that the worshipper's inward self would not simply adopt but deeply assimilate the formalized prayers of the church. And yet, whereas Cranmer explains this commitment to combining private and public devotion in terms of his desire to edify and unite the laity, for Hooker this shaping of the personal with collective forms responds to his perception of the individual's deepest spiritual needs.

This vision of human inwardness as a state of weakness in need of external props and aids, a vision that once again reveals Hooker's affinity to Calvin, culminates in Hooker's wonderfully complex and pragmatic response to Cartwright's complaint that the Prayer Book includes too many requests for "earthly" and not spiritual matters—"there shall be found more than a third part of the prayers," Cartwright protests, "which are not Psalms and texts of Scripture, spent in praying for, and praying against the commodities and incommodities of this life."[63] Hooker initially concedes that in a perfect world our prayers to heaven would "both in measure and number" exceed our earthly petitions to the same degree that heavenly objectives ought to outweigh our earthly needs. And yet, he continues, "it must be withal considered, that the greatest part of the world are they which be furthest from perfection." Because human worshippers are in fact far "better able to discern the wants of this present life, than by spiritual capacity to apprehend things above sense," Hooker contends that they are more likely to apply themselves vigorously to even the least significant petitions of public prayer "wherein their one particular is moved" (2:144).

By allowing the congregation to pray for those things that seem to represent their particular needs, Hooker does not imagine that a strictly earthly set of petitions will be performed. Instead, he concludes that through this process the worshippers will be more or less effortlessly led into praying for the spiritual things that they would otherwise never request:

> By this means there stealeth upon them a double benefit; first, because that good affection, which things of smaller account have once set on work, is by so much the more easily raised higher; and secondly in that the very custom of seeking so particular aid and relief at the hands of God doth by a secret contradiction withdraw them from endeavoring to help themselves by those wicked shifts, which they know can never have his allowance, whose assistance their prayer seeketh. These multiplied petitions of worldly things in prayer have therefore, besides their direct use a service whereby the church under hand, through a kind of heavenly fraud, taketh the souls of men as with certain baits. (2:145)

The startling metaphors of manipulation and theft that suffuse this passage, culminating in the notion of "heavenly fraud," convey Hooker's powerful commitment to the ends and not the means of Christian salvation. By sprinkling these prayers on the road to heaven, the Prayer Book not only encourages the worshippers' outward performance of devotion, but secretly and imperceptibly transforms their inward nature. Thus Hooker ultimately offers a powerful corrective to the non-conformists' account of the church service as a superficial and ineffectual practice: in the guise of soliciting little more than external conformity, the bait of common prayer catches nothing less than men's souls.

CHAPTER THREE

Prayer and Poetry

RHYME IN THE ENGLISH CHURCH

*I*n the centuries preceding the Reformation, there was no obvious distinction between lay prayer and devotional poetry. All of the prayers provided in the *Lay folks' Mass Book* were written in rhymed meter; many of the poems that we have received as medieval religious lyrics originated in vernacular primers or preaching manuals, where these metrical texts were intended as helpful examples of petitions and confessions. The intertwining of lay devotion and religious poetry can be traced in part to an ecclesiastical injunction issued by the Fourth Lateran Council of 1215, whereby parishioners were required not only to perform annual confession, but also to recite before the priest the Lord's Prayer and the Apostles' Creed. This imposition of learning was simplified, the clerics believed, by the use of English verse, which was mnemonically accessible to the unlearned in ways that both Latin and English prose were not. In these instances of liturgical and didactic translation, poetic form served a practical, not an aesthetic imperative: the more accessible the rhyme, the more likely the prayer was remembered.

When the Protestant Reformation introduced a vernacular Prayer Book into the Church of England, the mutually dependent relationship between poetic and devotional production was permanently unsettled. Once the public liturgy consisted only of comprehensible, English texts, the lay population no longer required easily digestible translations in order to learn their own prayers. These new vernacular texts were written entirely in prose and not verse, a decision that no doubt reflected both the practical exigencies of individual limitations— Cranmer laments that "Mine English verses lack the grace and facility that I would wish they had"—and more abstract prejudices against rhyme as symptomatic of an idolatrous relationship to language.[1] Moreover, because the Book of Common Prayer stipulated that "the Minister, Clerks and people" should utter many of the crucial prayers together, retaining metrical rhymes for average parishioners would have jeopardized the reformers' project of creating a liturgy sufficiently elevated for the voice of the minister as well as that of the congregation.

If verse no longer served as a primary vehicle for lay devotion and edification, what role did it assume in the liturgical culture of the sixteenth century? Or, to pose the question in reverse, what influence did the vernacular liturgy have upon the production of devotional poetry? In both of these cases, the answer turns on the prominence of the metrical Psalms. More than any other single text, the Book of Psalms represents the crucial site of transition between the mnemonic and didactic verse of the medieval period and the flourishing of original devotional poetry in the late sixteenth and early seventeenth centuries. Because the Psalms were understood to have been composed in Hebrew verse, the translation of prose Psalters into English meter did not represent a generic transformation or "poeticization" of Scripture, but instead meant returning these texts to an approximate original form. The explosion of Psalm translations in the years following the Edwardian Reformation reflected less the poetic impulses of individual authors than the devotional impulses of a liturgical culture interested in generating new texts for corporate worship.[2]

And yet, at the same time that metrical Psalters were primarily designed for liturgical use, over the course of the sixteenth century English Protestants began to consider the possibility that the devotional efficacy of the Psalms at least partly inhered in their status as poems. Within an ecclesiastical culture that had not clearly defined a place for poetry, the exception of the metrical Psalms as simultaneously poetic, liturgical, and scriptural texts provoked a new self-consciousness about the relationship between poetry and devotion. After a period of about fifty years following the Edwardian Reformation in which original (nonscriptural) devotional verse was regarded as an ambiguous and often suspicious genre of writing—a position confirmed by the dearth of such poetry written during these years—Protestant lyrics explode onto the scene in a manner entirely unprecedented in England. In this evolution of rhyme from a more or less automatic vehicle for lay worship in the late Middle Ages to an independent and immensely popular category of devotional language in the late Elizabethan period, Sir Philip Sidney's *An Apology for Poetry*, and his translation of the Psalms with his sister, Mary Sidney Herbert, the Countess of Pembroke, represent crucial interventions. By insisting that "heavenly poesy" ought to be acknowledged as a practice that is both separate from and ideally compatible with the devotional aims of the church, Sidney helps to articulate a place for poetry within the parameters of common prayer.

PRAYING IN RHYME

I know to God, full of might,
& to his mother maiden bright,
& to all halouse* here, [saints]

& to the father ghostly,* [spiritual]
that I have sinned largely,
In many sins sere:* [diverse]
In thought, in speech, & in delight,
In word, & work I am to wite* [know]
and worth to blame;
Therefore I pray saint Mary
and all halouse haly,* [holy saints]
In God's name,
and the priest to pray for me,
that God have mercy & pity,
for his manhood,
of my wretched sinfulness,
& give me grace & forgiveness
of my misdeed.[3]

These lines from the *Lay folks' Mass Book* are at once a confession of faith said before the Mass. They are also what we now regard as a poem. Unlike many of the lay prayers for the Mass, which, as we saw in chapter 1, freely depart from the Latin liturgy, here the English rhymes closely adhere to the clergy's *Confiteor*; what separates the priest from the people at this moment in the service lies not in the content but in the language of devotion. The difference between the two prayers is not simply that between English and Latin, however, but also between poetry and prose: the vernacular translation adopts a mnemonically easy rhyme in order to facilitate its use by the unlearned and illiterate laity. The near-absolute semantic equivalence between the two texts is formally severed by the imposition of verse.

Although the medieval laity was largely cut off from understanding or even hearing the priest's Latin Mass, catechetical instructions and sermons to the people were delivered in the vernacular tongue. According to the Lambeth Constitutions of 1281 issued by John Peckham, archbishop of Canterbury, which introduced the first systematic program of instruction in England following the Lateran decrees of 1215, all priests were expected to preach to their congregations at least four times a year on the essential texts of the Catholic faith: the Lord's Prayer; the articles of the Creed; the Ten Commandments; five senses; seven works of mercy; seven sacraments; and so on.[4] Parishioners were required to recite the first two of these as part of their annual confession and examination before their parish priest.[5] As an aid to the mandatory expositions of their catechetical texts, worshippers could find vernacular translations in Primers and devotional guides such as the fourteenth-century work known as the *Lay folks' catechism*, a translation of John Thoresby, archbishop of York's 1357 Latin In-

structions intended for the clergy. My point, however, is not to rehearse the well-documented role of the vernacular within medieval lay worship, but instead to draw attention to one feature of this practice that sits so visibly on the surface of things that it might easily be ignored.[6] As we can observe simply by looking at the pages of English Catechisms, Mass books, and Primers, a surprisingly large share of this vernacular literature was written in verse rather than prose. When parishioners rehearsed the Creed to the priest, prepared themselves for confession, or performed their own private prayers to God, the texts that they employed were often composed in rhyme.

The choice of verse over prose for vernacular devotion reflects a fundamentally didactic impulse. As Thoresby explains to the monk John Gaytrig, the people have fallen into enormous ignorance due to the "excessive subtleties of preaching"; therefore, religious instruction must be delivered in the clearest vernacular style. Because Gaytrig has been blessed with the "flowers of eloquence" (*"floribus eloquencie"*), Thoresby has chosen him for the task of preparing a vernacular translation of his *Instructions*, a task that Gaytrig fulfilled through the medium of alliterative verse.[7] Robert Mannyng articulates the strategic advantages of rhyme in his translation of the Anglo-Norman *Manuel des Pechiez* entitled *Handlyng Synne* (1303):

> For lewd men I undertook
> On english tongue to make this book.
> For many be of such manner,
> That tales and rhymes will blithely hear;
> In games and jests and at the ale,
> Men love to listen to trotouale:* [idle tale-telling]
> That may fall often to villainy,
> To deadly sin, or other folly;
> For such men have I made this rhyme
> That they may well spend here time,
> And therein somewhat for to hear
> To leave all such foul manner,
> And for to be able to know therein
> That they wene no sin be in.* [they know there is no sin inside (this book)][8]

If, Mannyng argues, the enthusiasm men feel toward hearing tales at the local tavern or gaming tables could be similarly aroused by metrical prayers, his confessional manual might be capable of converting its readers and listeners to good.

I refer to both readers and listeners, although Mannyng's characterization of his text seems to imagine only listeners: he hopes that just as "men love to listen to trotouale," so they might "hear" in his book the means "to leave all such foul manner." *Hear* rather than *read*: although Mary Carruthers's magisterial work on memory within the learned population of medieval Europe has taught us much about the visual mnemonic processes that were cultivated both in the mind and on the page, it has perhaps prevented us from grasping how aurally dependent most of the lay population would have been when learning its prayers.[9] As Thoresby's letter to Gaytrig as well as Peckham's original statutes clearly reveal, for the average medieval parishioners, the process of learning catechetical and confessional texts meant listening to expositions read aloud by the priest. So John Myrc (or Mirk) explains in his *Instructions for Parish Priests,* an instructional manual for inexperienced or unlearned clergy:

> The pater noster and the creed
> Preach thy parish thou must need,
> Twice or thrice in the year
> To thy parish hole and fere;* [well and strong]
> Teach them thus, and bid them say
> With good intent every day,
> "Father our that art in heaven,
> Hallowed be thy name" with meek stevene.* [voice][10]

The prayers that Myrc instructs the priest to read to the congregation are all in rhymed meter, as is the entirety of Myrc's own text. Thus Myrc explains to his clerical readers how to behave when shriving a woman:

> But when a woman cometh to thee,
> Look her face that thou not see,* [be sure you do not see her face]
> But teach her to kneel down thee by,
> And somewhat thy face from her thou wry,* [turn]
> Still as stone there thou sit,
> And keep thee well that thou ne spit. [be sure not to spit]
> Cough thou not then, thy thonkes,* [willingly]
> Nor wring thou with thy schonkes,* [legs]
> Lest she suppose thou make that far[e]* [lest she think you do so]
> For loathing what thou hearest there.
> But sit thou still as any maid
> 'Til that she has all I-sayde.* [until she has said all, finished] (lines 773–84)

"Still as stone there thou sit, / And keep thee well that thou ne spit": the priests are presumably imagined to remember these and similar pieces of pastoral advice more easily through the vehicle of rhyme. The didactic benefits of meter, it would seem, were not limited to the laity alone.

I want to return, however, to the prayers that Myrc supplies for lay instruction, prayers to be regarded as examples rather than officially prescribed texts.

Because there was no premium placed on creating uniformity in the laity's prayers, nor any sense of English as a sacred tongue whose efficacy depended upon strict adherence to scriptural or sacramental formulae, worshippers enjoyed an enormous freedom in terms of the particular language they could use in fulfilling their liturgical obligations. There was no privileged English version of the Lord's Prayer, for example, that was equivalent to the sacred status of the Vulgate Pater Noster. Instead, metrical Lord's Prayers range from close translations of the Vulgate to lengthy poetic expositions. "Our father in heaven rich / Thy name be hallowed ever i-liche [forever]" concisely renders the opening verse in one case, while an alternative extends the verse to a full stanza:

> Our father in heaven hallowed be thy name,
> As Jesus thy son taught us to say:
> Keep us thy children from sin and blame,
> That we may be saved at our last day.
> Thy name in us hallowed be may
> If we make clean our temple within.
> Now keep us, father, from deadly sin.[11]

In the first of these two examples, the lines stand in for the Latin, whereas the second is meant to explicate and dilate the prayer; the first seems intended for easy memorization and repetition, while the second aims to be absorbed and understood.

Rhymed verse was read from the pulpit not only for teaching the congregation its catechetical texts, but also as a device to sharpen the listener's affective experience of the priest's sermon.[12] A fourteenth-century homily on the verse *Ihesu, fili david, miserere mei* ("Jesus, son of David, have mercy upon me") attributed to John Sheppey, bishop of Rochester, includes these verses originally in southern English dialect:

> Jesus, that all this world hath wrought,
> have mercy on me! . . .
> David's son, full of might
> have mercy on me!
> David's son, fair to sight,
> David's son, that mixes mercy with right,
> have mercy on me, & make me meek to thee,
> & make me think on thee, & bring me to thee . . .
> Jesus [David's son!] *prosequatur sermo sic.** [let the sermon continue]
> Jesus that all this world had wrought,
> David's son, full of might,
> have mercy on me!

& make me meek to thee,

& *isto modo concludendo prosequitur sermo.** [In this manner concluding there
follows the sermon][13]

In its repeated invocations of Jesus' name and its multiple petitions for his
mercy, the poem seems designed to inspire the laity's devotion through simple
and accessible rhymes. Similarly, in a fourteenth-century commonplace book of
materials to be used by priests, the Franciscan friar John of Grimestone inter-
sperses metrical English verses among the Latin texts.[14] Grimestone's vernacular version of the popular Hours of the Cross, for example, is written in a
familiar second-person address to Christ—"At the time of matins, lord, thou
were taken"; "At underne [third hour of the day], lord, they began thee to cru-
cify"—thereby evincing both an intimacy and an immediacy to the laity's instruction in the sufferings of Christ.[15]

Apart from their frequent exposure to metrical texts that were included in
catechetical expositions or vernacular sermons, those parishioners having access to books would have encountered a wide range of devotional verse in the
pages of vernacular Primers. One of the most common genres of these metrical
texts was the "extended confession" that rehearsed the different components of
Peckham's original categories for Christian instruction—the seven deadly sins,
Ten Commandments, and so on—in order to help penitents examine their consciences before confessing to the priest.[16] In these exercises of formal contrition, the speaker proceeds through one or more categories of the so-called
confitendi formae in order to uncover the entirety of his or her sinfulness. A typical
poem from a fifteenth-century manuscript addresses the speaker's violation of
each of the Ten Commandments:

> The ten commandments I have broke
> Many a time with wicked skill;
> To false gods I have spoke
> And wrought against my lord's will.
> Many times I have take
> God's name in Idolship,
> Therefore I tremble, dread and quake.
> Mercy! God, for thy lordship . . .[17]

A lyric more ambitious in its affirmation of absolute sinfulness proceeds
through the entirety of the *formae*. On the seven deadly sins, the speaker declares:

> The seven deadly sins I cannot excuse:
> For I am guilty, in many different ways,
> With delectation, consent, and use;
> All now to rehearse I may not suffice;

> In Pride, Envy, wrath, Lechery, & covetousness,
> Sloth, and Gluttony, with all ther spices.
> Alas! all my life is full of vices!

The works of mercy are similarly catechized to acknowledge the sinner's infringement of each one:

> The works of mercy I have not fulfilled,
> After my power, as oft as I might:
> To help the poor I was not best willed,
> With meat and drink and clothing them dyght,* [provided]
> giving no harbor day or night,
> Helping no prisoners, nor visiting the sick;
> To bury the dead I was not meek.[18]

In their decidedly anonymous and impersonal tone, these verses do not reflect an individualized speaker so much as supply paradigms to facilitate the parishioners' confessional obligations.[19]

Not surprisingly, the church's program of instruction was not entirely successful. We need only consider William Langland's description of Sloth in *Piers Plowman*:

> "If I should die by this day," quoth he, "me list not to look.
> I can not perfectly my Paternoster as the priest it singeth
> But I can rhymes of Robin Hood and Raldolf Earl of Chester
> Ac neither of Our Lord nor of Our Lady the least that ever was maked."

> (Even if I should die this day, I have no desire to open my eyes, I do not know properly my Paternoster as the priest sings it, But I do know rhymes of Robin Hood and Randolph, earl of Chester, But neither of Our Lord nor of Our Lady the least that ever was made.)[20]

But whatever this allegorical figure can tell us about medieval devotion, one thing is strikingly clear: Sloth draws a connection between learning the rhymes of Robin Hood and the learning (or not learning) of his prayers. This connection is reinforced by Langland's use of the verb *maked*, which derives from the Middle English term *maker* or *makir* for *poet*, to describe the composition of the Pater Noster and the Ave Maria ("Our Lord" and "Our Lady").

In this brief sampling of medieval religious verse, I have not sought to represent the enormous range of this body of literature, whose complexities and achievements far surpass the lyrics that we have examined here.[21] However, I have meant to convey what Sloth's confession in *Piers Plowman* indirectly confirms: the broad use of verse as a liturgical tool in the centuries immediately preceding the Reformation. As we shall now see, it is precisely this unself-conscious relationship between metrical form and lay devotion that comes apart in the sixteenth century, when the genres of lay prayer and poetry sit less comfortably, or at least less obviously, together.

METRICAL PSALMS

For early sixteenth-century parishioners accustomed to the metrical rhymes printed in their Primers and expounded in their catechetical instruction, the lay prayers introduced by the newly reformed church must have been surprising. In the reformed Edwardian Primer issued in 1553, the only prayers presented in rhyme apart from the Psalms and scriptural songs are the "graces" to be recited before and after dinner, supper, and meat. (Versions of these texts are in fact first provided in lengthier prose versions, and then afterwards given mnemonic verse forms.) The Creed, Lord's Prayer, Collects, and occasional prayers, however, were printed in prose paragraphs.[22] The Elizabethan Primer of 1559, which reverted to the less reformed Edwardian Primer of 1551, did include a series of traditional hymns translated from the Latin into English meter. These hymns, taken almost entirely from the Catholic Sarum breviary, were to be used in daily domestic worship alongside the Psalms and scriptural songs that we find in the 1553 text. And yet, here too the Creed, Ten Commandments, Lord's Prayer, Collects, and the long series of occasional prayers are all delivered in prose translations.[23]

Although the handy verses that had facilitated learning these texts would no doubt have been equally effective for Protestants, no such efforts were made in either of these Primers or in the Book of Common Prayer. In place of the variety of verse translations that we find in medieval devotional books, the Protestant reformers established a single authoritative version for each prayer or confession of faith. The Lord's Prayer that is uttered repeatedly in the Prayer Book's Order for Morning and Evening Prayer and Order for Holy Communion as well as in the Primer's texts of private devotion remains the same:

> Our Father which art in heaven, Hallowed be thy name. Thy kingdom come. Thy will be done in earth, as it is in heaven. Give us this day our daily bread. And forgive us our trespasses, as we forgive them that trespass against us. And lead us not into temptation: but deliver us from evil. Amen.

Similarly, the rhymed versions of the Creed which proliferate in the pre-Reformation period are reduced to the lengthy prose formula that begins:

> I believe in God the Father Almighty, maker of heaven and earth: and in Jesus Christ his only Son our Lord, which was conceived by the holy Ghost, born of the

virgin Mary, suffered under Ponce Pilate, was crucified, dead and buried, he descended into hell, the third day he rose again from the dead, he ascended into heaven . . . Amen.[24]

Apart from the 1559 Primer, which printed these texts *as if* they were in verse, with single sentences or articles per line, the presentation of these texts as dense prose paragraphs did not facilitate the worshipper's quick visual memorization; nor do the sentences offer aural mnemonics so that listeners would quickly learn their prayers by heart. Once annual confession and its accompanying examination had been eliminated, there was no occasion in the Reformed church apart from children's catechism in which worshippers were "tested" in their prayers; Protestant reformers emphasized instead the laity's active participation in the liturgy. Whereas John Myrc had instructed priests to teach their congregations "the pater noster and the creed . . . twice or thrice in the year," English ministers sought to edify their parishioners through weekly services, ideally reinforced by domestic worship, in which devotional texts were recited and repeated aloud.[25]

The Protestants' decision to abandon verse as a vehicle for public devotion was marked by one significant exception: their use of metrical Psalms, and a number of scriptural songs, in the church.[26] More than any other single book of Scripture, the Book of Psalms occupied a central position in the Reformed liturgy. Beginning in 1552, Miles Coverdale's prose version of the Psalms from the Great Bible translation was appended to all of the smaller sized, domestic Prayer Books; by 1564 this translation was appended to the larger, folio editions that typically served as the church's own liturgical texts. This decision on the part of the reformers to include the Psalter within the Prayer Book reflects its frequent recitation in the service. The rest of the Old Testament was appointed to be read once over the course of every year, and the New Testament, with the exception of the Revelation of St. John, to be read three times annually, but the Book of Psalms was to be read through every month. There was nothing remarkable about this rate of recitation: in the pre-Reformation church, the full cycle of 150 Psalms was sung by religious and secular clergy during each weekly cycle of hours.[27] However, what differentiated the Reformed practice from its medieval counterpart was not only the adoption of an English (rather than Latin) Psalter for liturgical use, but the transformation of this Psalter into a text of common prayer.

For English Protestants, as for many centuries of Jewish and Christian theologians before them, the ability of the Psalms to embody a voice at once individual and representative, human and divine, rendered these texts the privileged source of praise and prayer.[28] The notion that the Psalms were inherently adaptable to the situation of any worshipper dates at least to the fourth-century the-

ologian St. Athanasius, whose description of the Psalms was reprinted in the
prefatory pages of Matthew Parker, archbishop of Canterbury's 1567 Psalter:

> There every one may see and perceive the motions and affections of his own heart
> and soul, both to see whereto he is inclined, and where he is strained and
> pinched, so that he may have a very good form of prayer therefore. . . . There be in
> other books words and sentences, which forbid diverse vices and enormities, but
> this book prescribeth a form, how a man may be clear of them, & how to avoid
> them. . . . Whosoever take this book in his hand, he reputeth and thinketh all the
> words he readeth to be as his very own words spoken in his own person.[29]

Athanasius's slightly younger contemporary, St. Basil, whose commentary upon
the Psalms is also included in Parker's brief anthology of ancient texts, similarly
remarks that "the revelation of all mysteries . . . be laid and couched up in the
Psalter book, as in a great treasure house common to all men."[30] Comparable
accounts pervade the writings of Protestant theologians and liturgists: John
Calvin, for example, exclaims that it is "not without cause [that] I am wont to
term this book the Anatomy of all the parts of the soul, inasmuch as a man shall
not find any affection in himself, whereof the Image appeareth not in this
glass"; and the Puritan divine Richard Bernard declares in *Davids Musick* (1616):
"there is no condition of any in prosperity or adversity, peace or wars, health or
sickness, inward or outward distress, with many particular causes in all these
kinds, but he shall find some Psalms, which he may think almost to have been
composed upon his own occasion."[31]

Within the regular practice of liturgical worship, English parishioners would
have encountered two different versions of the Psalms. As we have already observed, the Coverdale Psalms that were bound with most editions of the liturgy
were written in prose, and were read according to the "Table for the Order of
the Psalms, to be said at Morning and Evening Prayer" (frontispiece) that was
included in the prefatory pages of the Prayer Book. Because these Psalms were
meant to be recited aloud or sung in plainchant, and not simply to be read in
private, they were printed verse by verse in order to facilitate their congregational use.[32] In addition, by the early Elizabethan period, Coverdale's prose
translations were supplemented by metrical Psalms specifically designed for
congregational singing accompanied by music.[33]

The Church of England's tolerance for congregational song was not to be
taken for granted; Western Christianity had a long history of ambivalence surrounding scriptural music that can be traced to Augustine's famous account in
book 10 of the *Confessions*:

> Now in these sweet tunes which thy holy Scriptures give so lively a grace unto,
> when they be sung with the sweet voice of cunning men: I do confess that I am

somewhat delectably holden, but yet not for that I would dwell and abide still there. . . . For sometimes I think I esteem this musical harmony more highly than is convenient. . . . So again while that I eschew this subtle deceit of my senses, beyond due measure I err on the other wise, by overmuch sober gravity, yea so far otherwhiles, that I would all such sweet harmony of delectable singing, wherewith David's Psalter is used to be sung, utterly removed not from mine own ears only, but banished out of the church. . . . But more am I inclined and induced to allow this custom of singing in the church (although I speak not this as in sentence definitive) that the weaker sort of men, might by such delectation of the ear, rise up to godly affection and heavenly devotion. Notwithstanding, when I feel this in my self that the melody moveth me more than the matter of the ditty which is sung, I confess then that I offend mortally therein, & then wish I rather not to hear such singing than so to hear it.[34]

Calvin reduces similar sentiments to the declaration that "voice and singing" are to be "highly commend[ed] . . . so that they accompany the affection of the mind. For so they exercise the mind and hold it intentive in thinking upon God: which as it is slippery and rolling, easily slacketh & is diversely drawn, unless it be stayed with diverse helps."[35] He too concludes with a note of caution: "we must diligently beware that our ears be not more heedfully bent to the note, than our minds to the spiritual sense of the words."[36]

A far less guarded enthusiasm for sacred song as a devotional tool can be traced to Martin Luther, who actively participated in translating Latin Psalms and composing scripturally based hymns for his fellow Germans. As he explains in a 1522 letter to the court chaplain George Spalatin: "Following the example of the prophets and fathers of the church, I intend to make German psalms for the people, i.e. spiritual songs so that the Word of God even by means of song may live among the people."[37] In England, the Lutheran position was first adopted by Coverdale himself, who translated a selection of Luther's works into English in a printed volume entitled *Goostly Psalmes and spirituall songes drawen out of the holy scripture* (ca. 1535). Coverdale announces his purpose for these hymns in his prefatory verses:

> Go lytle boke, get the acquaintaunce
> Among the lovers of Gods worde
> Geve them occasyon the same to avaunce
> And to make theyr songes of the Lorde
> That they may thrust under the borde
> All other balettes of fylthynes
> And that we all with one accorde
> May geve ensample of godlynes.[38]

At this early moment in the English Reformation, Coverdale does not imagine that his vernacular songs will replace the Latin hymns still sung in the English church. And indeed, unlike their German counterparts, English Protestants did not in fact develop a tradition of singing vernacular hymns in church that only loosely paraphrased Scripture until the late seventeenth century. As I have already mentioned, the Prayer Book did not include the translated hymns from the Sarum rite that we find in the Edwardian Primer of 1551 and the Elizabethan Primer of 1559; nor were these traditional liturgical songs, many of which were ascribed to St. Ambrose, replaced with alternative Protestant hymns such as Coverdale's.[39] Instead, echoing a position that had recently been expressed by Erasmus in the 1516 preface to his Greek and Latin New Testament, and significantly anticipated in the early fourteenth-century confessional text by Mannyng, Coverdale hopes that his spiritual music will help to eradicate the worldly songs so popular among the common people in secular occupations:

> I would God that our minstrels had none other thing to play upon, neither our carters & ploughmen other things to whistle upon, save Psalms, hymns, and such godly songs as David is occupied withal. And if women sitting at their rocks, or spinning at the wheels, had none other songs to pass their time withal, than such as Moses' sister, Elchanas's wife, Debora, and Mary the mother of Christ have sung before then, they should be better occupied, than with hey nony nony, hey troly loly, & such like fantasies.[40]

The songs that Coverdale includes—"grounded on God's word, and taken some out of the holy scripture, specially out of the Psalms of David"—are meant both to teach and to delight. "Would God," he concludes, "that our Musicians would learn to make their songs: & that they which are disposed to be merry, would not . . . pass their time in naughty songs of fleshly love and wantonness, but with singing of Psalms and such songs as edify, & corrupt not men's conversation."[41] And yet, although Coverdale claims that his holy songs are designed to be sung at work and play rather than in church, his decision to include metrical versions of the Creed, the Pater Noster, the Ten Commandments, and the Nunc Dimittis (the song of Simeon) among his Psalm translations—along with his declaration in the dedicatory poem that his songs be sung "with one accord"—strongly suggest an interest in liturgical as well as secular applications.

Coverdale's Lutheran tunes were apparently not a favorite with the ever-vacillating Henry VIII, who, according to John Foxe, included *Goostly psalmes* on his list of banned books as part of a larger campaign in 1539 to halt evangelical reform.[42] When Edward VI came to the throne, and vernacular publications of Scripture and prayer flourished again without impediment, a new collection of metrical Psalms composed by one of the king's grooms, Thomas Sternhold, quickly gained ascendancy in the royal court. Although Sternhold's Psalms were published as early as 1549, they were not widely used outside of King Edward's household during this period. It was not until the Catholic reign of Mary I that English Protestants living abroad adopted the Continental habit of Psalm-singing in the church, and began to employ Sternhold's translations as part of their liturgical service.

Upon the Marian exiles' return to England in 1559, they brought with them an incomplete English Psalter of "One and Fiftie Psalmes of David" that had originally been published for congregational use in Geneva; this volume included all thirty-seven of Sternhold's Psalms as well as seven additional Psalms composed by John Hopkins, and seven new Psalms composed in Geneva by the minister William Whittingham.[43] Over the next few years the remaining Psalms were translated, so that in 1562 the queen's printer, John Day, could publish a complete version, entitled *The Whole booke of Psalmes, collected into Englysh metre by T. Starnhold, J. Hopkins & others.* This Psalter, which is commonly known as Sternhold-Hopkins, satisfied the seemingly contagious desire for metrical Psalms that had swept the English people.[44] Thus in a 1560 letter to Peter Martyr, John Jewel remarks with astonishment that "[y]ou may now sometimes see at Paul's Cross, after the service, six thousand persons, old and young, of both sexes, all singing together and praising God."[45] In some cases, the laity's excessive zeal may have interfered with the service itself: in December 1559 a group of Londoners accompanied by some of the Exeter locals apparently invaded the choir of Exeter Cathedral, and "usurp[ing] the places of the lay clerks . . . sang metrical Psalms at the early morning service, unbidden and unlicensed."[46]

Although the church required no single metrical Psalter, the Psalms of Sternhold-Hopkins quickly assumed the status of an official liturgical text.[47] As its 1567 title page announces, the volume was "allowed to be sung in all churches, of all the people together, before and after morning and evening prayer, as also before and after the sermon." Whereas the 1562 and 1565 title pages had merely declared, "Very meet to be used of all sorts of people privately for their solace & comfort," by 1567 Sternhold-Hopkins had openly laid claim to the public sphere of devotion.

The enormous success of Sternhold-Hopkins can largely be traced to its accommodations of Prayer Book worship. Sternhold-Hopkins's translations were heavily influenced by Coverdale's prose Psalms in the Great Bible, which, as we have seen, were already part of the church's daily services, and were therefore very familiar to English parishioners. The Great Bible's Thirty-eighth Psalm, for example, begins as follows:

> Put me not to rebuke (O Lord) in thine anger: neither chasten me in thine heavy displeasure. For thine arrows stick fast in me: and thy hand presseth me fore.

There is no health in my flesh because of thy displeasure: neither is there any rest in my bones, by reason of my sin.

In Sternhold-Hopkins, this text is faithfully transformed into the verses:

> Put me not to rebuke, O Lord,
> in thy provoked ire:
> Ne in thy heavy wrath, O Lord,
> correct me I desire.
> Thine arrows do stick fast in me,
> thy hand doth presse me fore:
> And in my flesh no health at all
> appeareth any more.

To facilitate the range of uses for the Psalms within the Prayer Book's services, Sternhold-Hopkins also includes multiple translations for heavily used petitions such as the Fifty-first Psalm (*Miserere mei Deus*), the most frequently recited Penitential Psalm, which occupied a central position in the Commination (Ash Wednesday) service. In its Great Bible translation, this Psalm begins: "Have mercy upon me, (O God,) after thy great goodness: according to the multitude of thy mercies, do away mine offences. Wash me thoroughly from my wickedness, and cleanse me from my sin." Sternhold-Hopkins provides two metrical versions, one of which, written by Hopkins, closely echoes Coverdale's prose:

> Have mercy on me (Lord) after
> thy great abounding grace:
> After thy mercies multitude
> do thou my sinnes deface.
> Yea wash me more from mine offence,
> And cleanse me from my sinne:
> For I do know my faults, and still
> my sinne is in mine eyn.
> Against thee, thee alone I have
> offended in this case:
> And evil have I done before
> the presence of thy face.

The other version of this Psalm, written by Whittingham, freely departs from the Great Bible translation:

> Lord consider my distresse, and now with speed some pitie take:
> My sinnes deface, my faultes redresse, good Lord for thy great mercies sake.
> Wash me, O Lord, and make me clean from this unjust and sinfull act,
> And purifie yet once again my hainous crime and bloudy fact.

In addition to their different sources and different musical settings, the two Psalms reflect spiritual emphases that are subtly distinct: while Whittingham focuses on the sinfulness of the carnal self—"my heinous crime and bloody fact"—Hopkins describes an internal, conscience-stricken guilt felt more directly in relation to God.

As a further sign of its efforts to satisfy all possible liturgical needs, Sternhold-Hopkins provides a series of metrical prayers and blessings that range from "the song of Zacharias, called *Benedictus*," "the Songe of Blessed Mary, called *Magnificat*," and "the Song of Simeon, called *Nunc dimittis*," to the Lord's Prayer and the Creed. Although there is little evidence that these metrical prayers were ever widely used in English congregations, William Whittingham, the author of many of the Sternhold-Hopkins Psalms as well as the probable editor of its first edition, was said to have introduced all of these materials into his church at Durham "to accommodate every part of the service to the psalmodic tone."[48]

Above all other factors, the success of Sternhold-Hopkins can perhaps best be explained by its simple metrical form. Whereas the French Psalter of Clement Marot and Théodor de Bèze (1562) compiled for use in Calvin's congregation at Geneva employs more than one hundred different meters, the English Psalter consistently employs a "common meter" of fourteeners—single lines of four and three beats, or alternating, shorter lines of eight and six beats.[49] In its ballad stanzas and doggerel rhymes, Sternhold-Hopkins reconceived of the Psalms as a collection of easy and familiar congregational songs. Indeed, if the popularity of this Psalter derived largely from its compatibility with the Prayer Book and its easily graspable lyrics, it did not depend upon its status as poetic verse. Despite audible complaints later on, there is very little evidence that this Psalter was poetically evaluated—either negatively or positively—throughout most of the Elizabethan period.

This lack of attention ought not to suggest, however, that English Protestants regarded Sternhold-Hopkins as generically different from what we would consider to be more poetically ambitious translations. In ways that their subsequent reception has largely obscured from critical view, English metrical Psalters were regarded as texts of devotion and not also as poems throughout most of the sixteenth century. Collections of poetry like Richard Tottel's *Songes and Sonnettes* do not include the Psalm paraphrases of Thomas Wyatt or Henry Howard, earl of Surrey within their selections from these authors; the popular Elizabethan miscellany, *The Paradyse of dainty devises* (1576), similarly omits the Psalm translations of one of its principal contributors, William Hunnis, who had published a volume of selected metrical Psalms in 1550.[50] Moreover, the title pages and prefatory materials for metrical translations during this period do not align the contents of religious verse with the practice of poetry. From John Hall's *Certayne Psalmes of David drawen in meter* to Wyatt's *Certayne Psalmes chosen out of the Psalter of David . . . drawen into englysche meter;* from William Hunnis's *Seven Sobs of A Sorrowful Soule For Sinne . . . framed into a forme of familiar praiers, and reduced into meeter* to Matthew Parker's *The whole Psalter translated into English Metre*, nowhere does the term *poesy* or any of its cognates appear.[51]

Even the recurring emphasis on meter does not seem to produce any associative links with poetry per se, but instead serves to separate these translations from their prose counterparts. Attention to the aesthetic dimension of these texts does quietly inform the ways in which translation is described: the past participles *framed, reduced,* and *drawn* all convey a sense of artful labor, an act of creating a carefully delineated object out of a more amorphous or formless original. And yet, although these clues suggest that something other than strict translation is at work, there was no explicit connection made during most of the sixteenth century between the composition of metrical Psalms and what we would now consider the poetic production of lyric.

"HEAVENLY POESY"

When Philip Sidney openly declares in *An Apology for Poetry* that "the holy David's Psalms are a divine poem," he makes an important polemical claim.[52] This is not to say that Sidney's identification of the Psalms as poetry is itself unique. The Psalms were understood as superior examples of lyrical verse by Jewish and Christian theologians throughout the ages; although the exact form of the Old Testament verse remained entirely unknown until the eighteenth century, when the nature of Hebrew parallelism was first understood, theologians and historians dating at least to the first century sought to locate in the Psalms classical forms of hymns and odes.[53]

In the medieval period, prominent European poets including Dante and Petrarch had experimented with original paraphrases of the Penitential Psalms; the first English Protestant versions belonged to Sir Thomas Wyatt, whose *terza rima* translation of these seven Psalms was composed sometime in the late 1530s.[54] There are also frequent references to David's status as a poet in sixteenth-century English accounts before Sidney's. Among other examples, Parker cites in his Psalter an excerpt from Eusebius that describes the "eloquent [Hebrew] orators, for they have verses and Poesies made by most exquisite art and cunning, as that great Canticle of Moses, & the 118. Psalm of David"; Parker's own prefatory poem "Of the virtue of Psalms" praises David as "the singing man: and poet muse"; and Thomas Lodge in his *Defence of Poetry, Music and Stage Plays* asserts that "[a]mong the precise Jews you shall find Poets, including David, Esay, Job and Solomon."[55]

What differentiates Sidney's argument from those of his contemporaries, however, and what marks the *Apology* as a significant intervention in England's reception of the Psalms, is its extended and polemically charged insistence on the Psalms' poeticality independent of their devotional content:

> Even the name of Psalms will speak for me, which being interpreted, is nothing but songs; then that it is fully written in metre, as all learned Hebricians agree, although the rules be not yet fully found; lastly and principally, his handling his prophecy, which is merely poetical: for what else is the awaking his musical instruments, the often and free changing of persons, his notable *prosopopoeias*, when he maketh you, as it were, see God coming in His majesty, his telling of the beasts' joyfulness and hills leaping, but a heavenly poesy?[56]

Of course, Sidney was interested neither in divesting the Psalms of their sacred status, nor in diminishing the stature of David by conjoining what many of his contemporaries understood as fundamentally antithetical enterprises: "But truly now having named him," he continues, "I fear me I seem to profane that holy name, applying it to poetry, which is among us thrown down to so ridiculous an estimation."[57] And yet, Sidney's purpose is not simply to affirm the Psalms' holiness—a hardly contestable point—but instead to defend poetry as a legitimate devotional practice. In a sentiment that we will return to later, Sidney concludes by appealing to those "with quiet judgements" who, looking "a little deeper into it [the name of poetry], shall find the end and working of it such as, being rightly applied, deserveth not to be scourged out of the Church of God."[58]

Sidney's *Apology for Poetry* participated in, and probably helped to provoke, a widespread rethinking of the distinction between poetry and devotion at the end of the Elizabethan period.[59] For the first time within the history of English poetry, writers of religious verse begin to think seriously about the relationship between original poems and metrical translations of the Psalms. Tensions over the possibilities for "heavenly poesy" surface above all in response to the emergence in the 1590s of Protestant sonnet series that are neither liturgically nor scripturally based, and that openly announce themselves as poems. From the perspective of English literary history, the impulse to produce these sonnets can easily be explained as a straightforward appropriation of a secular genre for devotional purposes.[60] Evidence for this argument is readily available in texts such as Barnabe Barnes's *Divine Centurie of Spirituall sonnets*, in which Barnes describes his poetic endeavors as a sign of his conversion from "lewde laies" in very much the manner that Miles Coverdale advocated (and John Donne will later imitate):

> No more lewde laies of Lighter loves I sing,
> Nor teach my lustfull Muse abus'de to flie . . .
> But my Muse fethered with an Angels wing
> Divinely mounts aloft unto the skie.[61]

And yet, our critical emphasis on the apparently simple shift of the sonnet series from a secular to a religious register does not acknowledge the significant challenge that this borrowing would have posed within mainstream religious culture, where to many the very name "spiritual sonnet" would have been a troubling designation.[62]

For authors interested in laying claim to both the religious and the poetic integrity of their sonnets, the difficult task was to justify how a predominantly secular and artificial form could be devotionally efficacious. A powerful instance of such an effort surfaces in Henry Lok's *Sundry Christian Passions, contained in two hundred sonnets*, in which Lok explains the challenge of composing these sonnets as one of legitimizing a clearly poetic form as a devotional medium. Lok begins by assigning to the sonnet an exemplary function similar to that which Athanasius or Calvin assigned to the Psalms. In his "Letter to the Christian Reader," the author grounds his hope that the sonnets will "serve for precedents for my self in the like future occasions: and not be altogether unprofitable for others to imitate" in a discussion of poetry's merits:

> As for the apt nature of Poetry, to delight, to contrive significatively in few words much matter, to pierce and penetrate affections of men, with the aptness thereof, for help of memory, I will not say much: but for my deducing these passions and affections into Sonnets, it answereth best for the shortness, to the nature, and common humor of men.[63]

Published alongside the 1597 edition of *Sundry Christian Passions* is Lok's translation of the Book of Ecclesiastes, which, unlike the metrical texts of Scripture issued earlier in the century, boldly announces its poetic claims: "*Ecclesiastes, Otherwise Called the Preacher,* Containing Solomon's Sermons or Commentaries (as it may probably be collected) upon the 49. Psalm of David his father. Compendiously abridged, *and also paraphrastically dilated in English poesy.*"

At the same time that figures such as Lok seek to justify the appropriateness of poetic form for devotional purposes, others cling tightly to the nonpoetic status of their metrical texts. In an effort to distance his translations of sacred hymns and songs from the creative labor of poetry that he himself practiced elsewhere, Michael Drayton explains in the dedicatory letter to *The Harmonie of the Church, Containing The Spirituall Songes and holy hymnes, of godly men, patriarkes, and Prophetes* (1591) that his texts should be "measure[d] . . . not by my ability, but by their authority: not as Poems of Poets, but prayers of Prophets."[64] Drayton's acute awareness of the tensions between poetry and prayer and his desire to align his poetic translations with Scripture rather than fiction are further elaborated in his letter "To the courteous Reader":

> Here I present thee with these Psalms or Songs of praise, so exactly translated as the prose would permit, or sense would any way suffer me: which (if thou shalt

be the same in heart thou art in name, I mean a Christian) I doubt not, but thou
wilt take as great delight in these, as in any Poetical fiction. (sig. b2)

The author's pains to distance himself from the act of invention do not cancel
out his desire to compete with those writers of "poetical fiction" for the ability
to please his readers. Instead, this simultaneous invocation and refusal of the
parallels between holy songs and poems, coupled with Drayton's earlier insistence that his texts should be read "not as Poems of Poets, but prayers of
Prophets," seems designed to rebuff the divine poeticality that Sidney proposes
without relinquishing the "delight" of strictly scriptural verse.

What Sidney has in mind, however, is more radical than what is seemingly
imagined in either Drayton's dismissal or Lok's affirmation of devotional poetry.
In the passage quoted earlier from the *Apology*, Sidney does not aim only to legitimize devotional poetry as a source for spiritual comfort, but instead means to
establish its rightful inclusion within the language of the church: "they that
with quiet judgements will look a little deeper into it, shall find the end and
working of it such as, being rightly applied, deserveth not to be scourged out of
the Church of God."

Now, in one sense the notion that poetry was in danger of being "scourged"
from Christian devotion could not have been a serious concern: metrical Psalters had been in regular use in English churches and cathedrals since the 1550s.
Moreover, the Protestant interest in the poetry of the Psalms for liturgical purposes dates to Luther's 1522 letter to Spalatin in which he explains his hope that
German Psalms and songs will be composed by gifted poets: "We are seeking
everywhere for poets, and since you are gifted with such knowledge of the German language and command so elegant a style, cultivated by much use, I beg
that you will work with us in the matter."[65] In England, however, because there
had been no similarly explicit identification of the metrical Psalms as poems,
there had also been no official recognition of poetry's place in the church. Once
Sidney assigns the label of poetry to this body of devotional texts, he forces a
new attention to the relationship between poetry and liturgy, a relationship that
was formerly unproblematic precisely because no one had demanded that
David's Psalms—however elaborately versified—be recognized as anything
other than texts of praise and prayer.

THE SIDNEY-PEMBROKE PSALTER

O all you landes the treasures of your joy
in mery shout upon the lord bestow:
your service cheerfully on him imploy,
with triumph song into his presence goe.

know first that he is god; and after know
this god did us, not we our selves create:
we are his flock, for us his feedings grow:
we are his folk, and he upholds our state.
with thankfulnesse, o enter then his gate:
make through each porch of his your praises ring.
all good, all grace, of his high name relate,
he of all grace and goodnesse is the spring.
Tyme in noe termes his mercy comprehends,
from age to age his truth it self extends.[66]

This simple song of thanksgiving and praise is the translation of the One
Hundredth Psalm by Mary Sidney Herbert, the countess of Pembroke. It is also
a perfect sonnet. The brief, joyful verses that constitute the Hebrew text are here
reconceived within the formal structures of Elizabethan poetry; the sonnet
maintains its traditional Petrarchan role as a vehicle for praise, but this praise is
now spoken on behalf of the community of worshippers, not the poet.

It is in the context of Sidney's insistence that "the holy David's Psalms are a
divine poem" and that poetry "deserveth not to be scourged from the Church of
God" that I want to situate the Psalter that he began, and that his sister completed and revised in the years following his death in 1586 (by then, Sidney had
composed the initial versions of the first forty-three Psalms; the Countess of
Pembroke revised his verses and translated Psalms 44 through 150).[67] As the
critical literature on this text reveals, there is little consensus on how these
Psalms ought to be read or received. For many scholars and editors, the collaborative text represents above all a sustained and theologically serious effort to
produce a faithful translation of the Psalms. Although the question of whether
either Pembroke or Sidney knew Hebrew remains unanswered, evidence suggests that they had access to the original language through either their own
limited knowledge or the help of learned friends.[68] As a sign of the authors'
commitment to producing a learned and distinctly Protestant text, the Sidney-
Pembroke Psalms are heavily inflected by both Continental and English biblical
scholarship, including the Geneva Bible; the Marot-Bèze Psalter; and the commentaries of Calvin and Bèze.[69]

At the same time that modern editors have well established the biblical
scrupulousness of the Sidney-Pembroke Psalter, attention to its accuracy as a
translation has often been overshadowed by critics interested in emphasizing its
poetic virtuosity. This emphasis turns on two largely implicit yet central definitions of poetic achievement. First, poetry as a display of formal, or technical excellence: the Sidney-Pembroke Psalter has long been praised for a range of
metrical invention and originality without parallel in sixteenth-century reli-

gious verse. In the words of Hallett Smith echoed by subsequent generations of critics, this text represents nothing less than a virtual "School of English Versification"; according to editorial calculations, there are only four instances in the entire collection where a single form and rhyme scheme are repeated.[70] Second, poetry as the expression of a personal and individualized voice: literary critics have sought to assimilate the formal accomplishments of these Psalms with a Petrarchan model of lyric. In place of the liturgical voice of the scriptural Psalmist, these Psalms are said to possess an introspective speaker whose words are more distinctly fictionalized and subjective.[71]

In chapter 4 we will consider the ways in which this characterization of lyric as the embodiment of a particular form of I has prejudiced readers against certain kinds of early modern poetry; for now, I want to show that the Sidney-Pembroke Psalter defies the critical assumption that formal excellence and private voice inevitably join, and that it does so specifically by applying poetic techniques to a simultaneously personal and liturgical model of devotion. Although this Psalter was not intended for church use—no musical settings were provided in any of the authoritative manuscripts, and Pembroke made no efforts to publish the volume, which did not see print until the nineteenth century[72]—its poetic achievements powerfully reflect many of the principles that shaped the established liturgy. The use of a paradigmatic or representative speaker; the non-specificity, and hence reiterability of the text; the commitment to formalized language as the ideal medium for communicating one's prayers: each of these aspects of common prayer resonates powerfully within the Sidney-Pembroke Psalms. The model of poetry that emerges from this text does not depend upon the presence of a fictionalized speaker who conveys a radically individualized experience—this may be the province of *Astrophil and Stella,* but it is not the "divine poem" that Sidney seeks to generate here.

The liturgical orientation of Sidney and Pembroke's approach can easily be grasped if we compare one of their Penitential Psalms to Wyatt's, whose paraphrases more clearly reflect what literary critics identify as "poetic" adaptations of these texts. This is not to deny the distinctly Protestant theology that pervades Wyatt's Psalms: he emphasizes God's grace over David's merit; he distinguishes between David's penitence and God's mercy as the vehicle for David's spiritual healing; and he shows an attention to the relationship between internal and external states of grief that cannot be traced to his primary source, the Italian paraphrase of these Psalms by Pietro Aretino, published in 1534. And yet, despite their theological affinities with the Reformed faith, Wyatt's highly introspective and complex translations remain decidedly outside of the devotional models for prayer that Cranmer introduced during the reign of Edward VI, who came to the throne five years after Wyatt's death in 1542.

After an elaborate narrative preface closely modeled after Aretino, conveying

David's state of anguished grief, Wyatt begins the Thirty-eighth Psalm:

> O LORD, as I the[e] have both prayd and pray,
> (Altho in the be no alteration
> But that we men, like as our sellfes we say,
> Mesurying thy Justice by our Mutation)
> Chastice me not, o lord, in thi furour,
> Nor me correct in wrathfull castigation.
> For that thi arrows off fere, off terrour
> Of sword, of sekenes, off famine and fyre
> Stikkes diepe in me. I, lo, from myn errour
> Ame plongid up, as horse owt of the myre
> With strok off spur: such is thi hand on me
> That in my fleshe for terrour of thy yre
> Is not on[e] poynt of ferme stabilite.[73]

Wyatt's taste for enjambment and parenthetical musings create a rhetorically as well as psychically complex petition that seems inherently unsuitable for congregational reiteration.

Philip Sidney, by contrast, creates a highly accessible and melodic lyric not dissimilar in tone from that of Sternhold-Hopkins:

> Lord, while that thy rage doth bide,
> Do not chide
> Nor in anger chastise me,
> For thy shafts have pierc'd me sore;
> And yet more
> Still thy hands upon me be.
>
> No sound part caus'd by thy wrath
> My flesh hath,
> Nor my synns lett my boanes rest;
> For my faults are highly spredd
> On my hedd,
> Whose foule weights have me opprest.[74]

The lack of a pronounced introspection on the part of the speaker, who describes things happening externally rather than internally (hence the repeated *mes* and absence of *I*s); the simple rhymes of "bide" and "chide," "spredd" and "head" in marked contrast to Wyatt's complex rhyme of "alteration," "castigation," and "mutation"; and the overall brevity of the lines combine to create more of a congregational hymn than a personal meditation.

It is not only through comparison to Wyatt that the Sidney-Pembroke Psalter reveals its affinities with the liturgical texts of the church: the formal design of these Psalms in many ways corresponds to that of metrical texts explicitly intended for congregational use. In keeping with their mostly English and French scriptural sources, Sidney and Pembroke do not individualize or stabilize the frequently shifting voice of the original Hebrew texts, which varies among a first-person singular, first-person plural, or third-person subject. In the Fifth Psalm, for example, the initial tone of personal petition gives way to a distanced, third-person pastoral voice:

> Ponder the wordes, O Lord, that I doe say
> Consider what I meditate in me:
> O harken to my voice which calls on thee
> My king, my God, for I to thee will play . . . $(1-4)$
> So shall all they that trust on thee doe bend,
> And love the sweete sound of thy name, rejoyce:
> They ever shall send thee their praising voice;
> Since ever thou to them wilt succour send.
> Thy work it is to bless, thou blessedst them;
> The just in thee, on thee and justice build:
> Thy work it is such men safe in to hemm
> With kindest care, as with a certain shield. (lines $33-40$)[75]

And in the Seventy-fifth Psalm, Pembroke emphasizes the transition from the corporate *we* to David's own *I* by including both voices within the first stanza:

> Thee god, o thee, wee sing, we celebrate:
> thy actes with wonder who but doth relate?
> so kindly nigh thy name our need attendeth.
> sure I, when once the chardg I undergo
> of this assembly, will not faile to show
> my judgments such, as justest rule commendeth.[76]

Sidney and Pembroke's interest in creating a series of texts that seems open to reiteration at both a personal and congregational level sheds light as well on the decision to eliminate all narrative frames from their translations. Not only do these Psalms conspicuously lack the elaborate prefaces that Wyatt provides, but they do not include even the brief "arguments" or superscriptions that we find in nearly all complete versions of the Psalms. The Geneva Bible, for example, provides the following preface to the Ninetieth Psalm, which is attributed to Moses:

> Moses in his prayer setteth before us the eternal favour of God towards his, Who are neither admonished by the brevity of their life, Nor by his plagues to be

thankful, Therefore Moses prayeth God to turn their hearts & continue his mercies toward them, & their posterity for ever.

By contrast, Pembroke includes only the first words of the Vulgate translation, "Domine Refugium," as her heading or title. In refusing to emphasize the Psalm's particularity as an Old Testament petition, she seems to encourage a specific kind of imaginative reclaiming by her readers, who are not asked to identify with Moses before assuming these words as their own. Although this impulse can in part be explained as an erasure of the Psalms' Jewish origins—as her editor Margaret Hannay notes, Pembroke's access to the Psalms was certainly "filtered through Christian eyes"—it seems at least equally motivated by a desire to purge the texts of historical or scriptural specificity.[77] Thus Pembroke resists all opportunities to incorporate contemporary polemical references of the sort that fill the Geneva Bible as well as the commentaries of Calvin and Bèze.[78] Far from representing, in the words of one critic, "a fictional reorientation" which "rubs out ritual, making it relatively difficult (as against the practices of their contemporaries) not only to sing the poems but to re-experience them," Sidney and Pembroke's Psalms seem designed to simulate a book of liturgical prayers.[79]

As I have already noted, the Sidney-Pembroke Psalter was never published during the countess's lifetime. In the two dedicatory poems that survive from one of the authoritative sixteenth-century manuscripts of her Psalms, Pembroke reveals no ambition for these texts to be circulated beyond a very limited circle: "Even now that Care" presents the Psalms to Elizabeth I for the queen's personal use, while "To the Angell Spirit of Sir Phillip Sidney" opens by declaring, "To thee pure sprite, to thee alone's addres't / this coupled worke."[80] And yet, notwithstanding the conventional topoi of exclusivity and privacy that both of these dedications express, it seems likely that Pembroke at least contemplated the possibility that her translations might serve a much wider audience.

First, her distant cousin and fellow poet John Harington, who acquired two manuscript copies of the Psalter, encourages her to publish the collection in his *Treatise on playe* (1597):

> seeing it already prophecied those previous leaves (Those hymns that she doth consecrate to heaven) shall outlast Wilton's walls, methinks it is pity they are unpublished, but lie still enclosed within those walls like prisoners, though many have made great suit for their liberty.[81]

Harington's desire to liberate Pembroke's Psalms from her home at Wilton, and his mention of similar "suit[s]" having already been made by others, suggest a community of readers eager to share rather than to hoard these holy "hymns." As if to establish the potential efficacy of these Psalms as devotional texts, both of the manuscripts that Harington possessed were in fact "rubricated" (prepared with hand-written insertions that coordinated the Psalms with rubrics from the Prayer Book) so that at least his versions of this Psalter could be used during the observance of Morning and Evening Prayer.[82]

Second, in an earlier draft of "To the Angell Spirit," Pembroke alludes to her Psalms as an improvement upon the English Psalter:

> That Israels King may daygne his owne transform'd
> In substance no, but superficiall tire:
> And English guis'd in some sort may aspire
> To better grace thee what the vulgar form'd.[83]

Although in the final version, these lines shift from an earthly to a heavenly register—"Israels King" becomes "heavens King," and the English congregation is replaced with "Angels . . . in their caelestiall quire"—the initial critique of the church's Psalms as the product of "vulgar" minds, together with the suggestion that they could be better "graced," conveys an underlying interest in the project of liturgical reform.[84]

The countess of Pembroke's brief (and excised) expression of disdain for Sternhold-Hopkins places her squarely among a growing number of English Protestants in the late sixteenth and early seventeenth centuries who seek to reform the church's Psalms by poetic means.[85] So Joseph Hall, later the bishop of Norwich and Exeter, explains his decision to translate "some few of Davids Psalms" in the dedicatory letter to his 1607 volume, *Some few of Davids Psalms Metaphrased*: "Indeed, my Poetry was long since out of date, & yielded his place to graver studies: but whose [hope] would it not revive to look into these heavenly songs? I were not worthy to be a Divine, if it should repent me to be a poet with DAVID."[86]

Far from signaling an occupation incompatible with ecclesiastical life, the label of poet has now become a "worthy" role for members of the English Protestant establishment interested in making both liturgical and career improvements:

> Neither do I see how it can be offensive to our friends, that we should desire our english Metaphrase bettered . . . since our whole Translation is now universally revised; what inconvenience or show of innovation can it bear, that the verse should accompany the prose? especially since it is well known how rude & homely our English Poesy was in those times, compared with the present; wherein, if ever, it seeth her full perfection.[87]

Produced only half a century earlier, the Sternhold-Hopkins Psalter has already become a relic from a primitive time before England's poetry reached its current levels of "perfection." This discrepancy between the poetry that the nation is ca-

pable of producing and the poverty of its current Psalter can only be blamed,
Hall argues, on "the negligence of our people which endure not to take pains
for any fit variety." Although "the French and the Dutch have given us worthy
examples of a diligence and exquisiteness in this kind," the English congregation has become so habituated to the lyrics and tunes of their inferior Psalter
that they resist the opportunity for change. The problem involves a lack of will
rather than a lack of talent: "Neither our ears, or our voices are less tuneable.
Here is nothing wanting, but will to learn."[88]

Hall's charge against the English people resonates throughout George Wither's
1619 prose tract, *A Preparation to the Psalter*, in which Wither attacks those "who allow of *Meter*, but will give way to no new *versions*":

> Among these I meet with some that put doubts not worth the answering; and
> some others again, that frame objections a little better deserving reply: such as
> these, that another Translation of the *Psalms* into *Numbers*, being admitted of in our
> Congregations were an Innovation not to be suffered, by reason of this inconve-
> nience; that, say they, every man almost, is so well exercised in the *Psalms* and tunes
> allowable in our Church, that he can make one of the Choir.[89]

However "convenient" the Sternhold-Hopkins Psalter may be, Wither insists
that its poor poetic quality bears directly upon on its efficacy in promoting the
people's devotions:

> Because the Elegancies of those Sacred *Poems* have in our Language been over-
> meanly expressed (or rather for that the praises of God make tedious Music in the
> ears of most men) they have seemed unto many but barren and simple *Poesy*, and
> the greater number take so small heed of their excellency, that, for ought I can per-
> ceive, they sing or read them with the same devotion, wherewith (as the Proverb
> is) Dogs go to Church.[90]

Why is it, Wither asks, that "the praises of God [should] make tedious Music"?
Instead of being attentive and appreciative worshippers, the congregation be-
haves like "dogs," or, to return to Cranmer's slur upon the Catholics, "pies or
parrots," performing their prayers without real understanding. For Wither, the
solution lies in eloquent poesy: just as Hooker describes common prayer as that
which "stealeth" into the "souls of men as with certain baits," so Wither imagines powerful verse as possessing "an enchanting sweetness, that steals into the
hearts of men before they be aware" (9).

If the congregation's devotional laziness results from its repeated exposure to
"barren and simple Poesy," Wither concludes that it can only be resolved by el-
evating the people's experience of the Psalms as poems. For although England
has on the whole become a nation of literary critics, few have been able to recover the literary achievement of the Psalms. Wither remarks that if he were to

enter into a conversation with a group of Englishmen concerning the poetic excellence of the Psalms, he would be met with a polite, but unenthusiastic response: "you may hear them perhaps, for fashion sake say, *They are good things*, or give them such slight commendations, as you may easily gather, they have neither true feeling of their power, nor sound opinion of their worth." And yet, if he were to ask the same gentlemen their feelings about Homer, Virgil, or Horace, they would instantly come to life:

> For in these they are Critics, and have ever one of them in their Pockets: you shall hear them, upon any slight occasion, break forth into their high commendations. They admire the extraordinary elegancy of this verse: the admirable facetiousness of that sentence; the unimitable expression of such a Simile; the singular proprieties that are in their words; the aptness of the Epithets; the rareness of their descriptions; the delicacy of their phrases; the depth of their inventions; the significance of their Metaphors; and the loftiness of their Hyperboles. (68)

If only, Wither concludes, the church's Psalter could capture the "unexpressible Poesy of these Psalms . . . [for] if we could be made capable of it, it were impossible that our ears should be touched with it, and our hearts insensible of a heavenly delight" (75).

By pointing to the efficacy of good poetry in the cultivation of faith, Wither offers a congregational justification for the use of poetic talent, or, to borrow a term introduced by Pembroke, the use of poetic *skill*. Pembroke employs this word in a striking departure from all of her sources in translating the opening verse of Psalm 111. In place of the Geneva Bible's "I will praise the Lord with my whole heart"; Coverdale's "I will give thanks unto the Lord with my whole heart"; Sternhold-Hopkins's "With heart I do accord / To praise and laud the Lord"; or Parker's "With all my heart I will: the Lord commend on high," Pembroke boldly declares: "At home, abroad, most willingly I will / Bestow on God my praises uttmost skill." "Uttmost skill": Pembroke's poetic craft is neither at odds with nor subordinated to her "whole heart," but serves as the highest medium for her devotional expressiveness. No longer an unremarked-upon vehicle to convey mnemonic or scriptural texts, poetry is now recognized as a separate category of devotional language whose formal achievements can be effectively deployed for liturgical ends. By the early seventeenth century, the act of writing a poem and rendering it skillfully in rhyme has become its own form of prayer.

CHAPTER FOUR

George Herbert and the
Devotional Lyric

*I*n his poem "Upon the translation of the Psalmes by Sir Philip Sydney, and the
Countess of Pembroke his Sister," written sometime following the countess
of Pembroke's death in 1621, John Donne explores the role that the Sidney-
Pembroke Psalms might play in reforming public devotion. Like Joseph Hall and
George Wither before him, Donne laments the poor quality of the Psalter used
in the established Church of England:

> When I behold that these Psalmes are become
> So well atttyr'd abroad, so ill at home,
> So well in Chambers, in thy Church so ill
> As I can scarce call that reform'd untill
> This be reform'd; Would a whole State present
> A lesser gift than some one man hath sent?
> And shall our Church, unto our Spouse and King
> More hoarse, more harsh than any other, sing?[1]

This initial complaint leads to Donne's proposal that the Sidney-Pembroke
Psalms, previously used only as private meditations in secret "chambers," replace Sternhold-Hopkins as the congregational Psalter. As if to make good upon
the rejected lines from the countess of Pembroke's dedicatory poem "To the Angell Spirit," in which she expressed her hope that her verses might better grace
the Psalms than "what the vulgar form'd," Donne anticipates the capacity of this
translation to glorify the prayers of the entire English people:

> Two that make one *John Baptists* holy voyce,
> And who that Psalme, *Now let the Iles rejoyce*,
> Have both translated, and apply'd it too,
> Both told us what, and taught us how to doe.
> They shew us Ilanders our joy, our King,
> They tell us *why*, and teach us *how* to sing. (lines 17–22)

The vehicle for this glorification lies in the repeated *how* in lines 20 and 22: the
Sidney-Pembroke Psalms should be adopted by the church because they dem-

onstrate the ideal way for the congregation to perform its praise and prayer. Whereas Sternhold-Hopkins was faulted for inadequately capturing the Psalms, this Psalter succeeds in conveying what Donne describes as "the highest matter in the noblest forme" (11).

Donne's claim that the liturgical efficacy of the Sidney-Pembroke Psalter lies in the power of its poetic forms neatly reflects the culmination of the position first articulated by Sidney in his *Apology for Poetry*: that poetry "deserveth not to be scourged out of the Church of God." This new appreciation of the role that poetry might play in heightening devotion not only affected seventeenth-century treatments of Sternhold-Hopkins and its competing Psalters, but also had substantial repercussions for the subsequent shape of original lyrics. For once metrical verse is valued within the church for the quality of its poetry, the devotional lyric emerges as a viable form of collective expression.

The notion that seventeenth-century poets often sought to create simultaneously personal and liturgical lyrics in a manner comparable to texts of public devotion directly contradicts our dominant critical account of this period's literature, an account that tends to identify private practices alone as capable of inspiring poetic expression. In his seminal work, *The Poetry of Meditation* (1954), Louis Martz argued that the "rapid upheavals and bitter controversies of the sixteenth-century's middle years" left England with a "deep inner need" that could be satisfied only by the individualized and private spiritual exercises associated with the Counter-Reformation, and not by the public devotions of the national church.[2] This understanding of England's devotional condition as both spiritually and textually bankrupt motivated Martz's account of the religious lyric, whose flourishing he attributes to the poet's effort to supplement the institutional utterances of the church with more personal and subjective devotion. The Catholic treatises, Martz contends, permeated not only the religious but also the literary imagination of the English people: the emphasis within these texts on achieving a heightened state of meditation encouraged a model of poetry whose aim was to evince such an act of contemplative withdrawal. Due to the clandestine nature of Catholic worship within an officially Protestant and Reformed nation, the religious lyric by extension becomes a strictly private devotional form.

So strongly did Martz's argument influence the critical conception of the devotional poet that even when it received its first formidable challenge, from Barbara Lewalski's *Protestant Poetics and the Seventeenth Century Religious Lyric* (1979), the association of the poet with meditative withdrawal escaped serious critique. Although Lewalski rejected Martz's alignment of the lyric with a Catholic tradition, she retained his assumption that the lyric originated in private devotional practices. Replacing the Counter-Reformation texts with their Reformed counterparts, Lewalski identified the Protestant practice of meditation on passages from Scripture, and the Calvinist emphasis on the worshipper's "painstaking analysis of the personal religious life," as responsible for shaping a new poetics in the seventeenth century. According to Lewalski, this model of poetry was "introspective [and] soul-searching"; the voice of the poet was one of spiritual interrogation, focusing on the particularity of individual sinfulness and the hope for individual redemption.[3]

In the decades following Lewalski's study, readers of seventeenth-century lyric have tended to construct impermeable boundaries between personal and liturgical poetry. Within this framework, "good" devotional poems are those that demonstrate their distance from the formalized examples of church worship. Anne Ferry, for example, compares the "formal, ritualistic liturgical" voice of Donne's "La Corona" sonnets with the more intimate and inward "Holy Sonnets," which, she contends, "do not strive for a representative public voice to utter what is in all hearts. In choosing for them a different mode, Donne freed their language from the kinds of constraints imposed by the liturgical style." The language of restriction that shapes this account of the so-called liturgical style demonstrates the common association of public worship with personal limitation; Ferry praises the "Holy Sonnets" for their loosening of the cords, their admission and exposure of the speaker's otherwise hidden "inward experience."[4]

As the preceding chapters have shown, this preference for poetry that seems private and original over that which seems formal and prescribed exactly mirrors Puritan attacks upon common prayer in the late sixteenth and early seventeenth centuries. The eventual poetic consequence of this contempt for formalized language lies in English Romanticism, for which we might simply recall Wordsworth's declaration in the preface to the *Lyrical Ballads*: "all good poetry is the spontaneous overflow of powerful feelings."[5] Although we may imagine ourselves to be detached from this late eighteenth-century definition of poetic creativity, the Romantic embrace of spontaneity has massively reinforced the Puritan antagonism toward set forms to create a dominant paradigm for reading early modern devotional verse, whereby we tend to assume that the poems we value reflect nonliturgical modes of expression.

If we shift our critical register from this privileging of private, spontaneous, and highly individuated voice toward poems that combine personal expression with what Donne identifies as the liturgical strengths of the Sidney-Pembroke Psalms, the seventeenth-century devotional lyric seems neither to anticipate the poetics of Wordsworth nor to derive its power exclusively from private meditational practices. Once we remove ourselves from our prejudices against liturgical language as artificial or insincere, we begin to see that what inspired many of the Protestant lyrics we most admire can be traced to the language used in the established church. When the two central principles that governed the texts of the Book of Common Prayer—the intertwining of the singular I and the collective we, and the absolute preference for formalized over spontaneous voice—are conjoined in the early 1600s with a belief in the liturgical power of eloquent verse, the possibility for a new form of poetry is released into the world.

Although there are a number of seventeenth-century poets who seem to be touched by this possibility, who feel its current, as it were, passing through their veins, it is most powerfully realized in George Herbert. For Herbert, writing devotional verse was simultaneously personal and communal, faithful and formal; in poem after poem of The Temple, the speaker intertwines the expression of his inner self with the creation of skillful texts that might be shared by fellow worshippers. The result of this poetic practice resembles neither the largely mnemonic and impersonal lyrics produced for lay worship in the late medieval church, nor the dauntingly complex and introspective Psalms like Thomas Wyatt's. For the first time in post-Reformation England, the devotional lyric discovers its inherent potential to become an act of common prayer.

"MORE DESIRE THAN SKILL"

In a 1625 sermon preached at St. Paul's Cross, Donne challenges the familiar Puritan notion that personal prayer can be generated through only original and extempore worship. "If [God] ask me an Idea of my prayers," he asks, "shall I not be able to say, It is that which thy word, and thy Catholic Church hath imprinted in me?" Praying spontaneously, Donne contends, not only severs the worshippers' ties to the church, but jeopardizes their chances for salvation:

> But if I come to pray or to preach without this kind of Idea, if I come to extemporal prayer, and extemporal preaching, I shall come to an extemporal faith, and extemporal religion; and then I must look for an extemporal Heaven, a Heaven to be made for me; for to that Heaven which belongs to the Catholic Church, I shall never come, except I go by the way of the Catholic Church, by former Ideas, former examples, former patterns.[6]

The triad of terms—"ideas," "examples," and "patterns"—which Donne characterizes as "imprinted" within him powerfully evokes the model of inwardness cultivated by the established church; the printed forms of the Prayer Book replace the untextualized and hence unreliable utterances of extempore prayer. "Let us not pray," Donne argues, "not preach, not hear, slackly, suddenly, unadvisedly, extemporally, occasionally, indiligently; but let all our speech to him, be weighed, and measured in the weights of the Sanctuary, let us be content to preach, and to hear within the compass of our Articles, and content to pray in those forms which the Church hath meditated for us, and recommended to us" (2:50). "Slackly, suddenly, unadvisedly, extemporally": far from representing, as Puritans maintained, the highest expression of the spirit, extempore prayer becomes a form of devotional sloth. For Donne, there ought to be no distinction between the petitions of the self and those of the church: "no prayer is so truly, or so properly mine," he elsewhere declares, "as that that the Church hath delivered and recommended to me" (9:218−19).

Donne's fervent insistence that liturgical forms supply the only appropriate language for speaking to God may seem to coincide with what many historians regard as the church's turn toward an Anglo-Catholic ceremonialism in the late 1620s and 1630s, when, under the leadership of William Laud, the Church of England began its program of revitalizing public devotion by reemphasizing the formal and sacramental aspects of religious practice.[7] Laud's commitment to restoring the "beauty of holiness" in the material church, most conspicuously manifested in his reintroduction of railed altars and stained glass, was accompanied by efforts to restore formalized prayer and the sacraments over the sermon at the center of public devotion. And yet, although Laud's emphasis on bowing, his attack on Sabbatarianism, and his redecoration of the church with devotional images certainly represented a marked departure from the dominant practices of the Elizabethan and Jacobean church, there was nothing particularly novel about the Laudian desire to secure liturgical worship at the center of devotional life. As we have repeatedly seen, the aversion to spontaneous prayers often associated with the decade immediately preceding the English civil war pervaded the established church, with varying degrees of intensity, from the midsixteenth century.

What is striking, however, about the early decades of the seventeenth century is a new self-consciousness about the role of rhetorical skill or eloquence in heightening the worshipper's devotion. Hence, when speaking to the congregation, Donne claims that the minister "shall not present the messages of God rudely, barbarously, extemporally; but with such meditation and preparation as appertains to so great an employment, from such a King as God, to such a State as his Church." For, he continues, it is the minister's obligation not only to preach truthfully or sincerely, but also "seasonably, with a spiritual delight," so that "by the way of such a holy delight, they may receive the more profit."[8] Behind Donne's opposition between rude and barbarous language on the one hand, and seasonable and premeditated speech on the other, lies the establishment's overwhelming presumption that spontaneity and eloquence were rarely if ever intertwined.

Surprisingly enough, this commitment to the efficacy of "delightful" forms was not limited to loyal adherents of the established church. Even John Milton, who so passionately advocates the power of exercising God's gift through immediate and extempore devotion in *Eikonoklastes*, later assigns the ability to pray both spontaneously and eloquently not to our world but to the world before the Fall. In the early books of *Paradise Lost*, Adam and Eve awake every morning to worship God in new and beautiful forms of praise:

> Lowly they bow'd adoring, and began
> Thir Orisons, each Morning duly paid
> In various style, for neither various style
> Nor holy rapture wanted they to praise
> Thir Maker, in fit strains pronounct or sung

Unmeditated, such prompt eloquence
Flow'd from thir lips, in Prose or numerous Verse
More tuneable than needed Lute or Harp
To add more sweetness. (5:144–52)

For this Edenic couple, prayer could be at once "unmeditated" and skillful—
what Milton neatly captures in the phrase "prompt eloquence."

In the postlapsarian world, however, Adam and Eve lose this capacity to produce beautiful prayers in either "prose or numerous verse." At the beginning of
book 11, the Son translates their wordless sighs and groans into language,
whose appeal he enhances with incense, before God can hear their fallen
prayers. "Now therefore bend thine ear / To supplication," the Son asks God,
"hear his sighs though mute / Unskilful with what words to pray, let mee / In-
terpret for him" (11:30–32). "Unskilful with what words to pray": no longer
the natural domain of human agency, the performance of prayer now depends
upon external mediation.[9]

The notion that spontaneous prayers cannot reliably achieve real eloquence
provides one of the period's central justifications for the necessity of formalized
prayers. Hence the Puritan divine Samuel Hieron begins his best-selling manual
for private prayer, *A Helpe unto Devotion* (1608), by announcing his aim to assist
"those who have more desire than skill to pour out their souls by petition unto
God."[10] This discrepancy between "desire" and "skill" once again contradicts
the notion that the most effective form of prayer would naturally pour out of
the worshipper's soul; despite the best intentions, Hieron argues, most worshippers "are not able to be their own messengers," a failing he attributes to
their "want of exercised wits, of knowledge in the Scriptures, and especially of
experience in the power of godliness, and of a lively sense and distinct conceiv-
ing of their own personal necessities" (sig. A3v–3r).

Hieron's aim in this popular text, which had reached its twenty-first edition
by 1639, is to teach those who have "as yet but stammering and lisping tongues,
until they shall be able, having tongues as fined silver, plainly and distinctly to
speak the language of Canaan." "There is a great deal more art in the carriage of
a suit to be put up unto God," Hieron assures his readers, "than every one,
though perhaps he have some good feeling and understanding in Religion, can
at the first attain unto." The cultivation of "art" that Hieron describes is not directly intended as a vehicle for pleasing God, whose tastes he does not venture
to guess. Instead, this skill is meant to generate devotional spirit in the petition-
ers, whose heightened awareness of what he describes as their "own personal
necessities" will help to produce more thoughtful performances of prayer. Far
from "straitening or bounding God's Spirit," the use of set forms or "moulds"
of prayer is a "means rather of quickening & stirring up of the spirit of him that
prayeth" (sig. A3r–A7r).

If skillful and formalized prayers represent the best means of "quickening &
stirring up . . . the spirit," then devotional poetry serves as an important vehicle
for such stirring. Despite the pretense of spontaneity in individual poems, there
is in fact no verbal art more carefully crafted than a perfect sonnet, a complex
hymn, or a set of rhymes that take the shape of an altar. We have already seen the
ways in which critiques of the Sternhold-Hopkins Psalter began to dwell upon
the poor quality of its translations: as Wither and Donne among others argued,
only when the church improves the poetry of the Psalms will the worshippers'
devotional practice improve. During the 1620s and 1630s, this notion that poetry could be employed to heighten devotion extends from the Psalms and
scriptural songs to original verse, whose practitioners awaken to the new opportunity to employ their poetic skill in the creation of liturgical texts.

In the case of Wither, the dream of writing devotional verse that might be used
for public worship was nearly realized. In 1623, he published his *Hymnes and Songs
of the Church*, which combined scriptural translations with a series of original
hymns. According to King James's appointment, Wither's volume was ordered to
be "inserted in convenient manner and due place into every English Psalm Book
in metre,"[11] an arrangement that was not merely a whim of the king, but clearly
reflected Wither's liturgical designs. Hence Wither explains in his dedicatory letter to James that the first part of his text, the "canonical hymns" and their ex-
planatory prefaces, are meant to be "properly applied also to the *Church's* particular occasions in these times"; the second part, containing his "spiritual songs," are
similarly designed for the "several times and occasions observable in the *Church of
England,*" whereby they shall become a "means both of increasing Knowledge, and
Christian Conformity within your Dominions." Because these songs are intended
to be used in church, he explains that his verses as well as the accompanying tunes
are suited throughout for the "common People's capacities."[12]

Moreover, in keeping with his concern in *A Preparation to the Psalter* that the
people's interest in the Psalms ebbed and flowed according to the skill of the
translation, Wither hastens to add at the end of his volume that he has provided
extra tunes for those who have "skill and are delighted with music" so that they
may "have the more variety to stir up the soon cloyed affections."[13] It is specifically this notion of stirring rather than cloying the worshipper's affections that
motivates Wither's liturgical project, a project that depends upon providing
both variety and delight through the medium of sacred song. Had it not been for
the interference of the Stationers' Company, with whom Wither fought, and
lost, a lengthy battle over the form of his text's publication, these new metrical
texts would have been appended to every copy of Sternhold-Hopkins, and
hence have become a more or less official part of the liturgy.

Because Wither's hymns were meant for use on liturgical occasions and holy
days in the Protestant calendar, and not also for private moments of prayer, he
does not attempt to intertwine personal modes of expression with liturgically

oriented verse. His texts consistently employ the plural *we* and not the singular *I*, and lack the kind of intimate and individualized voice that we associate with lyric poetry. The song for Lent, for example, maintains throughout the congregational tone with which it begins:

> The wondrous Fasting to record,
> And our rebellious flesh to tame,
> A holy Fast to thee, oh Lord,
> We have intended in thy Name:
> O sanctifie it, we thee pray,
> That we may thereby honor Thee,
> And so dispose us, that it may
> To our advantage also be. (lines 1–8)

Similarly, the hymn for Good Friday repeatedly affirms the community's collective guilt, culminating in the final (eighth) stanza:

> Our sinnes of spight were part of those that day,
> Whose cruell whips & thornes did make him smart;
> Our Lusts were those that try'de him in the way;
> Our want of love was that which pierc't his heart:
> And still when we forget, or sleight his paine,
> We crucifie and torture him againe. (lines 91–96)

Far from shattering our standard critical opposition between liturgical verse and lyric poetry, Wither's texts overwhelmingly confirm the distinction. And yet, notwithstanding their impersonal tone, the near-inclusion of these hymns in the Psalm Book suggests a religious climate that had begun to take seriously the possibility that new devotional verse could serve as forms of common prayer. When this possibility is imaginatively combined with the more personal and intimate traditions of lyric poetry, one of the results is Herbert's *Temple*.

THE COUNTRY PARSON

For Donne, the project of writing devotional verse that reflects a simultaneously individual and collective voice never seems to have materialized. Neither the impersonal and detached speaker of the "La Corona" sonnets nor the personal and often anguished voice of the nineteen "Holy Sonnets" offers a devotional paradigm for common expression. Despite the shared occasion that it commemorates, "Good Friday, 1613. Riding Westward" similarly does not strive to speak on behalf of Christian worshippers. Instead, it narrates the process through which the speaker learns to acknowledge his own sinfulness and accept the enormity of Christ's sacrifice, employing terms that could not easily be assimilated to the language of public devotion.

Even an ostensibly liturgical work like "The Litanie," which begins with personal invocations to the Father, the Son, the Holy Ghost, and the Virgin Mary, and then folds this singular speaker into a collective voice in the second half of the poem, does not ultimately offer prayers that one might plausibly imagine to be either read aloud by a congregation or read privately by anonymous worshippers. The refrain of "Lord deliver us" suggests Donne's efforts to speak on behalf of a larger community, and yet his consistently idiosyncratic and complex formulations for devotional relief seem entirely incompatible with the utterances of public worship. First, one need only consider the difficulties that average parishioners would face in comprehending, let alone pouring their hearts into, expressions like stanza 15:

> From being anxious, or secure
> Dead clods of sadnesse, or light squibs of mirth
> From thinking, that great courts immure
> All, or no happinesse, or that this earth
> Is only for our prison fram'd,
> Or that thou art covetous
> To them whom thou lovest, or that they are maim'd
> From reaching this worlds sweet, who seek thee thus,
> With all their might, Good Lord deliver us. (lines 127−35)

Second, the circumstances Donne describes often have little resonance for anyone beyond himself and perhaps a few of his like-minded peers. In the stanza we just examined, Donne grapples with his relationship to "great courts"; in the penultimate stanza, he focuses on his supremely personal sins of an excessive attachment to learning, beauty, and wit:

> That learning, thine Ambassador,
> From thine allegeance wee never tempt,
> That beauty, paradises flower,
> For physicke made, from poyson be exempt,
> That wit, borne apt high good to doe,
> By dwelling lazily
> On Natures nothing, be not nothing too,
> That our affections kill us not, nor dye,
> Hear us, weake ecchoes, O thou eare, and cry. (lines 226−34)

These, among many other moments in "The Litanie," are sufficient to warrant taking seriously Donne's account of the poem in a letter to Sir Henry Goodyer, in which he recounts:

> Since my imprisonment in bed, have made a meditation in verse, which I call a
> Litany. . . . I have met two Litanies in Latin verse, which gave me not the reason of

my meditations, for in good faith I thought not upon them then, but they give me a defense, if any man to a Lay man, and a private, impute it as a fault, to take such divine and public names, to his own little thoughts.

Whereas the Latin Litanies that he refers to were commanded by the pope "for public service in their Churches," Donne's own poem, he clarifies, is meant only "for lesser Chapels, which are my friends."[14]

Although the exact dating for most of Donne's religious lyrics remains unknown, it is reasonably clear that once he became a distinguished preacher in the church, he more or less abandoned the project of writing devotional verse. Donne may praise the Sidney Psalms for their potential efficacy in transforming church devotion, but he attempts no similarly ambitious feats of his own. The only evidence we have for Donne's liturgical use of one of his poems is Izaak Walton's claim in his *Life of Dr. John Donne* that Donne had his "Hymne to God the Father" set to music and "caused [it] . . . to be often sung to the *Organ* by the Choristers of St. *Paul's* Church, in his own hearing; and especially at the Evening Service." However, there is no sense in Walton's account that Donne intended this hymn for congregational rather than for private listening. Instead, Walton tells us only that Donne wanted it played for himself ("in his own hearing") and then recounts Donne's deeply personal response to hearing the hymn played: "[he] did occasionally say to a friend, *The words of this* Hymn *have restored to me the same thoughts of joy that possessed my Soul in my sickness when I composed it.*"[15] For the powerful spokesman of the ecclesiastical establishment, the preferred medium for speaking on behalf of a larger Christian community was neither the hymn nor the sonnet, but the sermon.

If for Donne poetry was a predominantly private enterprise distinct from his pastoral life in the church, for Herbert there was no comparable division. From the earliest stages of his adult life, Herbert displayed a profound commitment to combining his devotional and poetic practice. Unlike Donne, who in the third of his "Holy Sonnets" laments having wasted his poetic labors on what he now regards as idolatrous worship—"O might those sighes and teares return again / Into my breast and eyes, which I have spent / That I might in this holy discontent / Mourne with some fruit, as I have mourn'd in vaine" (lines 1−4)—Herbert declared his devotional calling as a poet at the age of sixteen or seventeen. As Walton recounts in his 1670 hagiographic *Life* of the author, the young Herbert sent a pair of sonnets to his mother along with a letter announcing his intention that "my poor abilities in poetry shall be all and ever consecrated to God's glory," an intention clearly announced in the opening lines of the first sonnet:

> My God, where is that ancient heat towards thee,
> Wherewith whole showls of *Martyrs* once did burn,
> Besides their other flames? Doth Poetry
> Wear Venus' livery? only serve her turn?

> Why are not sonnets made of thee? and layes
> Upon thine Altar burnt?[16]

This already familiar theme among devotional poets of appropriating erotic forms for religious purposes is further reinforced in the later lyric, "Jordan (I)," whose speaker begins by protesting the division of beautiful verse and religious expression: "Who sayes that fictions onely and false hair / Become a verse? Is there in truth no beautie?" (lines 1–2) The poem concludes by affirming Herbert's commitment to bringing "good structure" and simple eloquence to the project of devotional verse:

> Shepherds are honest people; let them sing:
> Riddle who list, for me, and pull for Prime:
> I envie no mans nightingale or spring;
> Nor let them punish me with losse of rime
> Who plainly say, My God, My King. (lines 11–15)

In this final invocation of the Psalms, whose formulaic "My God, My King" cleverly completes the final rhyme, Herbert reveals his indebtedness to David the poet at the same time that he realizes his intention to write beautiful poems of his own.[17]

Although Herbert did not publish his English lyrics during his lifetime, his reputation as a devotional poet seems to have been sufficiently established to warrant Francis Bacon's decision to dedicate his 1625 *Translation of Certaine Psalms into English Verse* to "his very good friend, Mr. George Herbert."[18] "It being my manner for Dedications," Bacon explains, "to choose those that I hold most fit for the Argument, I thought that in respect of Divinity, and Poesy, met, (whereof the one is the Matter, the other the Style of this little Writing) I could not make better choice."[19] Bacon's dedication of his Psalms to Herbert was in fact issued around the time of Herbert's ordination as deacon by the bishop of Lincoln, which occurred in late 1624 or early 1625, and marks the formal beginning of Herbert's professional life in the church. In 1630, after years plagued both by illness and indecision, Herbert was installed as rector in the rural parish of Fuggleston-cum-Bemerton, a position he held for three years before his death in 1633 at the age of forty. Despite the brevity of his tenure, Herbert's years at Bemerton have been famously memorialized in both Walton's *Life* and Herbert's own prose manual, *The Country Parson* (1652), texts that in different ways shaped our dominant image of Herbert as the church's ideal parish priest. As Herbert's friend Nicholas Ferrar succinctly concluded in his letter "to the Reader" that prefaced the first edition of *The Temple: Sacred Poems and Private Ejaculations,* Herbert's life was nothing short of a "pattern for the age he lived in."

The contemporary celebration of Herbert's pastoral piety is matched by an unprecedented number of poetic imitations in the years following his death.

George Harvey, whose book of poems, *The Synagogue: or the Shadow of the Temple* (1639), was for decades printed together with Herbert's *Temple* as a strategy, no doubt, for bolstering Harvey's sales, announces on his title page: "Sacred Poems, Private Ejaculations. In Imitation of Mr. George Herbert." Richard Crashaw's debts to Herbert pervade his 1646 *Steps to The Temple*, which, despite its use of Catholic rather than Protestant devotional forms, was both inspired by and modeled after Herbert's text; the anonymous "Preface to the Reader" boasts that Crashaw was "Herbert's second, but equal."[20] And Henry Vaughan, whose 1650 volume of poems, *Silex Scintillans: Sacred poems and private Ejaculations*, owes much more than his subtitle to *The Temple*, announces in his 1655 preface that "the first that with any effectual success attempted a diversion of this soul and overflowing stream (of secular verse) was the blessed man, Mr. *George Herbert*, whose holy life and *verse* gained many pious *Converts* (of whom I am the least)."[21] For these contemporary poets, as well as for Richard Baxter, and later for John Wesley, who reworked forty-two of the lyrics from *The Temple* in his 1739 *Hymns and Sacred Poems*, Herbert's pious verse was a source of enormous inspiration.

Given, then, this long tradition of admiring Herbert's piety in both its pastoral and poetic manifestations, it is striking how few efforts have been made to uncover the links between the liturgy that Herbert would have so deeply known and the language of his devotional lyrics.[22] Critics have usefully identified Herbert's literary debts to Scripture, particularly the wealth of his allusions to the Psalms, but have done very little to disclose the ways in which Herbert employed the devotional models of the Prayer Book—its habits of collective petitioning, praising, confessing—to shape his personal poetics.[23] Moreover, despite long-standing critical debate over Herbert's attention to his own artistry,[24] we have largely ignored the culture's broader preoccupation with poetic skill as a vehicle for enhancing devotional practice.

I want to begin by establishing what many readers of Herbert intuitively know, but too seldom figures in our accounts of his poetry: Herbert was deeply committed to the importance of common prayer. In "The Church Porch," the long, introductory poem to *The Temple*, Herbert declares unambiguously his preference for public over private devotion:

> Though private prayer be a brave designe,
> Yet publick hath more promises, more love.
> And love's a weight to hearts, to eies a sign.
> We all are but cold suitours; let us move
> Where it is warmest. Leave thy six and seven;
> Pray with the most: for where most pray, is heaven. (lines 397–402)[25]

This vision of the advantages of collective prayer shares with Hooker a sense of the enormous comfort one experiences when surrounded by fellow worshippers; the "love" that is aroused by praying publicly spreads contagiously when witnessing its presence in others.

As for Hooker and Donne, the power of public worship for Herbert does not lie strictly in the contagious enthusiasm that it helps to foster among the worshippers, but turns instead on the efficacy of common prayer in penetrating the inner self:

> Resort to sermons, but to prayers most:
> Praying's the end of preaching . . .
> In time of service seal up both thine eies,
> And send them to thine heart; that spying sinne,
> They may weep out the stains by them did rise:
> Those doores being shut, all by the eare comes in. (lines 409–10, 415–18)

In a manner entirely compatible with Thomas Cranmer's emphasis on the ears rather than the eyes as the key to experiencing the church service, Herbert imagines that hearing the liturgy ought to provoke the kind of internal scrutiny that Catholics identified with private prayer and confession. He therefore instructs his readers to empty their minds of all possible distractions: "Let vain or busie thoughts have there no part / Bring not thy plough, thy plots, thy pleasures thither / Christ purg'd his temple; so must thou thy heart" (lines 421–23). It is only when the worshippers actively strive to open their hearts, when they purge themselves of all secret "plots" and "pleasures," that they benefit from the service. As we shall see confirmed in his poems, there is absolutely no opposition for Herbert between liturgy and inwardness.

Herbert's strong belief that the laity must inwardly as well as outwardly engage with all aspects of the public service pervades *The Country Parson*, in which he directly confronts what we have seen to be one of the central questions raised by common prayer since its earliest inception: how can the minister best ensure that the practices of public worship will be effective in both reaching and ultimately shaping the worshippers' private selves? Because Herbert, like so many established churchmen, seems to affirm the causal relation between external behavior and internal change, he advises the minister to instruct his parishioners frequently on how to conduct themselves during the divine service in order to "exact of them all possible reverence." Ministers should by no means endure "either talking, or sleeping, or gazing, or leaning, or half-kneeling, or any undutiful behaviour in them," but instead must demand that all be seated or standing "in a straight and steady posture, as attending to what is done in the Church." Just as the congregation's physical posture should be straight, Herbert commands, so too should their liturgical utterances be clear and thoughtful: when they "answe[r] aloud both Amen, and all other answers [in the Prayer Book], they must not speak "in a huddling or slubbering fashion, gaping, or scratching the head, or spitting even in the midst of their answer." Instead, he insists that the congregation must answer the minister "gently and pausably, thinking what they say; so that while they answer . . . they meditate as they speak" (231).

Now, for anyone who has visited Herbert's parish at Bemerton, which still stands in the shadow of the massive Salisbury Cathedral, this detailed account of external manners assumes a real as well as a symbolic significance: given the remarkably small size of this church, whose narrow walls and single-aisled nave accommodate only eight short wooden pews on each side, the proximity of worshippers sleeping or gazing, let alone spitting, could disturb even the most pious minister's prayers. And yet, however important these external proscriptions may have been for maintaining order in the church, they ultimately reveal Herbert's more pressing concerns about the worshipper's internal condition. At the very end of this passage, Herbert makes clear that his interest lies not in eliminating the "huddling or slubbering" per se, but in producing the kind of worshippers whose liturgical responses reflect thoughtfulness and deliberation. Like Cranmer, Herbert wants the act of liturgical consent—and specifically, the act of saying "Amen"—to reflect real comprehension and reverence, and not to be uttered as a sloppy or automatic response. "This is what the Apostle calls a reasonable service," he declares, "when we speak not as Parrots, without reason . . . but when we use our reason, and apply our powers to the service of him, that gives them" (232). Although Walton himself concedes that "if [Herbert] were at any time too zealous in his Sermons, it was in reproving the indecencies of the people's behaviour in the time of divine Service,"[26] it is clear that for Herbert, the knowledge of "how to behave thyself in church" was by no means separable from the shaping of the inner soul.

In order to achieve the level of congregational thoughtfulness that Herbert regards as essential to a "reasonable service," the minister must seek to engage as fully as possible the attention of each member of his parish. In his discussion of "The Parson preaching," Herbert recommends that the parson should "procur[e] attention by all possible art, both by earnestness of speech . . . and by a diligent and busy cast of his eye on his auditors, with letting them know that he observes who marks, and who not."[27] The act of monitoring his parishioners is enhanced by the minister's "particularizing of his speech," so that his discourse moves "now to the younger sort, then to the elder, now to the poor, and now to the rich." "This is for you," he should indicate, "and This is for you." In addition to preaching from Scripture, Herbert recommends that the parson occasionally tell them "stories and sayings of others . . . for them also men heed, and remember better than exhortations; which though earnest, yet often die with the sermon." "Especially," he notes, "with Country people; which are thick, and heavy, and hard to raise to a point of Zeal and fervency, and need a mountain of fire to kindle them." "But stories and sayings," he knowingly concludes, "they will well remember" (233).

.

HERBERT'S POETICS OF COMMON PRAYER

> Thou, whose sweet youth and early hopes inhance
> Thy rate and price, and mark thee for a treasure;
> Hearken unto a Verser, who may chance
> Ryme thee to good, and make a bait of pleasure.
> A verse may finde him, who a sermon flies,
> And turn delight into a sacrifice. (lines 1−6)

Stories and sayings are not the only forms of kindling. In this address to the reader that begins "The Church Porch," Herbert declares poetry to be another means of firing up the resistant worshipper: "A verse may finde him, who a sermon flies." This notion that the reader might be "ryme[d] . . . to good" in a manner comparable to the effect of a great sermon implicitly corroborates the story that Walton tells of Herbert's deathbed provisions for his poems.[28] According to Walton's *Life*, the dying Herbert ordered the manuscript of *The Temple* to be delivered to Ferrar with the instructions that "if he can think it may turn to the advantage of any dejected poor soul, let it be made public; if not, let him burn it" (56). In choosing the first of these options, Ferrar may well have understood what centuries of subsequent readers have implicitly confirmed: the extent to which these poems succeed not only in penetrating their readers' souls, but in lending these souls a voice.

By exploring the ways in which the lyrics of *The Temple* seem designed to represent common devotional experiences, I do not mean to suggest that these lyrics are not powerfully and significantly personal. As he explains in "The Quidditie" (originally entitled "Poetrie"), writing verse was for Herbert the most intimate act of devotion:

> My God, a verse is not a crown,
> No point of honour or gay suit.
> No hawk, or banquet, or renown,
> Nor a good sword, nor yet a lute:
>
> It cannot vault, or dance, or play;
> It never was in *France* or *Spain*,
> Nor can it entertain the day
> With my great stable or demain:
>
> It is no office, art, or news,
> Nor the Exchange, or busie Hall;
> But it is that which while I use
> I am with thee, and *most take all*.[29]

Far from providing a form of courtly entertainment or a tool for political advancement, poetry is synonymous with the act of deepest personal prayer: "it is that which while I use / I am with thee." For Herbert, there was no obvious distinction between writing a poem and speaking to God.

And yet, although poetry was a profoundly intimate experience, it did not therefore represent a separate category of devotion from that which Herbert practiced in the church. As we saw in *The Country Parson*, Herbert firmly believed that no opposition ought to exist between outward worship and the cultivation of inwardness. In the pages that follow, I want to explore the crucial ways in which the principles that inform the language of common prayer manifest themselves in *The Temple*. This discussion is meant to be suggestive, not exhaustive: by showing Herbert's inventive use of liturgical modes in a number of exemplary poems, I hope to provide new critical tools for approaching his work as a whole.

The lyrics of *The Temple* begin with "The Altar," a poem that imagines the relationship between the speaker's internal self and the external poem in terms comparable to that between the individual worshipper and the texts of the public liturgy:[30]

> A broken ALTAR, Lord, thy servant reares,
> Made of a heart, and cemented with teares:
>   Whose parts are as thy hand did frame;
>   No workmans tool hath touch'd the same.
>   A HEART alone
>   Is suche a stone,
>   As nothing but
>   Thy pow'r doth cut.
>   Wherefore each part
>   Of my hard heart
>   Meets in this frame,
>   To praise thy Name:
>   That, if I chance to hold my peace,
>   These stones to praise thee may not cease.
> O let thy blessed SACRIFICE be mine,
> And sanctifie this ALTAR to be thine.

As Richard Strier has acutely observed, the complexity of the poem derives in part from its positing not one but two distinct "altars" as its subject.[31] First, there is the "altar" described in the opening two lines of the poem—"A broken ALTAR, Lord, thy servant reares, / Made of a heart, and cemented with teares"—and second, there is the altar that is formed by the poem, which is referred to for the first time in lines 9–12: "Wherefore each part / Of my hard heart / Meets in this frame, / To praise thy Name." What has escaped critical notice, however, is that the difference between the two altars neatly corresponds to the distinction between unskillful and eloquent devotion as it was repeatedly formulated in the early modern church. On the one hand, Herbert offers the equivalent of wordless sighs and groans; on the other hand, he proposes a formalized prayer composed in the shape of an altar.

How are we to understand the relationship between the broken altar made by the heart, and the altar that is "this frame"? And which altar does the poem mean to signify in its final petitionary lines, "O let thy blessed SACRIFICE be mine, / And sanctifie this ALTAR to be thine" (15–16)? If we assume, as a number of scholars have notably done, that Herbert adheres to an Augustinian or Puritan eschewal of human artistry, the answer would seem to lie in the initial altar, broken but sincere.[32] And yet, everything in the poem, as well as in the larger devotional culture that surrounded it, points to the opposite conclusion: namely, that the speaker *replaces* the first altar with the second, a replacement that might be explained by the church's commitment to the efficacy of formally crafted over extempore devotion. Like a prayer or Psalm, the altar that is formed by the poem promises to endure beyond the capacity of the poet's own voice: "if I chance to hold my peace, / These stones to praise thee may not cease." This hypothetical silencing of the speaker does not signify what Stanley Fish considers self-abnegation, or what Michael Schoenfeldt terms "self-immolation" so much as it suggests the speaker's substitution of a formalized offering—the newly designed "stones"—for his potentially idiosyncratic utterance.[33] In the end, just as Hooker recommends replacing the weak and unreliable utterances of the individual with the sturdy texts of the Prayer Book, the poet compensates for the weakness of his heart by subordinating himself to the poem that he has constructed.

For Herbert, as for many of his fellow churchmen, the spontaneous and unpremeditated expression of the self tends to produce an unnecessary spiritual discomfort rather than a welcome sensation of freedom; the metrical patterns of standardized texts do not restrain so much as encourage the attainment of devotional ease. Hence in "The Collar," the speaker's anger about his obligations to God and the church, conveyed with wonderful immediacy in his opening declaration—"I Struck the board, and cry'd, No more. / I will abroad" (1–2)—is poetically enforced by the irregular nature of his verse. As in the lyric "Deniall," which represents Herbert's inability to penetrate God's "silent ears" in terms of the poet's failure to sustain his rhyme scheme, the varied and erratic lines of "The Collar" enact the speaker's resistance to all forms of restriction:

> What? shall I ever sigh and pine?
> My lines and life are free; free as the rode,
> Loose as the winde, as large as store.
> Shall I be still in suit? (lines 3–6)

"My lines and life are free": the liberation that the speaker claims is experienced in both his poetry and his vocation. To be out of "suit" with God is precisely to be out of poetic discipline.

The frantic pace that the poem assumes, a pace that is rhetorically achieved by clustering defiant questions which are followed by brief assertions of self-encouragement, simulates the ranting of an unruly and rebellious spirit akin to the mood of the opening quatrains in several of Donne's "Holy Sonnets":

> Is the yeare onely lost to me?
>   Have I no bayes to crown it?
> No flowers, no garlands gay? all blasted?
>   All wasted?
> Not so, my heart: but there is fruit,
>   And thou hast hands.
> Recover all thy sigh-blown age
> On double pleasures: leave thy cold dispute
> Of what is fit, and not. Forsake thy cage . . . (lines 13−21)

This incitement to break out of the "cage" shows no signs of resolving itself internally; several lines later the speaker restates his initial claim, "I will abroad," an act of repetition that seems only to confirm the event's unlikeliness.

What breaks this pattern of spiritual and poetic thrashing about is not an internal resolution, but the perception of an external disruption:

> But as I rav'd and grew more fierce and wilde
>   At every word,
> Me thoughts I heard one calling, *Child!*
>   And I reply'd, *My Lord.* (lines 33−36)

God's apparent call to the speaker, a paternal mixture of love and reproach, not only effects the swift conclusion to the poem, but also brings instant regularity to its meter. It is no coincidence, moreover, that the meter Herbert adopts in these last two lines, a meter that the poem otherwise somewhat conspicuously avoids, is none other than the fourteeners so familiar to English congregations from the Psalms of Sternhold-Hopkins.[34] Once the poet submits to his relationship with God, his metrical idiosyncrasy vanishes; the "looseness" that he boasted at the beginning of the poem as a manifestation of his disobedience gets replaced by the comforting order of liturgy. For Herbert, the rhythms of church forms are not artificially imposed, but naturally expressive: when the poet answers God's private and intimate address, he responds in the so-called common meter.

Herbert's use of common meter at the end of "The Collar" embodies the hopes of established churchmen that the rhetorical models of the Prayer Book or Psalter would become one with the language of personal devotion. What is remarkably generous about Herbert's lyrics, and what in an important sense reflects the poetic fulfillment of common prayer, is their capacity to apply the skill and introspection that we traditionally associate with private meditations or erotic sonnets to poems that seem designed to be shared by others. Cranmer, we will recall, claimed not to possess the "grace and facility" to compose common prayers in verse; nearly one hundred years later, Herbert seems poised to do just that.[35]

As he describes in the lyric "Obedience," Herbert aims to establish a personal contract with God that would be enhanced, rather than diminished, if other like-minded worshippers were to pledge themselves as well. His written offer of "obedience" not surprisingly takes the form of poetry, which substitutes for a legal document representing the speaker's promise:

> My God, if writings may
> Convey a Lordship any way
> Whither the buyer and the seller please;
> Let it not thee displease,
> If this poore paper do as much as they.
>
> On it my heart doth bleed
> As many lines, as there doth need
> To passe itself and all it hath to thee.
> To which I do agree,
> And here present it as my speciall Deed. (lines 1–10)

Although the "speciall Deed" is composed with blood from the speaker's own heart, he insists that its terms be made available for all interested parties:

> He that will passe his land,
> As I have mine, may set his hand
> And heart unto this Deed, when he hath read;
> And make the purchase spread
> To both our goods, if he to will it stand. (lines 36–40)

Like the parishioner's knowing utterance of "Amen," Herbert's audience is asked first to read and then, if willing, to consent to the terms of this agreement: he "may set his hand / And heart unto this Deed, when he hath read."

As the last stanza makes clear, this "spread[ing]" of the "purchase" ultimately serves to strengthen the lyric itself:

> How happie were my part,
> If some kinde man would thrust his heart
> Into these lines; till in heav'ns Court of Rolls
> They were by winged souls
> Entred for both, farre above their desert! (lines 41–45)

For "some kinde man [to] thrust his heart / Into these lines," and for this now collective utterance to achieve "farre above [its original] desert," aptly describes the aim not only of Herbert's poetics, but also of common prayer.

There are many instances in *The Temple* of what I am describing as Herbert's devotional generosity: his implicit willingness to render available to his fellow worshippers his formalized expressions of faith, doubt, hope, and praise. Far from restricting their voice to the poet's own, these largely first-person lyrics seem filled with a longing to contribute their rhymes to the collective project of worship. Indeed, if we consider *The Temple* not merely as a book of poems, but also as a book of common prayers, we discover a wide range of devotional expressions consistent with liturgical worship. The most visible signs of this tendency are the many lyrics that explicitly address calendrical events or services of the established church. "Trinitie Sunday," for example, responds to the holy day of its title by offering what we might identify as a general confession spoken by a paradigmatic I:

> Lord, who hast form'd me out of mud,
> > And hast redeem'd me through thy bloud,
> > And sanctifi'd me to do good;
>
> Purge all my sinnes done heretofore:
> > For I confesse my heavie score,
> > And I will strive to sinne no more.
>
> Enrich my heart, mouth, hands in me,
> > With faith, with hope, with charitie;
> > That I may runne, rise, rest with thee.

In its modest assertion of man's origins "out of mud," and its humble request for divine cleansing, the poems seems to issue forth from the mouth of a Christian everyman. At the same time that the message of the lyric is immensely simple, its formal structure is quite complex: the poem delivers its common themes within highly crafted metrical manipulations of the Trinity—three 3-line stanzas that culminate with a series of petitions that each contains three separate parts ("heart, mouth, hand," "faith, hope, charitie," "runne, rise, rest"). And yet, none of this poetic sophistication detracts from the reiterability of the poem: we are left with exactly the kind of skillful yet repeatable petition that seventeenth-century churchmen so desperately sought in their liturgical texts.

In "Lent," Herbert directly pursues the possibility invoked in the opening lines of "The Church Porch," where he commands his reader to "hearken unto a Verser, who may chance / Ryme thee to good," by writing what can best be classified as a versified sermon. "Welcome deare feast of Lent," the poet-parson begins,

> > who loves not thee
> > He loves not Temperance, or Authoritie
> > But is compos'd of passion.
> > The Scriptures bid us *fast*; the Church says, *now*:

> Give to thy Mother, what thou wouldst allow
>
> To ev'ry Corporation. (lines 1–6)

The poem proceeds in a tone of ministerial authority to the would-be penitents, who are encouraged to participate wholeheartedly in their fast. Hence the speaker admonishes that "true Christians should be glad of an occasion / To use their temperance" (13–14); several stanzas later, he concedes the difficulty of the task—"It's true, we cannot reach Christ's forti'th day"—and yet assures his readers or listeners that "to go part of that religious way / Is better then to rest" (31–33).

What makes the homiletic tone most effective, and what corresponds to Herbert's advice in *The Country Parson* that "in preaching to others, [the minister] forgets not himself, but is first a sermon to himself," is the sudden eruption of the speaker's individualized voice in the penultimate stanza (p. 255). After the opening lines of impersonal pastoral comfort—"Who goeth in the way which Christ hath gone / Is much more sure to meet with him, then one / That travelleth by-wayes" (37–39)—the speaker shifts to an expression of personal hope: "Perhaps my God, though he be farre before / May turn, and take me by the hand, and more / May strengthen my decayes" (40–42). The humble and plaintive nature of these lines in which "my" replaces "our" does not diminish so much as heighten the affective force of the poem's final collective petition, whose *we* now seems affirmatively to include the speaker's first-person I:

> Yet Lord instruct us to improve our fast
>
> By starving sinne and taking such repast
>
> As may our faults controll:
>
> That ev'ry man may revel at his doore,
>
> Not in his parlour; banquetting the poore,
>
> And among those his soul. (lines 43–48)

What began as a somewhat detached act of preaching evolves into a common prayer.

If "Trinitie Sunday" produces a general confession, and "Lent" a versified sermon, a poem such as "Christmas" commemorates the holy day of its title by presenting a hymn of praise. This single lyric in the authoritative Bodleian manuscript of *The Temple* is composed of two previously separate lyrics in the earlier Williams manuscript; Herbert's decision to combine a sonnet upon Christ's birth with a sacred hymn meant to be sung aloud suggests a keen interest in supplementing personal meditations or supplications with more liturgical texts.[36]

The poet begins with a sonnet that describes an encounter with the holy infant lying in the manger:

> All after pleasures as I rid one day,
>
> My horse and I, both tir'd, bodie and minde,
>
> With full crie of affections, quite astray,

I took up in the next inne I could finde.

> There when I came, whom found I but my deare,
> My dearest Lord, expecting till the grief
> Of pleasures brought me to him, readie there
> To be all passengers most sweet relief?

The sestet shifts from narrative description to personal invocation:

> O Thou, whose glorious, yet contracted light,
> Wrapt in nights mantle, stole into a manger;
> Since my dark soul and brutish is thy right,
> To Man of all beasts be not thou a stranger:
> Furnish & deck my soul, that thou mayst have
> A better lodging then a rack or grave. (lines 1–14)

In this petition for divine intervention, the poem moves irreversibly inward, as the "thou" in the final couplet refers not simply to Christ, as it had in line 9, but to Christ's presence in the poet's own soul.

This personal sonnet, however, is followed by the speaker's open acknowledgement of the inadequacy of his private and silent manner of worshipping Christ, an acknowledgement that is provoked by his desire to join with the shepherds who celebrate the holy day in collective song. The hymn begins with a tone of self-chastisement—"The shepherds sing; and shall I silent be? / My God, no hymne for thee?" (15–16)—only then to establish the speaker's metaphorical claims to being a shepherd himself, who feeds his flock of "thoughts, and words, and deeds" (18). Having identified himself now as a rightful singer, he enters into the most vocal form of worship, promising to sing beyond the hours of the day reserved for this holy occasion:

> Shepherd and flock shall sing, and all my powers
> Out-sing the day-light houres.
> Then we will chide the sunne for letting night
> Take up his place and right:
> We sing one common Lord; wherefore he should
> Himself the candle hold. (lines 21–26)

"We sing one common Lord": however intimate and personal his experience of God may be, Herbert seeks to affirm his inclusion within a much larger devotional community.

The easy fluctuation between the singular and the plural voice in the remaining verses of the hymn reflects Herbert's new conjunction with an eager and pious sun—"a willing shiner"—who will gladly extend the day's hours with sacred song:

> I will go searching, till I finde a sunne
> Shall stay, till we have done;
> A willing shiner, that shall shine as gladly,
> As frost-nipt sunnes look sadly.
> Then we will sing, and shine all our own day,
> And one another pay:
> His beams shall cheer my breast, and both so twine,
> Till ev'n his beams sing, and my musick shine. (lines 27–34)

The final assertion of "my musick" has only been achieved through the speaker's willingness to seek out fellow worshippers, to expose his breast to others' beams, to join a pastoral choir.

Although the poems that I have just considered are directly connected to church forms or events, their primary liturgical characteristics—a commitment to formalized language that is at once metrically skillful and easily sung or repeated, and a fluctuation of singular and collective speakers, so that the first-person I is simultaneously affirmed and incorporated into a larger whole—are by no means limited to the explicitly "occasional" lyrics of *The Temple*. For once we tear ourselves away from the critical binaries that separate personal and liturgical verse, we discover how consistently Herbert sought to combine what F. E. Hutchinson describes as private "colloquies of the soul with God" with inclusive and paradigmatic modes of expression.[37] A substantial number of lyrics fit this general description, but the single example that perhaps most powerfully and unexpectedly achieves the interweaving of the personal and the universal is "The Flower," whose verses remain framed to this day on one of the walls of Herbert's former parish at Bemerton. In this poem relating the speaker's cycles of spiritual struggle, Herbert draws few, if any, boundaries around the story he tells. Even in what has long been recognized as one of Herbert's most personally compelling and eloquent lyrics, the voice never becomes exclusively the poet's.

"The Flower" employs the most common of metaphors for the rhythms of spiritual life: the growth and decline of flowers, whose life patterns depend upon natural phenomena entirely beyond their control. The speaker begins in a pastoral vein, carefully explaining the comparison between the pleasure of God's "returns" to mankind and the renewal of flowers in spring:

> How fresh, O Lord, how sweet and clean
> Are thy returns! ev'n as the flowers in spring;
> To which, besides their own demean,
> The late-past frosts tributes of pleasures bring.
> Grief melts away
> Like snow in May,
> As if there were no such cold thing.

The image of late snow not only quickly vanishing, but misleadingly taking with it all signs of its inevitable return—"as if there were no such cold thing"—supplies the context in which we are meant to understand the speaker's own recuperation from spiritual despair, as the poem shifts from this general and impersonal voice to one of startling intimacy in its second stanza:

> Who would have thought my shrivel'd heart
> Could have recover'd greennesse? It was gone
> Quite underground; as flowers depart
> To see their mother-root, when they have blown;
> Where they together
> All the hard weather,
> Dead to the world, keep house unknown. (lines 1–14)

"Who would have thought": the astonished, modest tone with which the speaker describes the transformation of his heart from a "shrivel'd" plant to a restored state of "greennesse" captures his overwhelming sense of the temporary and unpredictable nature of all spiritual conditions. His introduction of the first-person possessive pronoun my in line 8 does not signal an entry into a predominantly personal narrative; instead, the speaker shifts in the third stanza to a decidedly collective "we":

> These are thy wonders, Lord of power,
> Killing and quickning, bringing down to hell
> And up to heaven in an houre;
> Making a chiming of a passing-bell.
> We say amisse,
> This or that is:
> Thy word is all, if we could spell. (lines 15–21)

The straightforward assertion of God's tremendous power, which alone is responsible for human growth and decline, serves both as a general indictment of human error, and as a particular corrective for the speaker, who laments his futile ambition:

> O that I once past changing were,
> Fast in thy Paradise, where no flower can wither!
> Many a spring I shoot up fair,
> Offring at heav'n, growing and groning thither:
> Nor doth my flower
> Want a spring-showre,
> My sinnes and I joining together.
>
> But while I grow in a straight line,
> Still upwards bent, as if heav'n were mine own,

> Thy anger comes, and I decline:
> What frost to that? what pole is not the zone,
>> Where all things burn,
>> When thou dost turn,
> And the least frown of thine is shown? (lines 22–35)

The poem here takes on the tone of a cautionary tale or homily intended to warn the readers from similar acts of arrogance: we can no more control our own ascent to heaven, admonishes the poet-parson, than flowers can control their own growth. The presumption of the speaker's efforts to climb his way toward Paradise, a presumption that is watered, as it were, by the "spring-showre" that his sins manage to produce, is met only with God's devastating anger, which exceeds the metaphorical terms of the poem. "What frost to that?" Herbert laments, as if nothing that flowers might suffer could approximate the pain of divine reproof.[38]

These patterns of reaching upward and falling down, of assuming God's love and recognizing his anger, eventually give way in the penultimate stanza to a splendid description of the speaker's unexpected recovery that returns us to the tone of the poem's opening lines:

> And now in age I bud again,
> After so many deaths I live and write;
>> I once more smell the dew and rain,
> And relish versing: O my onely light,
>>> It cannot be
>>> That I am he
> On whom thy tempests fell all night. (lines 36–42)

The capacious metaphor of the self as flower with which this begins—"And now in age I bud again"—yields here to a less universal, more individualized account of the self as poet: it is not only that he lives, but that he writes; it is not only that he takes pleasure in the natural phenomena of dew and rain, but that he can once more "relish versing."

Although the affective power of these lines supplies a fitting closure to the speaker's personal story of spiritual crisis and recovery, the lyric does not end here. Instead, this momentary narrowing of focus to the speaker's poetic rebirth propels him outward toward a final expression of the common rhythms of spiritual life, and the "we" emerges once again:

> These are thy wonders, Lord of love,
> To make us see we are but flowers that glide:
>> Which when we once can finde and prove,
> Thou hast a garden for us, where to bide.
>>> Who would be more,

Swelling through store,
Forfeit their Paradise by their pride. (lines 43–49)

What is striking about this lyric is the perfect yoking of the quiet intimacy of the invocation to God—"O my onely light, / It cannot be / That I am he / On whom thy tempests fell all night"—with its tone of collective gratitude: "These are thy wonders, Lord of love, / To make us see we are but flowers that glide." "Us," Herbert insists, not "me." The deeply personal pleasure that Herbert takes in writing poems, a pleasure so beautifully announced in the enjambed line of the penultimate stanza—"I once more smell the dew and rain, / And relish versing"—cannot be separated from the pleasure of sharing his voice with others.

For Herbert, to be a lyric poet meant to participate in the century-long project of creating the most stirring, accessible, and eloquent forms to be used in praying to God. Nowhere is this more forcefully if somewhat paradoxically conveyed than in "The Forerunners," a long lyric near the end of The Temple that laments the speaker's loss of poetic skill in old age:

The harbingers are come. See, see, their mark,
White is their colour, and behold my head.
But must they have my brain? must they dispark
Those sparkling notions, which therein were bred?
Must dulnesse turn me to a clod?
Yet have they left me, Thou art still my God. (lines 1–6)

In bidding farewell to his talent, Herbert displays a strong resistance to abandoning his poetic project, a project he describes specifically in terms of bringing poetry into the church. Far from representing his lyrics as solely private petitions restricted to the ears of the divine, the speaker lays claim to a public role for his verse:

Farewell sweet phrases, lovely metaphors.
But will ye leave me thus? when ye before
Of stews and brothels onely knew the doores,
Then did I wash you with my tears, and more,
Brought you to Church well drest and clad:
My God must have my best, ev'n all I had.

Lovely enchanting language, sugar-cane,
Hony of roses, whither wilt thou flie?
Hath some fond lover tic'd thee to thy bane?
And wilt thou leave the Church, and love a stie?
Fie, thou wilt soil thy broider'd coat,
And hurt thyself, and him that sings the note. (lines 13–24)

The personal loss and the communal loss are hardly distinguishable here, for what is stripped from the poet ("will ye leave me thus?") and what is stripped from the church ("and wilt thou leave the Church, and love a stie?") are the same set of "sweet phrases," "lovely metaphors," and "lovely enchanting language." The loss is all the more painful, moreover, because of the speaker's own labors in bathing and dressing this otherwise debauched language so that it might enter the sacred sphere; now that his skill has been taken away, Herbert envisions his church bereft of poetry.

Although Herbert finally reconciles himself to the dullness of old age, this reconciliation comes only in the context of his withdrawal from the outside world:

> Yet if you go, I passe not; take your way:
> For, *Thou art still my God*, is all that ye
> Perhaps with more embellishment can say.
> Go birds of spring: let winter have his fee;
>   Let a bleak palenesse chalk the doore,
> So all within be livelier then before. (lines 31–36)

So long as "all within be livelier then before," the speaker imagines he can manage with the "bleak palenesse," the departure of spring birds, and the single line of Scripture that he has been left, *"Thou art still my God."*[39] Whether the poem suggests that the heightened inner liveliness will come here on earth in his newly reduced state or only in the aftermath of his imminent death, it seems clear that Herbert wishes to convey that he can ultimately do without poetry: however one reads the "perhaps" in line 33, poetry remains at heart "embellishment," a useful tool for enhancing devotion and not an essential feature of human faith.[40]

And yet, this recognition of poetry's status as *adiaphora* does nothing, finally, to diminish the poignancy of the speaker's reluctance to be stripped of his talent, a reluctance that is spectacularly reinforced by the poetic achievement of this lyric itself. With the exception of the deliberately awkward feminine rhyme in lines 11–12—"He will be pleased with that dittie; / And if I please him, I write fine and wittie"—neither "The Forerunners" nor the subsequent lyrics in the volume suggests that the poet has lost his poetic gift. In the end, Herbert seems determined to settle any doubts one might have that his piety can thrive without poetry, at the same time that he seems quietly to hope, both here and throughout *The Temple*, that his "lovely language" will have an enduring presence well beyond his chalked door.

PRINTED MATTER

If the argument I have proposed about the deep associations between poetry and liturgy reflects the realities of seventeenth-century devotion, why are there no visible traces in *The Temple* that indicate the volume's affinity with the church's liturgical texts? What kind of *material* evidence, in other words, can be invoked to support the claims I have made for the formative relationship between the Book of Common Prayer and Herbert's book of poems?

These questions can only be answered if we pull ourselves away from our contemporary volumes of Herbert and return to *The Temple*'s first edition, where my claims seem to be borne out by the physical text itself. First published several months after Herbert's death in 1633, *The Temple* quickly became one of the best-selling books of the midseventeenth century, reaching its sixth edition by 1641. The success of the volume did not depend, however, upon Herbert's fame as either poet or parson. Far from emphasizing the identity of the author or lamenting his recent death, the title page of *The Temple* emphasizes the title and even the subtitle of the volume over Herbert's name, and fails to mention either his career as a parson or his tenure as a Cambridge Orator (p. 113). Apart from the lyrics themselves, the book of *The Temple* includes only some dedicatory lines from the poet to God; a table of contents listing the poem titles in alphabetical order; and Ferrar's "to the Reader," which dismisses any expectations on the part of the reader for a courtly publication of poetry:

> The dedication of this work having been made by the Author to the Divine Majesty only, how should we now presume to interest any mortal man in the patronage of it? Much less think we it meet to seek the recommendation of the Muses, for that which himself was confident to have been inspired by a diviner breath than flows from Helicon. The world therefore shall receive it in that naked simplicity, with which he left it, without any addition either of support or ornament, more than is included in it self.[41]

Ferrar's boast that the volume lacks any "support or ornament" differentiates *The Temple* from most contemporary editions of verse, which were textured with an array of dedicatory poems, portraits of the author, and, in the case of a posthumous volume, elegies and commendatory verses in honor of the deceased.

No book is completely "naked," however, and Herbert's *Temple* is no exception. If we ignore conventional wisdom and allow ourselves to judge this book by its cover (or at least by its title page), we make a remarkably unsuperficial set of discoveries. Unlike the lyrics of Donne or Francis Quarles, both published roughly simultaneously by the commercial printer John Marriot, Herbert's poems were published by the printers at Cambridge University. This fact alone is significant, as almost all seventeenth-century verse was published within the busy world of the London presses, and *The Temple* would have represented an important departure from Cambridge's usual list. In the fifty years since printing first began at Cambridge in 1583, the English poetry published by the University Press was limited to the work of King's College Fellow Giles Fletcher and his two sons, Giles and Phineas.[42] Apart from these titles, Cambridge's publications had consisted mainly of almanacs, Greek and Latin grammars, theological trea-

Title page from George Herbert, The Temple (Cambridge, 1633). By permission of the Houghton Library, Harvard University.

tises, commendatory verses for the king and his family, and liturgical texts including the Bible, the Book of Psalms, and the Book of Common Prayer.

This last group of titles represented more of an achievement than may be immediately apparent, for the license to print the official volumes of the established church was extremely difficult to obtain. Upon his accession to the throne, King James had both strengthened the already powerful Company of Stationers, which controlled the patents for all varieties of publication in England, and increased the monopoly of his private royal printers in the publica-

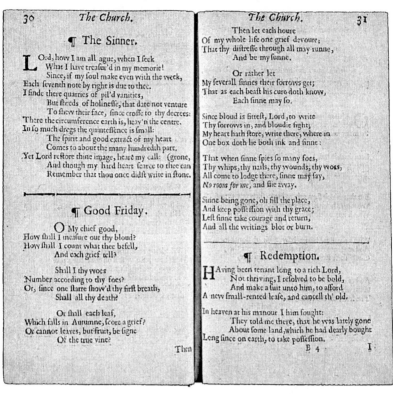

"The Sinner" and "Good Friday" from *The Temple* (1633 ed.). By permission of the Houghton Library, Harvard University.

tion of sacred books.[43] The king's printers were responsible for financing as well as printing the Authorized Version of the Bible, and held the exclusive patent for publishing the Bible, the Psalter, and the Prayer Book.[44] Cambridge University Press had long sought to compete in this highly lucrative market: in the late 1580s and 1590s, the university printer John Legate had illegally printed both the Bible and the Sternhold-Hopkins Psalter, for which he was officially penalized after a grievance was filed by the Stationers' Company. His successor, Cantrell Legge, tried unsuccessfully to enter the Bible market in the 1610s, and seems to have printed a series of small Psalm books in the early 1620s, which eventually brought him before the Privy Council in 1623.[45] Although the council did not authorize Legge to print Bibles or Psalters at this time, it did begin a gradual loosening of the obstructive monopolies by authorizing Cambridge to "comprint" with the Stationers all privileged titles except for Bibles, Prayer

THE COLLECTS.

¶ The xviii. sunday after Trinity.
The collect.
LOrd we beseech thee grant thy people grace to avoid the infections of the devil, and with pure heart and minde to follow thee the only God, through Jesus Christ our Lord.

The epistle. 1.Cor.1.
I thank my God alwayes verse 4.unto verse 9.

The gospel. Matth.22.
But when the Pharisees had verse 34 unto the end.

¶ The xix. sunday after Trinity.
The collect.
OGod, forasmuch as without thee we are not able to please thee, grant that the working of thy mercy may in all things direct and rule our hearts, through Jesus Christ our Lord.

The epistle. Ephes.4.
This I say therefore, and testifie verse 17.unto the end

The gospel. Matth.9.
Then he entred into a ship verse 1.unto verse 9.

¶ The xx. sunday after Trinity.
The collect.
ALmighty and mercifull God, of thy bountifull goodnesse keep us from all things that may hurt us, that we being ready both in body and soul, may with free hearts accomplish those things that thou wouldest have done, through Jesus Christ our Lord.

The epistle. Eph.5.
Take heed therefore, that ye verse 15.unto verse 22.

The gospel. Matth.22.
The kingdome of heaven is verse 2.unto verse 15.

¶ The xxi. sunday after Trinity.
The collect.
GRant we beseech thee, mercifull Lord, to thy faithfull people pardon and peace, that they may be cleansed from all their sins, and serve thee with a quiet minde, through Jesus Christ our Lord.

The epistle. Eph.6.
Finally my brethren, be strong verse 10.unto verse 21.

The gospel. Joh.4.
And there was a certain ruler verse 46.unto the end.

¶ The xxii. sunday after Trinity.
The collect.
LOrd we beseech thee to keep thy houshold the church in continuall godlinesse, that through thy protection it may be free from all adversities, and devoutly given to serve thee in good works, to the glory of thy name, through Jesus Christ our Lord.

The epistle. Phil.1.
I thank my God having verse 3.unto verse 12.

The gospel. Matt.18.
Then came Peter to him verse 21.unto the end.

¶ The xxiii. sunday after Trinity.
The collect.
GOd our refuge and strength, which art the authour of all godlinesse, be ready to heare the devout prayers of thy church, and grant that those things which we ask faithfully, we may obtain effectually, through Jesus Christ our Lord.

The epistle. Phil.3.
Brethren, be followers of me verse 17.unto the end.

The gospel. Matth.22.
Then went the Pharisees and verse 15.unto verse 23.

¶ The xxiiii. sunday after Trinity.
The collect.
LOrd we beseech thee, assoil thy people from their offences, that through thy bountifull goodnesse we may be delivered from the bonds of all those sinnes, which by our frailty we have committed, Grant this,&c.

The epistle. Colos.1.
We give thanks to God verse 3.unto verse 13.

The gospel. Matth.9.
While he thus spake verse 18.unto verse 27.

¶ The xxv. sunday after Trinity.
The collect.
STirre up we beseech thee, O Lord, the wills of thy faithfull people, that they plenteously bringing forth the fruit of good works, may of thee be plenteously rewarded, through Jesus Christ our Lord.

The epistle. Jer.23.
Behold, the dayes come verse 5.unto verse 9.

The gospel. John 6.
Then Jesus lift up his eyes verse 5.unto verse 15.

¶ If there be any moe sundayes before Advent sunday, to supply the same, shall be taken the collect, epistle and gospel of some of those sundayes which were omitted between the Epiphanie and Septuagesima.

¶ S. Andrews day.
The collect.
ALmighty God, which didst give such grace unto thy holy apostle S. Andrew, that he readily obeyed the calling of thy Sonne Jesus Christ, and followed him without delay: grant unto us all, that we being called by thy holy word, may forthwith give over our selves obediently to

C 2   follow

Collects from the Book of Common Prayer (Cambridge, 1630). By permission of the Houghton Library, Harvard University.

Books, Psalters, Primers, grammars, and common law books. Finally, in new legislation passed in April 1629, the university press won the right to print the Bible (although in folio and quarto only, and not in the smaller, more popular sizes), the Book of Common Prayer, and the metrical Psalter.[46]

The exception made for Cambridge in 1629 is most easily understood as a political favor reflecting a climatic change both at the university and at the royal court. The accession of Charles I in 1625 was marked by a rapid intensification of censorship, focusing especially on those presses and texts unsympathetic to the English church. Although the Cambridge University Press had been strongly affiliated with non-conformist publications during the late sixteenth and early seventeenth century, the election in 1626 of one of the king's closest allies, the duke of Buckingham, as university chancellor, and the appointment of the conservative brothers Thomas and John Buck as university printers, signaled a royalist turn that no doubt encouraged Charles's favor.[47] However they obtained the license, the Bucks, soon joined by their partner Roger Daniel, began to compete in the market for publishing ecclesiastical texts. The *Short Title Catalogue* list of books published in these years still shows a nearly uninterrupted flow of the king's printers in the list of liturgical titles, yet it is occasionally and significantly interrupted by the Cambridge University imprint.[48]

For printers interested in retaining their hard-earned privilege of publishing sacred texts, all decisions to publish nonliturgical devotional texts must have undergone enormous scrutiny. In 1633, Herbert's was the only volume of this type published by Cambridge, and in the two preceding years, such volumes seem to have been limited to a book on Christian hospitality and a translation of Protestant meditations that was first published in Latin in 1627. Cambridge was not, in other words, cultivating a side industry in English poets, but on the contrary seems to have made an exception in taking on Herbert's *Temple*.

It is crucial to recognize that *The Temple*'s publication by two printers who had recently obtained the right to print the Bible, the Book of Psalms, and the Book of Common Prayer, was hardly coincidental: the complex thematic affinities that we have seen between *The Temple* and the church liturgy find material confirmation in the physical texts themselves. First, the aforementioned lack of attention in the volume to Herbert's personal life, and the related lack of dedicatory or commemorative materials, creates a textual apparatus more similar to liturgical texts than poetic works. The only personally inflected moment in the entire apparatus of the first edition is a brief account of Herbert's piety in Ferrar's letter "to the Reader":

> His obedience and conformity to the Church, and the discipline thereof was singularly remarkable. Though he abounded in private devotions, yet went he every morning and evening with his family to the Church; and by his example, exhortations, and encouragements drew the greater part of his parishioners to accompany him daily in the public celebration of the Divine Service. (¶2v)

This account of Herbert's devotional practice could easily be confused with an advertisement for regular churchgoing, a piece of ecclesiastical encouragement that reveals the Bucks' and Daniel's understanding of Herbert's work as a private companion to the liturgical titles that Cambridge had recently won the right to print.

Second, the decorative ornaments framing the pages of *The Temple* are interchangeable with those that frame Cambridge's edition of the Book of Common Prayer, and the poems themselves are separated from one another by the pilcrow (¶), an icon used in the Prayer Book to divide the Collects and the weekly readings from scriptural passages (pages 114 and 115).[49] Using the pilcrow to separate poems seems to have been unique to *The Temple*: volumes of seventeenth-century verse published either in London or Cambridge typically employ this symbol only to number prefatory pages bound before signature A, or to introduce the publication date and location at the bottom of the title page.[50]

Third, the duodecimo-size pages of *The Temple* represent an anomaly for the seventeenth-century publication of poetry. Single-author volumes, like Marriot's editions of Donne and Quarles, were typically published in quarto format, whereas the very small duodecimo was usually reserved for inexpensive copies of the Prayer Book or Psalter so they could be slipped into a pocket for ready access in times of spiritual need.[51] To a seventeenth-century worshipper, Cambridge's editions of Herbert's *Temple* would have visually conjured up the liturgical texts of everyday life. Holding the book, absorbing its exquisite poems, the reader could have experienced the perfect fusion of personal and universal voice that common prayer sought to achieve.

CONCLUSION

The Bay Psalm Book

FROM COMMON PRAYER TO COMMON POEMS

When Nicolas Ferrar brought Herbert's manuscript to Cambridge University Press, following the poet's deathbed instructions that "if he can think it may turn to the advantage of any dejected poor soul, let it be made public," the press's conservative licensers approved the entire volume for publication with the exception of two lines from the long, prophetic poem, "The Church Militant": "Religion stands a tip-toe in our land / Readie to passe to the *American* Strand." Here is Izaak Walton's account of the meeting between Ferrar and Cambridge's vice-chancellor:

> When Mr. Ferrar sent [*The Temple*] to Cambridge to be licensed for the press, the Vice-Chancellor would by no means allow the two so much noted verses, "Religion stands a Tip-toe in our Land/Ready to pass to the American Strand" to be printed; and Mr. Ferrar would by no means allow the book to be printed and want them: but after some time and some arguments for and against their being made public, the Vice-Chancellor said, "I knew Mr. Herbert well and know that he had many heavenly speculations and was a divine poet; but I hope the world will not take him to be an inspired prophet, and therefore I license the whole book."[1]

Walton's regard for these verses as "much noted" no doubt confirms the worst of the vice-chancellor's suspicions: by the time Walton published his *Life of Mr. George Herbert* in 1670, New England Puritans had moved well beyond the already threatening doctrines they had first cultivated in England during the 1620s and early 1630s, hurling the Protestant faith into territory hardly assimilable to the High Church commitments of the Cambridge press. And along with Bibles and theological treatises, one of the books that seems to have traveled across the Atlantic was Herbert's *Temple*, a 1634 edition of which can be traced to the early collections of Harvard College, founded in 1636.[2]

If the Bible and *The Temple* were two Cambridge titles that made the journey to New England, the Book of Common Prayer was one emphatically left behind. Although there is mention of a Prayer Book in the possession of John Winthrop Jr., the son of the Massachusetts governor, its inclusion in his library was unintentional, and its condition, as fate would have it, something less than pristine. According to the senior Winthrop's diary entry for October 15, 1640,

> Mr. Winthrop the younger . . . having many books in a chamber where there was corn of diverse sorts, had among them one wherein the Greek testament, the psalms and the common prayer were bound together. He found the common prayer eaten with mice, every leaf of it, and not any of the two other touched, nor any other of his books, though there were above a thousand.[3]

Mice in New England were apparently discerning non-conformists, but however fabricated Winthrop's tale may be, it neatly captures the antiliturgical spirit of the Puritan colonists. Not only in the separatist colony at Plymouth founded by English pilgrims from Holland, but also in the officially nonseparatist churches of the Massachusetts Bay Colony, public devotional services were performed entirely without a liturgy.

The 1640s were, on the whole, difficult years for the Book of Common Prayer.[4] In 1644, under the authority of the mostly presbyterian Westminster Assembly (the synod appointed by the Long Parliament to reform the Church of England), the Prayer Book was officially banned from either public or private worship.[5] In its place, the Westminster Assembly put together a new guideline for ministers entitled The Directory for Public Worship (1645), which closely resembled the Elizabethan non-conformist liturgy so detested by the established churchmen in the 1580s. Like its Elizabethan counterpart, the Directory did not offer mandatory forms so much as helpful examples; lengthy prayers are provided, but always with loose instructions that the minister should "pray to this or the like effect."[6]

However, far from leaving things entirely to the minister's discretion, the Westminster divines require that their text be used "for all the parts of Public Worship, at Ordinary and Extraordinary times."[7] And although it was printed in six separate editions in its first year of publication, congregations were apparently slow to adopt the new text. An ordinance passed in August of 1645 warns both ministers and parishioners:

> If any person or persons whatsoever shall at any time or times hereafter use or cause the aforesaid Book of Common Prayer to be used in any Church, Chapel, or public place of worship, or in any private place or family . . . that then every such person so offending therein; shall for the first offense forfeit and pay the sum of 5 pounds.[8]

Whereas in England the rejection of the Book of Common Prayer was not accompanied by a rejection of liturgy per se, even the flexible structures of a manual like the Directory, let alone the confining texts of the Prayer Book, were deemed unsuitable for the churches of the Massachusetts Bay Colony. According to John Cotton, the teacher of the First Church in Boston and the primary exponent of New England ecclesiology in the 1640s:

> We conceive it . . . to be unlawful to bring in ordinarily any other Books, into the public worship of God, in the Church, besides the Book of God, and therefore do see no more warrant to read out of a Prayer-Book, the public Prayer of a Church: than out of a book of Homilies to read the public Sermons of the Ministers of the Church.[9]

Cotton's position ultimately rests on a suspicion of reading in either sermons or in prayer, a position that we have seen articulated in attacks upon the Prayer Book since the 1570s: "If it could be proved," he argues, "that the reading of a prescript form of prayer upon a Book were an ordinance of God, sanctified for the edification of the Church (as the reading of the Scriptures is) we might ordinarily expect the like assistance and blessing" (7).

For English Puritans interested in sustaining close ties with their Massachusetts brethren, this harsh condemnation of liturgical forms was an occasion for real alarm. In his *Tryall of the New-Church Way in New England and in Old*, the English minister John Ball exclaims:

> It never entered into us to persuade you to a set Liturgy, much less to complain that you had not accepted ours. But that all stinted Liturgies should be condemned as devised worship, and so condemned as that none may lawfully be present at, or partake of the Sacraments administered in a stinted or devised form, this we call a new opinion.[10]

The "new opinion" of public worship in New England was organized around two principles diametrically opposed to the traditions of the Church of England: a commitment to original and spontaneous prayer, and a privileging of the individual voice of the minister over the collective voice of the congregation. These principles of devotional spontaneity and individuality were by no means accompanied, however, by a rejection of public worship in favor of private prayer. On the contrary, the sixteenth-century reformers' desire to create public practices that would not only engage the congregation's full attention during the service, but also shape their private worship, remained at the center of New England piety. As Perry Miller has convincingly argued, American Puritans of the early seventeenth century were dominated by the rigorous conditions of their public religious life; "private meditation was demanded," Miller explains, "but meditation chiefly upon last Sunday's sermon or Thursday's lecture; reading of the Bible was required, but reading of it in the light of the exposition."[11]

What was dramatically different about worship in New England when compared with the ecclesiastical practices of the English church turned on the extent to which worshippers participated in the service. In an intensified version of what English non-conformists would have likely experienced, the central activity of New England worship was the sermon, which was typically delivered every Thursday and Sunday and could last several hours.[12] The congregation did not contribute to the prayers that preceded the sermon, which were extemporaneous performances ranging anywhere from very brief to ninety-minute exhortations. Nor were there General Confessions, Collects, or responsive readings that engaged the churchgoers in collective petitions. In the churches of the Massachusetts Bay Colony, the individual's experience of the service was almost entirely consumed by the act of listening.

There were several important exceptions to the dominance of the minister's voice in the midseventeenth-century public church of New England. One such exception, well documented by historians and literary critics, was the performance of personal conversion narratives in order to gain church membership.[13] According to the Cambridge (Massachusetts) Platform of 1648, the church was obliged to "make trial of the fitness of such who enter," with allowances made only for those who "through excessive fear, or other infirmity, be unable to make their personal *relation* of their spiritual estate in public." In these exceptional cases, it is deemed "sufficient that the Elders having received private satisfaction, make *relation* thereof in public before the church, they testifying their assents thereunto."[14] In these personal "relations," aspiring church members would offer confessional accounts of their experiences as a means to prove their conversion; the "visible saints," as church members were called, voted whether to accept the new candidate.

Although the conditions of these performances varied—in some cases, they were made strictly before the elders in private, and in others before the "mixed" congregation of elect and nonelect worshippers—the experience of hearing these narrations seems to have been encouraged as part of the larger process of edification. Thus Roger Clap, one of the founders of Dorchester, remarks in his memoirs:

> Many were converted, and others established in Believing: many joined unto the several Churches where they lived, confessing their faith publicly, and showing before all the Assembly their Experiences of the Workings of God's Spirit. . . . And many Hearers found very much Good by, to help them to try their own Hearts, and to consider how it was with them.[15]

Increase Mather similarly defends the use of personal testimonies against the attacks of Solomon Stoddard in 1680 by declaring that "some have been converted by hearing others relate the story of their conversion, others have been comforted, and edified thereby."[16]

A second exception to the congregation's largely silent role in church, and one that involved communal rather than individual participation, lies in the singing of metrical Psalms. Psalm-singing was by no means an innovation of the New England Puritans: English Protestants had adopted this Continental practice during the Marian exile, and by the early Elizabethan period, the Church of England had incorporated metrical Psalms into its regular services. However, despite the great affinity of High Churchmen with the singing of Psalms, it was the Puritans who were consistently criticized in the seventeenth century for their excessive attachment to this practice, an attachment that seems to have been transported to New England without slackening at all in intensity. The mocking exhortation in the 1639 song "The Zealous Puritan"—"stay not among the Wicked / But let us to *New England go* . . . / We will not fear our entry / The Psalms shall be our musick"—aptly describes the musical conditions of the midseventeenth-century New England church, where nothing apart from the unison singing of Psalms was likely to be heard.[17]

Early American scholarship has focused enormous attention on those devotional practices whose texts were not prescribed and hence varied from day to day: the minister's original prayers and sermons; the weekly lectures; the aspiring members' conversion narratives; and so on. But it has largely ignored the significance of the far less sensational practice of singing Psalms, a tradition that was unique in engaging the entire body of worshippers in vocal and uniform devotion. The reasons for this lack of scholarly attention no doubt derive in part from the familiar critical tendency to underestimate the force of paradigmatic and standardized practices in favor of individualized and spontaneous behavior; and in part from the more specific problem that the use of Psalms poses for scholars interested in constructing a coherent narrative of religion in New England. For however committed the American Puritans may have been to abolishing the Prayer Book of their English past, they were equally serious about maintaining the congregational traditions surrounding the metrical Psalms. In a church shorn of all liturgies, the presence of a standardized Psalter represents a peculiar and compelling aberration.

I began this book by describing the production of the Book of Common Prayer, a text designed to create a single language of public devotion for the minister and congregation alike. In concluding, I want to explore the ways in which the issues that preoccupied the Church of England in justifying common prayer unexpectedly resurface in the decisively nonliturgical world of New England. Although the Common Prayer Book itself has been left behind, the fierce negotiations that it provoked—between original and standardized worship, individual and collective utterances, poetry and devotion—resonate in the discourse surrounding the so-called Bay Psalm Book, the first book to be printed on American soil.[18]

These resonances, moreover, did not escape the notice of either the English or the Massachusetts Bay Puritans. At the same time that Bay Colonists such as Cotton sought to push aside English liturgical traditions, they found themselves forced to defend their use of a Psalter intended to create uniformity in sacred song. How could these New Englanders so vehemently oppose set forms of prayer at the same time that they actively sought to implement set forms of Psalms? In a series of tracts published in the 1640s, the answer that Cotton offers does not primarily lie in what seems to be his strongest defense: that the Prayer Book was humanly authored, whereas the Psalms were texts of Scripture. Instead, he and his fellow divines adopt a surprising explanation for why the Psalter demands a different treatment from other devotional texts. It is because of the Psalms' status as poetry.

"LINING OUT"

In his 1645 treatise, *The Way Of The Churches Of Christ In New England*, John Cotton recounts to his English brethren the reasons for creating a metrical Psalter in the Massachusetts Bay Colony:

> Before Sermon, and many times after, we sing a Psalm, and because the former translation of the Psalms doth in many things vary from the original, and many times paraphraseth rather than translateth; besides diverse other defects (which we cover in silence) we have endeavored a new translation of the Psalms into English meter, as near the original as we could express it in our english tongue, so far as for the present the Lord hath been pleased to help us, and those Psalms we sing, both in our public Churches, and in private.[19]

According to the Bay Psalm Book preface, which Cotton is likely to have written, none of the printed Psalters available for use was ideally suited for the new Puritan congregations.[20] The Sternhold-Hopkins Psalter was regarded as an unfaithful "paraphrase" rather than a strict translation; although the preface acknowledges its indebtedness to God "for the religious endeavors of the translators of the psalms into meter usually annexed to our Bibles," it proceeds to explain that "it is not unknown to the godly learned that they have rather presented a paraphrase than the words of David translated according to the rule 2 chron. 29.30."[21] By contrast, the rigorously Hebraist version produced by Henry Ainsworth, the pastor of the English church in Amsterdam, was not only difficult to sing, as the preface declares, but also strongly affiliated with the separatist Pilgrims at Plymouth, from whom the Bay Colonists wanted to distance themselves.[22]

As Winthrop records in his journal entry for March 1, 1639, the task of publishing the new Psalm Book followed quickly upon the arrival of the first printing press in Massachusetts: "A printing house was begun at Cambridge by one

Daye, at the charge of Mr. Glover, who died on sea hitherward. The first thing which was printed was the freemen's oath, the next was an almanac made for New England by Mr. William Peirce, mariner; the next was the Psalms newly turned into meter."[23] Whether the presence of a local press motivated the production of the Psalter or whether its arrival fortuitously coincided with the project's completion remains unknown. Approximately sixty years later, Cotton Mather recounts in his massive ecclesiastical history of New England, *Magnalia Christi Americana*:

> About the Year 1639 the New-English Reformers . . . though they blessed God for the Religious Endeavors of them who translated the Psalms into the Meter usually annexed at the End of the Bible [Sternhold-Hopkins], yet they beheld in the Translation so many Detractions from, Additions to, and Variations of, not only the Text, but the very Sense of the Psalmist, that it was an Offense unto them. Resolving then upon a New Translation, the chief Divines in the Country, took each of them a Portion to be translated.[24]

The exact identity of the translators involved in this collaborative enterprise has long been a subject of historical debate, occasioned by the comic jingle written by the Cambridge pastor Thomas Shepard and recorded in Cotton's *Magnalia*:

> You Roxb'ry Poets, keep clear of the Crime,
> Of missing to give us very good Rhime.
> And you of Dorchester, your Verses lengthen,
> But with the Texts own Words, you will them strengthen.[25]

Shepard's coded description of Thomas Weld and John Eliot of Roxbury, and Richard Mather of Dorchester, has given prominence to the involvement of these three figures, but many others are likely to have participated, including John Cotton; John Wilson, the original minister and pastor of Boston's First Church; and the English poet Francis Quarles.[26] Notwithstanding several centuries of conjecture, the anonymity of this Psalter was clearly a desired effect: unlike the Sternhold-Hopkins volume, which prints the author's initials with each of the Psalms, both the preface to the Bay Psalm Book and the Bay Psalms themselves are printed without authorial attribution.[27]

Although the Massachusetts Bay Puritans sought to eliminate the liturgical uniformity they had so passionately opposed in the Church of England, the creation of the Bay Psalm Book paradoxically reproduced many of the challenges that the English churchmen had faced in disseminating the Book of Common Prayer. In particular, the problem arose in New England, as it had in England during the previous century, as to how to make a devotional text available to a population with vastly different degrees of literacy and access to books. The Bay Colony churches, like their English counterparts, did not supply their congregations with copies of the Psalms, so that only worshippers who owned their own Psalters would have the text to guide them through the service. In an effort both to minimize costs and maximize portability, the Bay Psalm Book was printed on very small pages; after the first edition, which seems to have been printed in "small octavo," the size of the text was standardized to duodecimo, the popular size for Bibles and Prayer Books in England.[28]

However, as had been the case with the Prayer Book in England, neither book ownership nor literacy was a prerequisite for learning the new metrical Psalms.[29] Instead, the Massachusetts Bay Puritans followed their English brethren in the practice that came to be known as "lining out," in which the Psalms were read aloud verse by verse by the minister or parish clerk before they were sung by the congregation. According to the Westminster *Directory*, the reading of Psalms before singing was recommended as a temporary solution until such a time when all worshippers could read from their own Psalters: "But for the present, where many in the Congregation cannot read, it is convenient that the minister or some other fit person appointed by him and the other Ruling Officers, do read the psalm, line by line, before the singing thereof" (40).

Although some historians have claimed that "lining out" was not firmly established in New England until the second or third generation of colonists, whose lack of religious zeal extended to their poor knowledge of the metrical texts, the practice was certainly in some degree of regular use by 1647 when John Cotton argues:

> It is doubted by some, and concluded by others, that reading of the *Psalms* is not to be allowed in order to singing. We for our parts easily grant, that where all have books and can read, or else can say the *Psalm* by heart, it were needless there to read each line of the *Psalm* before hand in order to singing.

Until such a time of literacy and wealth, however, Cotton recommends that it is "a necessary help, that the words of the *Psalm* be openly read before hand, line after line, or two lines together, that so they who want either books or skill to read, may know what is to be sung, and join with the rest in the duty of singing."[30] In response to those who condemn the reading of Psalms before singing as an "unwarrantable invention of man," Cotton likens this habit of reading to the role that scaffolds play in the New England meeting-house: "no express precept," he argues, "nor example in Scripture calleth for them; and yet the light of Nature easily suggesteth it, that they help to hearing, and so to edification, in as much as they draw multitudes of people to sit within the Minister's voice." So too, Cotton concludes, must "reading in order to Singing" be tolerated as a "necessary or convenient help, either to the hearing or understanding of what is said in the worship of God" (62).

At the heart of Cotton's defense of "lining out" in particular, and of the standardized Psalter in general, lies a categorical distinction between reading prayers and singing Psalms. In response to accusations of inconsistency from English Puritans such as Ball, who argues that "the reasons you bring against a set form of prayer or Liturgy do hold as strong against . . . [the] singing of Psalms," Cotton explains that in order for the congregation to participate in prayer, there is nothing required beyond their listening silently, and at the end of the minister's prayers, "expressing their consent in voice, by saying *Amen*, 1. Corinth. 14.16." By contrast, in the case of the Psalms, the people of God are meant to sing together with one voice, as stated in the Book of Isaiah, chapter 52, verse 8, "which putteth a necessity upon a set form of *Psalms*, else one should sing one thing, and another another thing, which would instead of harmony, breed confusion."[31]

Cotton's argument turns on two seemingly definitive injunctions concerning the different acts of vocal worship: Isaiah's prophetic call for song, "Thy watchmen shall lift up the voice; with the voice together shall they sing"; and Paul's description of prayer: "Else when thou shalt bless with the spirit, how shall he that occupieth the room of the unlearned say Amen at thy giving of thanks, seeing he understandeth not what thou sayest?" And yet, as Cotton is no doubt well aware, this separation of prayer and song is in many respects artificial, not least because the preceding verse from Paul explicitly joins them together: "I will pray with the spirit, and I will pray with the understanding also: I will sing with the spirit, and I will sing with the understanding also" (1. Cor. 14:15). The problem that the New England divines face is ultimately resolved not through invocations of isolated moments in Scripture, but on poetic grounds.

MINISTERIAL GIFTS

In lines that have frequently been repeated as the foundational expression of the New England "plain style," the preface to the Bay Psalm Book declares:

> If therefore the verses are not always so smooth and elegant as some may desire or expect; let them consider that God's Altar needs not our polishings: Ex. 20. for we have respected rather a plain translation, than to smooth our verses with the sweetness of any paraphrase, and so have attended Conscience rather than Elegance, fidelity rather than poetry, in translating the hebrew words into english language, and David's poetry into english meter. (sigs. **3v–**4r)

This description of the new Psalms as unhewn stones seems simultaneously to invoke and reverse Herbert's use of the same passage from Exodus—"And if thou wilt make me an altar of stone, thou shalt not build it of hewn stone: for if thou lift up thy tool upon it, thou hast polluted it"—in "The Altar." Unlike Her-

bert, the Bay Psalm Book preface declares its opposition to forging poetic artifacts out of its devotional sacrifices—"let them consider," the author contends,
"that God's Altar needs not our polishings." And yet, despite this firm disavowal
of poetic ambitions, elsewhere in the preface as well as in related publications
the Bay Puritans explicitly align the Psalms with poetry that requires special
skills, if not aesthetic polishings. In the arguments launched to exempt the Bay
Psalter from New England's general prohibition of standardized devotional
books, Cotton and his fellow divines rely upon a distinction between the difficulty of creating poems versus the ease of creating prayers.

Whereas every good minister by virtue of his election possesses the gift of
prayer, the Bay Psalm Book preface concedes there is no comparable assurance
that ministers will possess the gift of poetry. In response to the anticipated ob-
jection—"Ministers are allowed to pray conceived [newly invented] prayers,
and why not to sing conceived psalms? must we not sing in the spirit as well as
pray in the spirit?"—the preface provides three reasons. First, the minister cannot rely on creating conceived psalms in the manner he can depend upon creating conceived prayers because "every good minister hath not a gift of spiritual
poetry." Second, even if the minister is blessed with this gift, as some exceptional figures were, the congregation is meant to sing together "with joint consent and harmony of all the Church in heart and voice," and therefore needs to
have a standardized Psalm translation that is not spontaneously generated or al-
tered according to the minister's will. Finally, the Book of Psalms is "so complete a System" of holy songs, invented by the Holy Ghost himself in order to
"suit all the conditions, necessities, temptations, affections, &c. of men in all
ages," that even if the minister's new psalms could successfully be implemented
in church worship, they would never achieve the devotional power of the Old
Testament texts.[32]

Now, the notion that the congregation cannot sing together in spontaneous
forms is an argument that dates to late sixteenth-century churchmen's justifications of common prayer; as we saw in chapter 2, Whitgift and Bancroft criticized the non-conformists' liturgy specifically for its dependence upon extempore prayers that the congregation would not be able to follow. And
similarly the argument that the Book of Psalms is a perfect "system" of prayers
can be traced at least to the patristic theologian Athanasius, who described the
Psalms as a book in which "every one may see and perceive the motions and affections of his own heart and soul." But what is novel about the explanation the
preface gives for why ministers should not create new psalms lies in the first of
its three reasons: that "every good minister hath not a gift of spiritual poetry."
However dependable their skills may be in prayer, holy ministers cannot be
guaranteed to possess poetic talent.

This poetic inability is neither regarded as a deficiency in individual ministers, nor is it applauded as a liberation from a suspicious or even idolatrous form of art. Instead, the difficulty of replacing David's Psalms with original songs is meant to confirm the special quality of the Old Testament texts, whose duplication is prevented by God himself:

> Therefore by this the Lord seemeth to stop all men's mouths and minds ordinarily to compile or sing any other psalms (under color that the occasions and conditions of the Church are new) &c. for the public use of the Church, seeing, let our condition be what it will, the Lord himself hath supplied us with far better. (sig. *4)

The reassurance that the Lord actively interferes in the creative process by "stop[ping] all men's mouths and minds" relieves the minister from imagining that he ought "ordinarily" to be capable of composing spiritual poetry. As Cotton argues in *A Modest and Cleare Answer*: "Many a good Minister that is able to express the necessities of the people or the doctrine of salvation in a form of words devised and studied by himself; is not able so to dictate and compose a *Psalm* to be sung by the people every several occasion, no, though he should meditate and study hard for it." "Poetry is not every good scholar's faculty," Cotton concludes, "nor the penning of holy *Psalms* the skill of every good Minister" (31).

What is startling about this account is precisely what it aims to dismiss: the unprecedented and seemingly unwarranted expectation that the minister would possess the special "skill" of the poet. However, this ostensibly unnecessary and elaborate defense of the minister's lack of poetic talent is ultimately revealed as part of a larger strategy to justify what seem to be contradictory positions about poetry's role in the church. On the one hand, Cotton argues for the inappropriateness of using original poems as part of public worship:

> Though many of God's people have gifts to compose spiritual Songs, as well as carnal Poets carnal Sonnets, and Drunkards profane Sonnets; yet that will not argue, that the spiritual Songs, which many of God's people have gifts to compose, are fit to be sung in the public holy Assemblies of the Saints, no more than the carnal and profane Sonnets of drunken Poets are fit to be sung in civil Assemblies. Let drunken carnal Poets sing their carnal Sonnets in their Taverns and Alehouses, and such of God's people as have received a gift to compose a spiritual Song fit for their private solace, sing it in their private houses. (32)

On the other hand, at the same time that Cotton rhetorically aligns spiritual songs with "carnal sonnets," he remains committed to the use of vernacular rhymes and meters—to the use, that is, of English poetry—as the ideal vehicle for translating the Psalms. Far from being "scourged out of the Church of God," as Philip Sidney had warned against, the poetry of the Psalms is celebrated as an important tool for collective worship:

> If God commands the people to join together as well in voice as in heart, to sing
> Psalms, and to sing them with understanding, singing Psalms are a kind of holy
> Poetry, even as Grammar will be a necessary help to translate the Psalms into English;
> So Poetry will be requisite to translate the English into verse. (17)

"The Scriptures cannot be translated into our Mother Tongue," Cotton declares, "without the help of Grammar, nor the Psalms into verse and meter without the help of Poetry" (34).

The specific form of poetry that Cotton recommends bears little resemblance to the "plain style" that we have come to associate with Puritan poetics. In his subsequent work, *Singing of Psalmes a Gospel Ordinance*, Cotton asserts that just as "it is an artificial elegancy which the holy Penmen of Scripture used [when] they penned the Psalms," so it is merely "a sacrilegious niceness, to think it unlawful lively to express all the artificial elegancies of the Hebrew Text, so far as we are able to imitate the same in a translation." For Cotton, there is no inherent opposition between "artificial elegancies" and a faithful translation. Here Cotton's language strikingly echoes that of Wither, who, we will recall, lamented that the "elegancies of those sacred poems have in our language been over-meanly expressed." Indeed, in a sentiment that we might expect from Wither or Donne, and not from the teacher of Boston's church, Cotton concludes: "it were a part of due Faithfulness in a Translator . . . to express lively every elegancy of the Holy Ghost (as much as the vulgar language can reach) that so the people of God may be kindly affected, as well with the *manner* as with the *matter* of the holy Scriptures."[33]

"THEIR OWN COUNTRY POETRY"

When the preface to the Bay Psalm Book declares its commitment to "fidelity rather than poetry," it rehearses a standard disclaimer of poetic ambition that pervades religious verse. This is not to deny the awkward rhymes and tortured syntax of many of these translations; any reader familiar with the Psalms of Sternhold-Hopkins, let alone those of the Sidney Psalter, will recognize the poetic failings of the Bay Psalms, which I do not intend to catalogue here. But regardless of the Psalter's lyric shortcomings, the Bay Psalm Book preface reveals a commitment to poetry much more consistent with Cotton's subsequent accounts than this isolated binary between "fidelity" and "poetry" might suggest. Just as Cotton combines the "faithfulness" of the translator with the "lively elegancy of the Holy Ghost," so too does the preface affirm the inseparability of a faithful and a poetic translation.

In addition to this famous disclaimer in its final paragraph, the preface contains an alternative account of the Bay Psalter's poetic aspirations. This account is far less prominently displayed in the pages of the preface, and far less consonant with the image of New England poetry that we have so powerfully inherited. Buried deep within the thirteen-page text, the author of the preface responds to the question of whether the Psalms ought to be sung "in their own words, or in such meter as english poetry is wont to run in" with the seemingly simple declaration:

> If in our english tongue we are to sing them, then as all our english songs (according to the course of our english poetry) do run in meter, so ought David's psalms to be translated into meter, that so we may sing the Lord's songs, as in our english tongue so in such verses as are familiar to an english ear which are commonly metrical. (sigs. ** 1 v–** 2r)

The choice of English meter not only accommodates the "english ear," and therefore facilitates congregational song, but also reflects God's own design:

> But the truth is, as the Lord hath hid from us the hebrew tunes, lest we should think our selves bound to imitate them; so also the course and frame (for the most part) of their hebrew poetry, that we might not think our selves bound to imitate that, but that every nation without scruple might follow as the graver sort of tunes of their own country songs, so the graver sort of verses of their own country poetry. (sig. ** 2r)

The failure of Old Testament scholars to understand the formal properties of the Psalms is cleverly manipulated into a divine mandate for vernacular poetry: God has kept secret the nature of Hebrew verse in order to enable his worshippers to pursue their own poetic forms in their translations of Scripture.

In addition to liberating vernacular poets from their futile search for the mysteries of Hebrew verse, an objective others have had before, these sentences contain within them early hints of New England's eventual quest for independence. For as its rhetoric unfolds, the initial emphasis on the linguistic category of English shifts to denote a geographic and political category: God's obfuscation is meant to enable the production of Psalms not for every tongue, but for "every nation." The repetition of the phrase "their own country" within the context of a Psalter explicitly created for use in the Bay Colony sets New England distinctly apart from the England it left behind. And if the sixteenth-century Protestant reformers chose common prayer as the crucial language for reforming the country's devotion, the seventeenth-century divines of Massachusetts Bay build their congregational worship upon a foundation of common poems.

Notes

Introduction

1. William Shakespeare, *Hamlet*, in *The Norton Shakespeare*, ed. Stephen Greenblatt (New York: W. W. Norton and Co., 1997). This and subsequent references are to act, scene, and line.

2. Although Claudius's notion that his external posture will assist his internal condition distinctly reflects what we will discover to be the Reformed English position, his appeal to angels for assistance one line earlier—"Help, angels!"—seems to invoke a Catholic understanding of devotional intercession. However, Shakespeare perhaps unwittingly hits on a subject of much ambiguity within English doctrine: while article 22 of the Thirty-nine Articles does forbid the invocation of saints as "a fond thing, vainly invented, and grounded upon no warranty of Scripture, but rather repugnant to the word of God," there is no specific ruling against the invocation of angels (Charles Hardwick, *A History of the Articles of Religion* [Deighton, Bell and Co., 1859], 305). Richard Hooker conjoins angels and saints as heretical objects of devotion; in a sermon on Matthew, chapter 7, verse 7, he instructs against "invocation of any other than God alone," explaining "that whereas God hath in scripture delivered us so many patterns for imitation when we pray . . . there is not one no not one to be found directed unto Angels or saints or any saving God alone" (*The Folger Library Edition of the Works of Richard Hooker*, ed. W. Speed Hill, 6 vols. [Cambridge, Mass.: The Belknap Press of Harvard University Press, 1977–93], 5:386, lines 20–27). Whatever its doctrinal status, Claudius's ostensibly heretical plea to the angels is certainly not unique in Reformed devotion; even the pious conformist George Herbert laments the church's position in his poem "To All Angels and Saints":

> Not out of envie or maliciousnesse
> Do I forbear to crave your speciall aid:
>   I would addresse
> My vows to thee most gladly, Blessed Maid,
> And Mother of my God, in my distresse . . .
> But now, alas, I dare not; for our King,
> Whom we do all joyntly adore and praise,
> Bids no such thing.

(*The Works of George Herbert*, ed. F. E. Hutchinson [Oxford: Oxford University Press, 1941], 7–10, 16–18).

3. A. C. Bradley, *Shakespearean Tragedy* (New York: Ballantine Books, 1991), 115.

4. Samuel Johnson, *Selections from Johnson on Shakespeare*, ed. Bertrand H. Bronson (New Haven, Conn.: Yale University Press, 1986), 334.

5. Francis Bacon, "Certain Observations Made upon a libel Published this Present Year, 1592, entitled 'A Declaration of the true causes of the great Troubles, presupposed to be intended against the Realm of England,'" in Bacon, *Works*, 8 vols., ed. James Spedding (London: Longman, 1861), 1:178.

6. Patrick Collinson, "The Elizabethan Church and the New Religion," in *The Reign of Elizabeth I*, ed. Christopher Haigh (Basingstoke, England: Macmillan, 1984), 178.

7. Katharine Eisaman Maus, for example, contends that this moment in *Hamlet* speaks to a larger trend within Renaissance texts, which consistently distinguished between the individual's "unexpressed interior" and "theatricalized exterior"; "the point of such distinction," Maus claims, "is normally to privilege what is classified as interior" (*Inwardness and Theater in the English Renaissance* [Chicago: University of Chicago Press, 1995], 2). Maus's argument is itself a response to those critics who deny altogether the internality of the early modern subject: as Maus acutely observes, Catherine Belsey's contention that the "unified subject of liberal humanism" emerged only in the late seventeenth century, or Francis Barker's characterization of the English Renaissance as a period of "pre-bourgeois subjection," sweepingly reduces all apparent manifestations of inwardness in Tudor-Stuart England to mere instances of critical anachronism, with Hamlet in act 1 as a jarring but remarkable exception. (Catherine Belsey, *The Subject of Tragedy* [New York: Methuen, 1985]; Francis Barker, *The Tremulous Private Body* [New York: Methuen, 1984].)

8. For further discussion of these issues in *Hamlet*, see my article "The Performance of Prayer: Sincerity and Theatricality in Early Modern England," *Representations* 60 (fall 1997): 49–69.

9. *The Basic Works of Aristotle*, ed. Richard McKeon (New York: Random House, 1941), 952.

10. Augustine, *Confessions*, trans. R. S. Pine-Coffin (London: Penguin Books, 1961), 207.

11. William Tyndale, *Doctrinal Treatises and Introductions to different portions of the Holy Scripture*, ed. Rev. Henry Walter (Cambridge: Cambridge University Press, 1848), 255. I am using Tyndale's translation of the Book of Matthew here to facilitate my discussion of Tyndale's *Exposition on Matthew* in the pages that follow.

12. Tyndale, *Doctrinal Treatises*, 257.

13. Martin Luther, *Luther's Works*, ed. Jaroslav Pelikan and Helmut Lehman, 55 vols. (St. Louis: Concordia Publishing House, 1955–), 21:142–43.

14. Lancelot Andrewes, *Works*, 11 vols. (Oxford: John Henry Parker, 1843), 5:325. This sermon is not dated. For a definitive calendar of Andrewes's court sermons, see the diskette included with Peter E. McCullough's illuminating study of court preaching under Elizabeth and James, *Sermons at Court: Politics and Religion in Elizabethan and Jacobean Preaching* (Cambridge: Cambridge University Press, 1998).

15. Thomas Becon, *The Catechism, with other pieces*, ed. Rev. John Ayre (Cambridge: Cambridge University Press, 1844), 125.

16. *Five Pious and Learned Discourses . . . by Robert Shelford of Ringsfield in Suffolk. Priest* (Cambridge: Cambridge University Press, 1635), 24. I am indebted to Peter Lake's groundbreaking article, "The Laudian Style: Order, Uniformity and the Pursuit of the Beauty of Holiness in the 1630s" (in *The Early Stuart Church, 1603–42*, ed. Kenneth Fincham [Basingstoke, England: Macmillan, 1993], 161–85), for references to Shelford, Browning, and Robarts.

17. Foulke Robarts, *Gods Holy House and Service* (London, 1639), 61–62.

18. John Browning, *Concerning Publicke-Prayer; And the Fasts of the Church. Six Sermons, or Tractates* (London: Richard Badger, 1636), 25.

19. Thomas Browne, *Religio Medici*, ed. James Winnow (Cambridge: Cambridge University Press, 1963), 5.

20. John Bulwer, *Chirologia: Or the Natural Language of the Hand, and Chironomia: Or the Art of Manual Rhetoric*, ed. James W. Cleary (Carbondale, Ill.: Southern Illinois University Press, 1974), 23.

21. Augustine, *The City of God against the Pagans*, trans. William M. Green, 7 vols. (Cambridge, Mass.: Harvard University Press, 1972), bk. 22, chap. 8, pp. 213, 219.

22. Robarts, *Gods Holy House and Service*, sig. 3v.

23. Browning, *Concerning Publicke-Prayer*, 25.

24. Ibid.

25. Philip Sidney, *The Countess of Pembroke's Arcadia* [known as the *New Arcadia*], ed. Maurice Evans (London: Penguin Books, 1977), 464.

26. John Milton, *Eikonoklastes*. In *Complete Prose*, ed. Merritt Y. Hughes, 6 vols. (New Haven, Conn.: Yale University Press, 1962): 3:362. There is a long history of debate over Milton's possible role in the publication of Pamela's prayer in *Eikon Basilike*; in 1693, Milton was charged with forgery, a charge that Dr. Johnson, among others, later accepted. Hughes's full analysis of these circumstances persuasively exonerates Milton, or at least casts sufficient doubt on the evidence against him (*Complete Prose*, 3:152–59).

Chapter One

1. *The Letters of Stephen Gardiner*, ed. James Arthur Muller (Cambridge: Cambridge University Press, 1933), 355.

2. Ibid.

3. In Thomas Frederick Simmons, *The Lay folks' Mass Book*, hereafter LFMB (Oxford: Oxford University Press, 1879), 365.

4. Ibid., 364; emphasis mine.

5. In addition to his position as prebendary, Harding was the chaplain and personal confessor to Bishop Gardiner.

6. In *The Works of John Jewel*, ed. John Ayre, 3 vols. (Cambridge: Cambridge University Press, 1845–50), 1:332.

7. *Miscellaneous Writings and Letters of Thomas Cranmer*, ed. John Edmund Cox (Cambridge: Cambridge University Press, 1846), 180.

8. Jewel, *Works*, 1:323–24.

9. Diarmaid MacCulloch, *Thomas Cranmer, A Life* (New Haven, Conn.: Yale University Press, 1996), 223. I am indebted to this magisterial biography, which greatly contributed to my understanding of Cranmer and the ecclesiastical world in which he lived.

10. Ibid., 223, 224.

11. For an informative overview of the production of the Prayer Book and its uses of earlier materials, see A. G. Dickens, *The English Reformation*, 2d ed. (London: B. T. Batsford Ltd., 1989), 242–55. See also Leighton Pullan, *The History of the Book of Common Prayer* (London: Longmans Green & Co., 1900); Daniel Rock, *The Church of Our Fathers*, ed. G. W. Hart and W. H. Frere, 4 vols. (London: John Murray, 1905); and Francis Procter, *A New History of the Book of Common Prayer*, revised and rewritten by Walter Howard Frere (London: Macmillan, 1902).

12. Here I echo the argument made by John N. Wall, whose introductory chapters in *Transformations of the Word: Spenser, Herbert, Vaughan* (Atlanta: The University of Georgia Press, 1988) represent one of the most serious and sustained considerations of the Prayer

Book's influence upon early modern religious community. Wall rightly protests the tendency among scholars to emphasize the abstract theological commitments and debates that surround the Prayer Book over the more palpable transformations it brought to the social and devotional lives of English Protestants. "Thus it was," he claims, "that in the reigns of Edward, Elizabeth, James, and Charles the Church of England came to understand itself and to understand Christianity less in terms of assent to doctrine than in terms of behavior" (43). Although Wall does not dwell upon Hooker's contribution to this project, his focus on devotional behavior rather than theology has been very useful to me in considering book 5 of The Lawes.

13. Patrick Collinson, for example, focuses on the central role of obedience as the "weapon of episcopacy" in The Religion of Protestants: The Church in English Society, 1559–1625 (Oxford: Clarendon Press, 1982). Although Collinson acknowledges that "the 'multitude' doubtless conformed in great numbers to the prayer book religion of the parish church" (191), he never imagines that this obedience might have had a profound influence upon the people's devotional lives. Peter Lake's Anglicans and Puritans?: Presbyterianism and English Conformist Thought from Whitgift to Hooker (Boston: Allen & Unwin, 1988) documents the church's struggle with, and (temporary) triumph over, early forms of presbyterianism in the late Elizabethan period; in this account, conformity is likewise imagined as a largely ecclesiastical and Erastian rather than a devotional project, in which Richard Hooker serves as the crucial figure in the construction of an "Anglican" polity. The one significant exception to this tendency among historians is Judith Maltby's elucidating and intelligent new study, Prayer Book and People in Elizabethan and Early Stuart England (Cambridge: Cambridge University Press, 1998), which documents the depth of devotional commitment to the Prayer Book among mainstream English Protestants. Maltby's detailed analysis of the court records and petitions filed in favor of the Prayer Book in the years 1640–42 decisively shows that commitments to the liturgy cannot be explained away as superficial conformity. Her argument offers a strong challenge both to Collinson's overarching focus on Puritanism as the most vigorous and devotionally serious branch of early modern English Protestantism, and to Christopher Haigh's contention that the Church of England was filled with so-called parish Anglicans who were merely holding on to whatever traces of Catholic practice and ritual they could find in the reformed rite (Haigh, Reformation and Resistance in Tudor Lancashire [London: Cambridge University Press, 1975], and English Reformations: Religion, Politics, and Society under the Tudors [Oxford: Clarendon Press, 1993]).

14. Haigh neatly encapsulates this position at the end of his study, English Reformations, as follows: "The endowments and equipment of traditional worship were confiscated by governments, and comfortable old rituals were scrapped, and replaced by the sterilized services of the Book of Common Prayer. The instruments of popish superstition had thus been destroyed, but the attitudes which had sustained them had not" (288). See Eamon Duffy, The Stripping of the Altars: Traditional Religion in England 1400–1580 (New Haven, Conn.: Yale University Press, 1992) and John Bossy, Christianity in the West 1400–1700 (Oxford: Oxford University Press, 1985).

15. The Complete Works of Thomas More, vol. 9, The Apology, ed. J. B. Trapp (New Haven, Conn.: Yale University Press, 1979), 103.

16. William Maskell, Monumenta Ritualia Ecclesiae Anglicanae, 3 vols. (Oxford: Clarendon Press, 1882), 1:xi–xiii.

17. F. E. Brightman, *The English Rite*, 2 vols. (London: Rivingstons, 1921), 1:36. All references to the Book of Common Prayer are from this edition.

18. Duffy, *The Stripping of the Altars*, 213.

19. Ibid., 215.

20. Anne Hudson, *The Premature Reformation* (Oxford: Clarendon Press, 1988), 166–68.

21. *Acts and Monuments of John Foxe*, ed. George Townsend, 8 vols. (New York: AMC Press, 1965), 4:580–81. For an account of the church's persecution of Lollards in the early sixteenth century, see John A. F. Thomson, *The Latter Lollards, 1414–1520* (Oxford: Oxford University Press, 1965). For a brief discussion of Harding's case, see p. 92.

22. According to Margaret Deanesly, *The Lay folks' Mass Book* was originally written by the archdeacon of Rouen, Jeremias, about 1150; the French version was probably used in England until the fourteenth century, when it was first translated into northern English. As Deanesly establishes, this manual confirms that the Bible was read exclusively in Latin during the Mass (*The Lollard Bible and Other Medieval Biblical Versions* [Cambridge: Cambridge University Press, 1920; reprint, 1966], 212–14).

23. This particular rubric is from the York Order of the Mass, reprinted in Simmons, *LFMB*, 100.

24. Ibid., text B, 26.278–86. This and subsequent references are to page and line.

25. Lyndwood's Latin instruction is "ne impediatur populus orare." Cited in Duffy, *The Stripping of the Altars*, 117.

26. Simmons, *LFMB*, text B, 44–46.480–95.

27. This moment in the Canon is described more fully in a contemporary manual written for use in convents, *The Myroure of Oure Ladye*:

> After the sacring the priest sayeth the Pater noster, all aloud that the people may hear it & pray the same in their hearts. And therefore he beginneth with *Oremus*, That is to say, pray we. For in this time ye ought to hear the priest and to pray with him. (Quoted in Simmons, *LFMB*, 292).

28. Simmons, *LFMB*, text B, 56.600–606.

29. Duffy, *The Stripping of the Altars*, 98.

30. *Articles to be enquired of in the generall visitation of Edmonde [Bonner] Bisshoppe of London, exercised by him the yeare of oure Lorde 1554* (London, 1554), article 32.

31. J. Eric Hunt, *Cranmer's First Litany, 1544 and Merbecke's Book of Common Prayer Notes, 1550* (London: SPCK, 1939), 86.

32. Wilhelm Pauck, ed., *Melancthon and Bucer* (Philadelphia: Westminster Press, 1969), 14; Edmund Hooper, *Later Writings of Bishop Hooper*, ed. Charles Nevinson (Cambridge: Cambridge University Press, 1852), 122–23, 146; and Walter H. Frere, ed., *Visitation Articles and Injunctions of the Period of the Reformation*, 3 vols. (London: Longmans Green & Co., 1910), 3:166–67.

33. Maskell, *Monumenta*, 1:xxv.

34. *The Remains of Edmund Grindal*, ed. William Nicholson (Cambridge: Cambridge University Press, 1843), 133.

35. This was originally printed on the last page of the 1549 Book of Common Prayer (Brightman, *The English Rite*, 2:926).

36. Andrew Gurr, "The Shakespearean Stage," in *The Norton Shakespeare*, ed. Stephen

Greenblatt (New York: W. W. Norton, 1997), 3285. See also Lawrence Stone, *Family and Fortune* (Oxford: Clarendon Press, 1973), 59–61.

37. Hunt, *Cranmer's First Litany*, 86.

38. Maskell, *Monumenta*, 1:ccviii.

39. Ibid., 1:ccix.

40. One of the many strengths of Maltby's study lies in her profitable use not only of visitation articles, which she rightly calls "the church's machinery of enforcing discipline," but also of the church wardens' required reports about their own ministers to the consistory courts (*Prayer Book and People*, 33–34). Hence, as she convincingly shows, the disciplining mechanism worked in both directions.

41. Cranmer, *Miscellaneous Writings*, 161; Hooper, *Later Writings*, 141–42.

42. James Raine, ed., *Depositions and other Ecclesiastical Proceedings from the Courts of Durham*, vol. 21, *The Publications of the Surtees Society* (London, 1845), 231.

43. Cranmer, *Miscellaneous Writings*, 169–70.

44. Ibid., 449–50; emphasis mine.

45. In *De Regno Christi*, Cranmer's friend and advisor Martin Bucer advises that the Protestant worshippers "should not only listen to the prayers with the greatest attention but they should also reply to the minister: and not only Amen but also those other things which are customarily said in reply to ministers." "For these responses," he explains, "are not the concern of the clergy only, any more than the prayers themselves are, but of the whole people" (144).

46. The four lines are from Psalm 50:17 ("Priest" and "Answer"), Psalm 37:23, and Psalm 69:2, respectively. In the 1549 text, the service is still called by its Latinate name, "matins"; this is changed in 1552 to "morning prayer."

47. MacCulloch, *Thomas Cranmer, A Life*, 217.

48. *Sermons and Remains of Hugh Latimer*, ed. George Elwes Corrie (Cambridge: Cambridge University Press, 1844), 179–80.

49. The 1563 Homily on Repentance likewise affirms the individual's right to share doubts of conscience with a curate or pastor or godly man, but insists that "it is against the true Christian liberty that any man should be bound to the numbering of his sins" (cited in Frere, *Visitation Articles*, 2:298).

50. Latimer, *Sermons and Remains*, 180.

51. Brightman, *The English Rite*, 2:656–58.

52. See Thomas N. Tentler, *Sin and Confession on the Eve of the Reformation* (Princeton, N.J.: Princeton University Press, 1977), 349ff.

53. This same text is included in the 1549 Prayer Book, but comes later in the service.

54. MacCulloch, *Thomas Cranmer, A Life*, 510; Hooper, *Later Writings*, 125.

55. *The Two Liturgies with other Documents set forth by authority in the Reign of King Edward The Sixth*, ed. Rev. Joseph Ketley (Cambridge: Cambridge University Press, 1844), 382.

56. Ibid., 383.

57. Following this version of the General Confession, the Primer provides an additional prayer, listed with the instruction "Add to this confession this Prayer." Hence the individualized version of the General Confession is clearly the "confession of thy sins" indicated in the initial rubric, while the instruction to add "the prayer following" points to a separate text, which begins: "Almighty God, the Father of our Lord Jesus Christ, which desirest not the death of a sinner, but rather that he may turn from his wickedness and live . . ." (ibid.).

Chapter Two

1. John Milton, *Eikonoklastes*, in *Complete Prose*, ed. Merritt Y. Hughes, 6 vols. (New Haven, Conn.: Yale University Press, 1962), 3:505.

2. Ibid., 506.

3. W. H. Frere and C. E. Douglas, eds., *Puritan Manifestoes* (London: Society for Promoting Christian Knowledge, 1907), 21.

4. Ibid.

5. For the relationship between theatrical and liturgical performances, see Jeffrey Knapp, "Players and Preachers in Shakespeare's England," *Representations* 44 (fall 1993): 29–59 and Targoff, "The Performance of Prayer," *Representations* 60 (fall 1997): 49–69.

6. 1 Cor. 14:15.

7. Frere and Douglas, *Puritan Manifestoes*, 114–15.

8. Ibid., 29.

9. *Miscellaneous Writings and Letters of Thomas Cranmer*, ed. John Edmund Cox (Cambridge: Cambridge University Press, 1846), 180.

10. See p. 26 above.

11. Frere and Douglas, *Puritan Manifestoes*, 115.

12. *Oxford English Dictionary*, 2d ed., s.v. "intend."

13. Cited in John Whitgift, *The defense of the answere to the Admonition* (London, 1574), 501.

14. Ibid.

15. This rubric is from the General Confession; see p. 33 above.

16. Whitgift, *The defense of the answere to the Admonition*, 502.

17. Ibid., 501–2.

18. Ibid., 533.

19. *Certain Sermons or Homilies* (1547) and *A Homily against Disobedience and Wilful Rebellion* (1570), ed. Ronald B. Bond (Toronto: University of Toronto Press, 1987), 55–56.

20. Ibid., 57.

21. *Iniunctions Geven By The Quenes Maiestie* (London: R. Jugge and J. Cawood, 1559), article 3.

22. Christopher Haigh, ed., *The Reign of Elizabeth I* (London: Macmillan, 1984), 185. See also Christopher Hill, *The Economic Problems of the Church, from Archbishop Whitgift to the Long Parliament* (Oxford: Clarendon Press, 1956), 108–9, 250, and passim.

23. Haigh, *The Reign of Elizabeth I*, 186.

24. Thomas Cooper, *An Admonition To The People Of England: Wherein Are Answered, Not Onely The slanderous untruethes, reprochfully uttered by Martin the Libeller, but also many other Crimes by some of his broode, obiected generally against all Bishops* (London: Christopher Barker, 1589), 115.

25. Martin Marprelate [pseud.], *O read over D. John Bridges, for it is a worthy worke: Or an epitome of the first Booke of that right worshipfull volume written against the Puritanes* (Printed overseas in Europe within two furlongs of a Bouncing Priest at the cost and charges of M. Marprelate, gentleman), 33, 34.

26. Cooper, *An Admonition To The People Of England*, 115.

27. See Haigh, *The Reign of Elizabeth I*, 183.

28. For a history of Grindal and his role in the Elizabethan church, see Patrick Collinson, *Archbishop Grindal, 1519–1583: The Struggle for a Reformed Church* (Berkeley: University of California Press, 1979).

29. Unlike the Homilies, the Book of Common Prayer was translated into Welsh in

1567. See Albert Owen Evans, *A Chapter in the History of the Welsh Book of Common Prayer*, 3 vols. (Bangor, Maine: Jarvis & Foster, 1922). For Penry's text to Parliament, see *A Treatise containing the Aequity of An Humble Supplication . . .*, in *An Introductory Sketch to the Martin Marprelate Controversy, 1588–1590*, ed. Edward Arbre (London, 1880), 62. According to the arguments launched by the Protestant reformers against the Latin liturgy that we examined in chapter 1, Penry's complaint about the use of a largely foreign tongue in Wales would seem completely legitimate: Cranmer's aim was not to elevate English per se, but to render the liturgy comprehensible to all worshippers. By the time James came to the throne, Penry's arguments seem to have prevailed: the first volume of Homilies in Welsh was published by the King's printer, Robert Barker, in 1606.

30. Marprelate, *O read over D. John Bridges*, 30.

31. Martin Marprelate [pseud.], *Hay any worke for Cooper* (Printed in Europe not farre from some of the Bouncing Priestes), 46.

32. Anonymous, "The Lamentable Complaint of the Commonalitie," in *Parte of a Register, contayninge sundrie memorable matters, written by divers godly and learned in our time* (Edinburgh: Waldegrave, 1593), 211.

33. See Patrick Collinson, *The Elizabethan Puritan Movement* (Berkeley: University of California Press, 1967) and *The Religion of Protestants* (Oxford: Clarendon Press, 1982).

34. Marprelate, *Hay any work for Cooper*, 17–18.

35. *A booke of the forme of common prayers, administration of the Sacraments, &tc. agreable to Gods worde, and the use of the reformed Churches* (Edinburgh: Waldegrave). The first passage is from the 1584 edition; the second, from 1587.

36. John Strype, *The Life and Acts of John Whitgift*, 4 vols. (Oxford: Clarendon Press, 1822), 3:188.

37. Maltby mentions, for example, the case of a group of Suffolk parishioners who "brought their own copies of the Prayer Book to divine service in order to note more accurately their non-conformist minister's deviation from the liturgy" (*Prayer Book and People in Elizabethan and Early Stuart England* [Cambridge: Cambridge University Press, 1998], 28).

38. Strype, *The Life and Acts of John Whitgift*, 188–89.

39. 1 John 4:1.

40. Richard Bancroft, *A Sermon Preached At Paule's Crosse the 9. of Februarie, being the first Sunday in the Parleament, Anno 1588. by Richard Bancroft D. of Divinitie* (London, 1588), 62.

41. Ibid., 63.

42. Maltby provides evidence of parishioners in Lincolnshire in the 1590s, for example, who registered formal complaints against their minister for reading too hastily and refusing to let them participate in the service (*Prayer Book and People*, 42).

43. Bancroft, *A Sermon Preached At Paule's Crosse*, 63.

44. Ibid., 65.

45. For further discussion of the peculiar conditions surrounding the efficacy of "amen" as a devotional speech-act, and its potential complications of J. L. Austin's models of performative language (Austin, *How to Do Things with Words*, 2d ed. by J. O. Urmson and Marina Sbisà [Cambridge, Mass.: Harvard University Press, 1975]), see my forthcoming article, "'Dirty Amens': Coercion and Consent in *Richard III*."

46. See Peter Lake, *Anglicans and Puritans?: Presbyterianism and English Conformist Thought from Whitgift to Hooker* (Boston: Allen & Unwin, 1988), 227.

47. John E. Booty, introduction to book 5 in the *Lawes*, in *The Folger Library Edition of the*

Works of Richard Hooker, ed. W. Speed Hill, 6 vols. (Cambridge, Mass.: The Belknap Press of Harvard University Press, 1977–93), vol. 6, pt. 1, p. 202.

48. Hooker, *Works*, 2:112.

49. *Oxford English Dictionary*, 2d ed., s.v. "probable."

50. Hooker, *Works*, 1:33.

51. See Shuger's fine essay, "Society Supernatural," in *Religion and Culture in Renaissance England*, ed. Claire McEachern and Debora Shuger (Cambridge: Cambridge University Press, 1997). See also Shuger's brilliant account of Hooker in *Habits of Thought in the English Renaissance: Religion, Politics, and the Dominant Culture* (Berkeley: University of California Press, 1990).

52. Cited in Lake, *Anglicans and Puritans?* 39–40.

53. Jon. 3:5–8.

54. St. John Chrysostom, *On the Incomprehensible Nature of God*, trans. Paul W. Harkins (Washington, D.C.: Catholic University of America Press, 1984), 112.

55. "Prayer (I)," in *The Works of George Herbert*, ed. F. E. Hutchinson (Oxford: Oxford University Press, 1941), 5.

56. Hooker, *Works*, 2:112.

57. *The Sermons of John Donne*, ed. George R. Potter and Evelyn M. Simpson, 10 vols. (Berkeley: University of California Press, 1953–62), 5:13.

58. These passages from Hooker and Donne rehearse the fear of private prayer that pervades many late sixteenth- and seventeenth-century writings. Although there was certainly no injunction against praying privately, and in fact private prayer was always encouraged as an important complement to public devotion, English conformists generally considered what the Sermon on the Mount refers to as the "secret closet" of prayer to be a far riskier devotional site than its public counterpart. For a rich and provocative account of the devotional manuals that were written specifically for the "prayer closet," see Richard Rambuss, *Closet Devotions* (Durham, N.C.: Duke University Press, 1998), 103–35. As Rambuss shows, unlike the public liturgy of the church, the manuals written for closet prayer, with titles like *Enter into thy Closet, The Duties of the Closet*, and *The Privy Key of Heaven*, encourage an interiorized and often eroticized devotion that depends upon both bodily and spiritual searching of the self. Most of the works that Rambuss examines were published in the latter half of the seventeenth century, and seem likely to reflect changes in devotional climate in the aftermath of the Restoration.

59. Cited in William Bouwsma, *John Calvin: A Sixteenth Century Portrait* (New York: Oxford University Press, 1988), 89.

60. Hooker, *Works*, 2:148.

61. "The Church Porch," in *The Works of George Herbert*, 439–40.

62. Hooker, *Works*, 2:116.

63. Cited in Hooker, *Works*, 2:143.

Chapter Three

1. Diarmaid MacCulloch, *Thomas Cranmer, A Life* (New Haven, Conn.: Yale University Press, 1996), 331.

2. According to Rivkah Zim, more than seventy separate English Psalters were published between 1530 and 1600, although many of these were in prose (Zim, *English Metrical Psalms: Poetry as Praise and Prayer, 1535–1601* [Cambridge: Cambridge University Press,

1987], 2). For a complete list of metrical Psalms published during this period, see Zim's instructive appendix (211ff), to which I am enormously indebted.

3. Thomas Frederick Simmons, *The Lay folks' Mass Book* (Oxford: Oxford University Press, 1879), text B, 8–10. Reprinted in Frank Allen Patterson, *The Middle English Penitential Lyric* (New York: Columbia University Press, 1911). In the case of these medieval lyrics, I have modernized the spelling except when the modernization affects the rhyme of the verse.

4. For the Latin text of Peckham's program of instruction, often referred to as the "Ignorantia sacerdotum" (the first words of this article in the 1281 Canons), see F. M. Powicke and C. R. Cheney, *Councils and Synods* (Oxford: Clarendon Press, 1964) vol. 2, pt. 2, 900–905.

5. G. R. Owst, *Preaching in Medieval England: An Introduction to Sermon Manuscripts of the period c. 1350–1450.* (Cambridge: Cambridge University Press, 1926), 281–82.

6. For further exploration of the role of the vernacular in medieval culture, see Jocelyn Wogn-Browne, Nicholas Watson, Andrew Taylor, and Ruth Evans, eds., *The Idea of the Vernacular: An Anthology of Middle English Literary Theory 1280–1520* (University Park, Pa.: Pennsylvania State University Press, 1999); Nicholas Watson, "Censorship and Cultural Change in Late Medieval England: Vernacular Theology, the Oxford Translation Debate, and Arundel's Constitutions of 1409," *Speculum* 70 (1995): 822–64; Margaret Aston, "Wycliffe and the Vernacular," in Aston, *Faith and Fire: Popular and Unpopular Religion, 1350–1600* (Rio Grande, Ohio: Hambledon Press, 1993), 27–72; and A. J. Minnis, ed., *Latin and Vernacular: Studies in Late Medieval Texts and Manuscripts* (Cambridge: D. S. Brewer, 1989). For literary studies that specifically address the status of verse in the lay prayers of the pre-Reformation era, see, among others, Margaret Deanesly, *The Lollard Bible and Other Medieval Biblical Versions* (Cambridge: Cambridge University Press, 1920; reprint, 1966), 213–16 and passim; Derek Pearsall, *Old English and Middle English Poetry* (London: Routledge and Kegan Paul, 1977), 103–4; and N. F. Blake, *Middle English Religious Prose* (Evanston, Ill.: Northwestern University Press, 1972), 7.

7. For a copy of the letter that Thoresby sent to Gaytrig, with an English translation, see R. N. Swanson, "The Origins of the Lay folks' Catechism," *Medium Aevum* 60, no. 1 (1991): 92–100. See also David A. Lawton's discussion of Gaytrig's text in "Gaytryge's Sermon, Dictamen, and Middle English Alliterative Verse," *Modern Philology* (May 1979): 329–43.

8. Robert Mannyng, *Handlyng Synne and its French original,* ed. Frederick Furnivall (London: Kegan Paul, Trench Trubner & Co., 1901), lines 42–56.

9. Mary J. Carruthers, *The Book of Memory: A Study of Memory in Medieval Culture* (Cambridge: Cambridge University Press, 1985), 82.

10. *Instructions for Parish Priests by John Myrc,* ed. Edward Peacock (London: Kegan Paul, Trench Trubner & Co., Ltd. 1868), lines 404–11, 413. The date for this work is unknown; according to Peacock, the oldest manuscript is from circa 1450, and the *Dictionary of National Biography* (London: Oxford University Press, 1921–22) lists Myrc (spelled here "Mirk") as flourishing about 1400.

11. Both lyrics are included in Frank Patterson, *The Middle English Penitential Lyric* (New York: Columbia University Press, 1911), 108.

12. For the use of verse in sermons, see Owst, *Preaching in Medieval England.* For more recent work on this subject, see, among others, H. Leith Spencer, *English Preaching in the Late*

Middle Ages (Oxford: Clarendon Press, 1993); and Siegfried Wenzel's *Verses in Sermons: "Fasciculus Morum" and Its Middle English Poems* (Cambridge, Mass.: Mediaeval Academy of America Publications 87, 1978).

13. From the Merton College MS, collection of John Sheppey; printed in Carleton Brown, *Religious Lyrics of the Fourteenth Century*, 2d ed., revised by G. V. Smithers (Oxford: Clarendon Press, 1952), 51. Sermons such as this were usually preserved in manuscript in Latin, a translation that reflects not only the status of Latin as the preeminent written language, but also the desire among medieval ecclesiastics to facilitate the use of sermons outside of the local dialects in which they may have been originally delivered. The poems that are scattered throughout these manuscripts, however, often remain in their vernacular form.

14. Brown, *Religious Lyrics of the Fourteenth Century*, xix.

15. Grimestone's was one of many vernacular translations of the Latin *Horae de Sancta Cruce*; see Simmons, *The Lay folks' Mass Book*, 85–87 for the Latin text, and 346–53 for explicatory notes.

16. Patterson, *The Penitential Lyric*, 21; Eamon Duffy, *The Stripping of the Altars: Traditional Religion in England 1400–1580* (New Haven, Conn.: Yale University Press, 1992), 61.

17. Brown, *Religious Lyrics of the Fourteenth Century*, 211–12, lines 1–8, 13–20, 25–28.

18. Patterson, *The Penitential Lyric*, 48ff, lines 29–35, 43–49.

19. Although literary critics have rightly tended to read these poems as anonymous, impersonal, and paradigmatic, there are important exceptions to this general rule. See Lee Patterson's persuasive and original account in *Chaucer and the Subject of History*, in which he argues that the critical prejudice against these lyrics has caused us to ignore a number of significant, idiosyncratic poems in which the speaker fails to produce an "authorized penitential language" (Madison: University of Wisconsin Press, 1991, pp. 374–89).

20. William Langland, *The Vision of Piers Plowman*, ed. A. V. C. Schmidt (London: Everyman, 1991) text B, passus 5, lines 394–96.

21. The critical literature on medieval religious lyric is too vast to catalogue here. For an introduction to the field, see Rosemary Woolf's authoritative study, *The English Religious Lyric in the Middle Ages* (Oxford: Clarendon Press, 1968). For a sampling of this literature, see Carleton Brown's anthologies, *Religious Lyrics of the Fourteenth Century* and *Religious Lyrics of the Fifteenth Century* (Oxford: Clarendon Press, 1939). For a broader European context, see Patrick Diehl, *The Medieval European Religious Lyric: An Ars Poetica* (Berkeley: University of California Press, 1985).

22 See Rev. Joseph Ketley, ed., *The Two Liturgies with other Documents set forth by authority in the Reign of King Edward The Sixth* (Cambridge: Cambridge University Press, 1844), 372–75, 384, 391, 439–82.

23 William Keatings Clay, ed., *Private Prayers Put Forth by Authority during the Reign of Queen Elizabeth* (Cambridge: Cambridge University Press, 1851), 13–44.

24. The Holy Communion service departs here from the morning and evening prayer and the catechism texts, which all adhere to this translation of the Creed. In its place, the Holy Communion offers a lengthier version, which seems to have been recited by the minister alone. In morning prayer, by contrast, the rubric reads: "then shall be said the Creed, by the minister and the people, standing."

25. We can still find traces of Myrc's instructions in the Second Royal Injunctions of

Henry VIII issued nearly ten years before the liturgical innovations of Cranmer and his fellow reformers. Thus article 4 stipulates:

> Item, that ye shall every Sunday and holy-day through the year, openly and plainly recite to your parishioners, twice or thrice together, or oftener, if need require, one particle or sentence of the *Pater Noster*, or Creed, in English, to the intent that they may learn the same by heart; and so from day to day to give them one like lesson or sentence of the same, till they have learned the whole *Pater Noster* and Creed in English, by rote. And as they may be taught every sentence of the same by rote, ye shall expound and declare the understanding of the same unto them, exhorting all parents and householders to teach their children and servants the same, as they are bound in conscience to do. (Walter H. Frere, ed., *Visitation Articles and Injunctions of the Period of the Reformation*, 3 vols. [London: Longmans Green & Co., 1910], 2:36)

26. Thus the use of hymns from the Sarum rite was limited to the realm of domestic prayer: only Elizabeth's Primer, but not her revised Book of Common Prayer, also issued in 1559, includes these texts in its daily orders. For an accessible and learned edition of the text, which is not included in Brightman, see John Booty, ed., *The Book of Common Prayer 1559: The Elizabethan Prayer Book* (Charlottesville, Va.: The University Press of Virginia, 1976), 53–58. In addition to the Book of Psalms, the other books of Scripture that were understood to have been originally composed in verse, and were frequently translated into English meter, were Ecclesiastes, Job, Proverbs, and the Song of Solomon. See Barbara Lewalski's invaluable work, *Protestant Poetics and the Seventeenth-Century Devotional Lyric* (Princeton, N.J.: Princeton University Press, 1979), 32ff.

27. Mary Kay Duggan, "The Psalter on the Way to the Reformation: The Fifteenth Century Printed Psalter in the North," in *The Place of the Psalms in the Intellectual Culture of the Middle Ages*, ed. Nancy Van Deusen (Albany, N.Y.: SUNY Press, 1999), 153.

28. See Lewalski's illuminating discussion of the Psalms' simultaneously individual and representative voice (*Protestant Poetics*, 232–45).

29. Reprinted under the heading "Athanasius in Psalmos" (Matthew Parker, *The whole Psalter translated into English Metre* [London, 1567], sig. Ci–ii).

30 Ibid., sigs. Eii–iii. See Anne Lake Prescott's fine article, "King David as a 'Right Poet': Sidney and the Psalmist" (*English Literary Renaissance* 19, no. 2 [spring 1989]: 131–51), which persuasively argues for Sidney's use of both Basil and Athanasius in developing his defense of poetry as a "speaking picture." Prescott also shows that Sidney is likely to have relied upon Parker's version of the Psalms as one of the sources for his own translation.

31. "John Calvin to the godly Readers sendeth greeting" (prefatory letter), in *The Psalmes of David and others. With M. John Calvins Commentaries*, trans. Arthur Golding (London, 1571) and "The Epistle to the Reader," in *David's Musick: or psalmes of that Royal Prophet, once the sweete Singer of that Israel. . . . by R. B. and R. A.* (London, 1616), sig. A2b.

32. In contrast, we find unbroken prose in midsixteenth-century Great Bibles, where the verses of the Psalms were separated only by a slightly enlarged space or an occasional asterisk.

33. A similar set of circumstances surrounds the collection of scriptural hymns or canticles that were included in the Prayer Book, and had long formed part of the Christian liturgy: the Te Deum, the Benedicite, the Nunc Dimittis, the Benedictus, the Magnifi-

cat, and so on. These petitions were all provided in nonmetrical versions in the liturgy, but were rendered in rhyme, with accompanying tunes, in Sternhold-Hopkins, which I discuss at length later in this chapter.

34. I have used the translation that Renaissance readers would have found in Matthew Parker's reprinting of this passage in the prefatory pages to his Psalter (Parker, *The whole Psalter translated into English Metre*, sig. Fii–iii).

35. Calvin, *The Institution of the Christian Religion*, trans. Thomas Norton (London, 1574), fols. 274r–275v. I owe this reference to Annabel Patterson's eloquent account of the status of the Psalms, and of Psalm-singing in particular, in the context of Marvell's devotional poetry (Patterson, "'Bermudas' and 'The Coronet': Marvell's Protestant Poetics," *English Literary History* 44 (1977): 479–82).

36. Calvin, *The Institution of the Christian Religion*, fol. 275v.

37. *Luther's Works*, ed. Jaroslav Pelikan and Helmut Lehman, 55 vols. (St. Louis: Concordia Publishing House, 1955–), 53:221.

38. Miles Coverdale, *Goostly Psalmes and spirituall songes drawen out of the holy scripture* (London, 1535?).

39. See Louis Benson, *The English Hymn: Its Development and Use in Worship* (New York: Hodder & Stoughton, 1915). The production of so many original hymns in the early modern period was not part of a liturgical project for public worship, but instead seems to have been intended for domestic and non-ecclesiastical gatherings. Walton, for example, famously describes both Donne's and Herbert's pleasure in singing hymns apart from their liturgical duties. (For Donne's desire to hear his own hymns performed, see p. 94 below.) Walton tells us that Herbert's "love to Music was such, that he went usually twice every week on certain appointed days, to the *Cathedral Church in Salisbury*," where he would "usually sing and play his part, at an appointed private Music-meeting; and to justify this practice, he would often say, *Religion does not banish mirth, but only moderates and sets rules to it*" (Walton, *The Life of Mr. George Herbert*, in Herbert, *The Temple* [London, 1674], 41). The emphasis here on the "private" nature of the meeting, and of the need for justification, suggests the lack of liturgical tradition supporting this practice. As Benson and others confirm, there were no Hymnals published for liturgical use until after the Restoration.

40. Coverdale, "Myles Coverdale unto The Christen Reader," in *Goostly Psalmes*, ii–iii (2–3). Hence Erasmus declares in *Paraclesis*: "I disagree very much with those who are unwilling that Holy Scripture, translated into the vulgar tongue, be read by the uneducated. . . . I would that even the lowliest women read the Gospels and the Pauline Epistles. And I would that they were translated into all languages so that they could be read and understood not only by Scots and Irish but also by Turks and Saracens. . . . Would that, as a result, the farmer sing some portion of them at the plow, the weaver hum some parts of them to the movement of his shuttle, the traveller lighten the weariness of the journey with stories of this kind!" (Erasmus, *Christian Humanism and the Reformation: Selected Writings*, ed. John C. Olin [New York: Harper & Row, 1965], 97.) See also Langland's attack on court minstrels and entertainers, which in the C text follows immediately after the aforementioned passage from Sloth (Derek Pearsall, ed., *Piers Plowman by William Langland* [Berkeley: University of California Press, 1982], passus 7, lines 82–119.) In the B text, this passage is much later in the poem (passus 13, lines 421–456).

41. Coverdale, "Myles Coverdale unto The Christen Reader," iv–v.

42. According to John Foxe, Henry's list of banned books included Tyndale's *Obedience*

of a Christian Man; Becon's *Davids Harpe, Newes out of Heaven*, and several other of Becon's works; new translations of the Bible; English catechisms; and many English translations of the Psalms. This list appears only in the 1563 edition of Foxe's *Actes and Monumentes* (John Foxe, *Acts and Monuments of John Foxe*, ed. George Townsend, 8 vols. [New York: AMC Press, 1965], 5:565–68).

43. *One and Fiftie Psalmes of David in Englishe metre, whereof .37. were made by Thomas Sterneholde: and the rest by others* (Geneva: John Crespin, 1556). Hopkins's seven Psalms included in this volume had in fact originally been appended to Sternhold's thirty-seven in a volume published soon after Sternhold's death in 1549.

44. *The Whole booke of Psalmes, collected into Englysh metre by T. Starnhold, J. Hopkins & others* (London, 1562). This expanded Psalter was compiled by Hopkins, Whittingham, and a number of other contributors. See Zim for a detailed listing of the translators for each of the 150 Psalms (*English Metrical Psalms*, 232).

45. In *The Zurich Letters, Comprising the Correspondence of Several English Bishops and Others, with some of the Helvetian Reformers, during . . . the Reign of Queen Elizabeth*, ed. Hastings Robinson (Cambridge: Cambridge University Press, 1842), 71.

46. Frere, *Visitation Articles*, 3:42. According to Frere, the singers were warned by the chapter that they were violating Elizabeth's Act of Uniformity, but they refused to stop, calling instead upon the vicar's chorale to help them "in these their godly doings." The unresolved situation was ultimately brought before the Ecclesiastical Commissioners, who decided in favor of the Psalm-singers.

47. English visitation articles from this period do not prescribe the use of Sternhold-Hopkins, but demand only that each church possess a copy of the Psalms. Thus Grindal states in his 1571 Injunctions for York that all parishes must have "the book of Common Prayer, with the new calendar, and a Psalter to the same" (*The Remains of Edmund Grindal*, ed. William Nicholson [Cambridge: Cambridge University Press, 1843], 133). Robert Horne, bishop of Winchester, likewise inquires in his 1570 Articles "whether your parishes have a Bible of their own, of the largest volume, the book of common prayer, [and] a Psalter" (*Articles to be ministred by the right Rever'd in Christ, Robert by Gods providence Bishop of Winchester* [London, 1570]).

48. Cited in Benson, *The English Hymn*, 55, from Thomas Warton, *History of English Poetry*, Hazlitt's ed., vol. 4 (n.p., 1871), 130.

49. According to Waldo Selden Pratt, there are 110 different meters in the Marot-Bèze Psalter (*The Music of the French Psalter of 1562* [New York: Columbia University Press, 1939], 26). I owe this reference to Hallett Smith, "English Metrical Psalms in the Sixteenth Century and Their Literary Significance," *Huntington Library Quarterly* 9, no. 3 (May 1946): 269.

50. See Hunnis, *Certayne Psalmes chosen out of the Psalter of David and drawen furth into Englysh meter* (London, 1550). An imitation of *The Paradyse* entitled *A Gorgeous Gallery of Gallant Inventions*, first published in 1578, also fails to include any metrical Psalms.

51. The word *poem* or its cognates was used during this period in secular volumes of verse; among other examples, see Thomas Howell's volume called *The Arbor of Amitie; wherein is comprised pleasant Poems and pretie Poesies* (London, 1568) or George Gascoigne's *A hundreth sundrie flowres bounde up in one smale poesie* (London, 1573), followed by a revised edition entitled *The posies of George Gascoigne esquire* (London, 1575).

52. Sir Philip Sidney, *An Apology for Poetry*, ed. Geoffrey Shepherd (Manchester, England: Manchester University Press, 1973), 99.

53. First described by Robert Lowth in 1753 as *parallelismus membrorum*, or the parallelism of cola, in which two or more sequences of syllables (cola) compose the poetic line (*The New Princeton Encyclopedia of Poetry and Poetics*, ed. Alex Preminger and T. V. F. Brogan [Princeton, N.J.: Princeton University Press, 1993], s.v. "parallelism"). In his notes to the *Apology*, Shepherd cites the first-century historian Flavius Josephus, who claimed in his *Antiquities of the Jews* that the Psalms contained classical odes and hymns in both trimeter and pentameter; and St. Jerome (ca. 342–420), who argued for "iambic, alcaic and sapphic verse in the Psalms similar to those of Pindar and Horace" (Sidney, *An Apology for Poetry*, 152).

54. There is much critical debate over the composition date of the Psalms, with critics arguing alternately for 1536 or 1541. See *Sir Thomas Wyatt, The Complete Poems*, ed. R. A. Rebholz (London: Penguin Books, 1978; reprint, 1988), 455.

55. Parker, *The whole Psalter translated into English Metre*, sig. Fv; Thomas Lodge, *Defence of Poetry, Music and Stage Plays*, reprinted in *Elizabethan Critical Essays*, ed. G. Gregory Smith, 2 vols. (Oxford: Clarendon Press, 1904), 1:71.

56. Sidney, *An Apology for Poetry*, 99.

57. Ibid. As Prescott has powerfully shown, Sidney's assignment of David to the category of "divine poets" as opposed to the "right poets" that Sidney seeks to defend is by no means entirely sustained in the *Apology*, which also registers a "rival tradition in which the psalmist, besides his other advantages, was also a 'right poet'" (Prescott, "King David as a 'Right Poet,'" 134). Although my interest here is not in David's status within Sidney's classifications of divine, philosophical, and right poets so much as in the generic classification of the Psalms themselves, Prescott's attention to Sidney's ambivalence over David's position, and his tendency to "subpoena him [from the temple of divine poets] from time to time to testify on poetry's behalf" (147) helps to confirm my sense of the nervous and self-conscious rethinking of the relationship between scriptural prayer and poetry in the 1580s and 1590s.

58. Sidney, *An Apology for Poetry*, 99.

59. It is difficult to assess how widely Sidney's manuscript copies of the *Apology* circulated before its eventual posthumous publication in 1595 in two separate editions: one as *A defence of poesie*, entered in the Stationers' Register in November 1594 by William Posonby; then in April 1595 the same work was registered as *An apologie for poetrie* by Henry Olney. Although the date of composition is also uncertain, editors generally believe the *Apology* was written sometime between 1580 and 1583; as late as 1585, suggests Duncan-Jones. Unfortunately, only two known manuscripts survive. See H. R. Woudhuysen, *Sir Philip Sidney and the Circulation of Manuscripts 1558–1640* (Oxford: Clarendon Press, 1996), 410–11. According to Woodhuysen, manuscript circulation of the *Apology*, unlike that of *Astrophil and Stella* and the *Old Arcadia*, was "kept on a tight rein" (211); "even if as many as five or six manuscripts of the work existed at one time (and there may have been more) it does not appear that Sidney wanted it to circulate widely" (234). Olney's announcement in his 1595 publication that those who have only heard of this work but not yet read it will "praise me, as the first public bewrayer of Poesies Messias" does suggest that the essay had achieved a certain notoriety (Woodhuysen, *Sir Philip Sidney and the Circulation of Manuscripts*, 232). Whatever its broader circulation may have been, the *Apology* was certainly known within literary circles.

60. This is the position adopted by Lily Campbell in her influential book, *Divine Poetry and Drama in Sixteenth-Century England* (Cambridge: Cambridge University Press, 1959).

61. Barnabe Barnes, *A Divine Centurie of Spirituall Sonnets* (London, 1595), sonnet 1, lines 1–4.

62. The term *sonnet* had strong associations with the secular poetry of Petrarch and his English imitators, such as Wyatt and Surrey, who do not use the sonnet form to write their devotional verse. The term was also used as a synonym for lyrics in volumes such as Tottel's *Songes and Sonnettes*, or Barnabe Googe's 1563 *Eglogs, Epytaphes, and Sonnettes*. It is as a corrective to this loose understanding of the "sonnet" that Gascoigne writes in his "Certayne notes of Instruction concerning the making of verse" appended to his *Posies* (1575): "Some think that all Poems (being short) may be called Sonnets. . . . I can best allow to call those Sonnets which are of fourteen lines, every line containing ten syllables." There is no record, however, of the term *spiritual sonnet* in an English publication of verse until Barnes.

63. Henry Lok, *Sundry Christian Passions Contained in two hundred Sonnets* (London, 1597), ¶4. In *Christs Victorie, and Triumph in Heaven, and Earth, over, and after death* (Cambridge: Cambridge University Press, 1610), the poet Giles Fletcher similarly defends the use of poetry against its detractors in his prefatory letter "To the Reader": "There are but few of many that can rightly judge of Poetry, and yet there are many of those few, that carry so left-handed an opinion of it, as some of them thinke it half sacrilege for profane Poetry to deal with divine and heavenly matters, as though *David* were to be sentenced by them, for uttering his grave matter upon the harp" (¶1r).

64. Michael Drayton, *The Harmonie of the Church, Containing The Spirituall Songes and holy hymnes, of godly men, patriarkes, and Prophetes* (London, 1591), sig. b1. As its title suggests, Drayton's volume contains "songs" from Moses, Solomon, Jeremiah, Tobias, and Judith, among others. He does not include any of the Psalms. Drayton's "spiritual" productions are generically separated from his publication of his collected *Poems* in 1605.

65. Cited in Campbell, *Divine Poetry and Drama in Sixteenth-Century England*, 29.

66. *The Collected Works of Mary Sidney Herbert, Countess of Pembroke*, ed. Margaret P. Hannay, Noel J. Kinnamon, and Michael G. Brennan, 2 vols. (Oxford: Clarendon Press, 1998). All references to Pembroke's Psalms (Ps. 44–150) are from this edition. As Zim acutely observes in her discussion of this Psalm, the Countess of Pembroke "represented this psalm's lyric mode of praise and prayer by exploiting a form more traditionally associated with a secular convention for praise and devotion: the sonnet." And yet, the transformation of the sonnet, typically used in both secular and devotional contexts as a vehicle for first-person, subjective expression, into a corporate form represents a more significant innovation than Zim acknowledges here (*English Metrical Psalms*, 196).

67. For an account of the countess of Pembroke's composition, see M. Herbert, *Collected Works*, 2:3–32.

68. See Theodore L. Steinberg, "The Sidneys and the Psalms," *Studies in Philology* 92, no. 1 (winter 1995): 1–17. Steinberg makes a strong case for the countess of Pembroke's use of the Hebrew texts. See also M. Herbert, *Collected Works*, 2:16–19.

69. For a discussion of these sources, see J. C. A. Rathmell, *The Psalms of Sir Philip Sidney and the Countess of Pembroke* (New York: Anchor Books, 1963), xvii–xx and M. Herbert, *Collected Works*, 2:9–32 and passim. All quotations of the First through the Forty-third Psalms come from Rathmell's edition.

70. Smith, "English Metrical Psalms," 269; Rathmell, *The Psalms of Sir Philip Sidney*, xvii.

71. The best example of this trend in criticism is Roland Greene's essay, "Sir Philip

Sidney's *Psalms*, the Sixteenth-Century Psalter, and the Nature of Lyric," *Studies in English Literature* 30 (1990): 19–40.

72. Pembroke's Psalms 51 and 130 can be found in a fragmentary manuscript with musical accompaniments for treble voice and lute. (Rathmell, *The Psalms of Sir Philip Sidney*, xxvii; M. Herbert, *Collected Works*, 2:28.)

73. *Collected Poems of Sir Thomas Wyatt*, ed. Kenneth Muir and Patricia Thompson (Liverpool, England: Liverpool University Press, 1969), lines 325–37. The preface to this Psalm reads:

> He then Inflamd with farr more hote affect
> Of god then he was erst of Bersabe,
> His lifft fote did on the yerth erect,
> And just thereby remaynth the tother kne;* [the other knee]
> To his lifft syde his wayght he doth direct.
> Sure hope of helth, and harpe agayne takth he;
> His hand, his tune, his mynd sowght his lay,
> Wyche to the Lord with sobre voice did say (lines 317–24)

74. Rathmell, *The Psalms of Sir Philip Sidney*, lines 1–12.

75. Compare, for example, Bèze's paraphrase:

> 1. Hear what I say O Lord, understand mine inward meditation.
> 2. Give ear unto my cry, my king and my God: for thou art he to whom I do present my prayers.
> 3. Hear my voice early in the morning. For daily in the morning will I prepare my self to pray unto thee . . .
> 11. Then shall they all rejoice that flee unto thee for succor, and in that thou doth defend them, they shall triumph for ever: and all that fear thy name shall praise thee with joy.
> 12. Because thou hast showed thy favor to the innocent O Lord: and hast defended him with the shield of thy mercy.

(Gilby: *The Psalmes of David, Truely Opened and explaned by Paraphrases . . . set foorth in Latine by that excellent learned man Theodore Beza. And faithfully translated into English, by Anthonie Gilbie* [London, 1580], 6–8.)

76. The Geneva Bible, for example, offers this translation:

> We will praise thee, o God, we will praise thee, for thy Name is near:
> therefore they will declare thy wondrous works.
> When I shall take a convenient time, I will judge righteously.

In the Marot-Bèze Psalter, the verses read as follows:

> 1. O Seigneur, loué sera, Loué sera, Loué sera ton renom: Car la gloire de ton Nom Près de nous s'approchera: Et de nous seront chantez Les hauts faits de tes bontez.
> 2. Estant mon terme venu, Je jugerai droitement: Du pais le fondement.

(*The Bible and Holy Scriptures Conteyned in the Olde and Newe Testament. Translated According to the Ebrue and Greke, and conferred with the best translations in divers langages* [Geneva, 1560]; *Les Pseaumes mis en rime Francoise, Par Cl. Marot, & Theodore de Bèze* [Lyon, 1563]).

77. Hannay, Kinnamon, and Brennan note, for example, that Pembroke follows Calvin and Bèze in translating the "anointed one" and the "messiah" as "Christ" in Psalms 89 and 132 (M. Herbert, *Collected Works*, 2:19).

78. Ibid., 2:25-26.

79. Greene, "Sir Philip Sidney's *Psalms*," 36-37.

80. M. Herbert, *Collected Works*, 1:110, lines 1-2. These poems appear in the Tixall manuscript, which is likely to have been copied from the Penshurst manuscript by John Davies of Hereford, and prepared for presentation to the queen. William Ringler first speculated that the Penshurst manuscript was not ultimately presented to the queen "because the many corrections made in the process of copying marred its appearance" (M. Herbert, 2:312). In all, there are seventeen extant manuscripts of these Psalms.

81. Cited in Woudhuysen, *Sir Philip Sidney and the Circulation of Manuscripts 1558-1640*, 344-45. Wilton was the home of the earl of Pembroke, where the countess cultivated what her biographer Margaret P. Hannay describes as her own private court (*Philip's Phoenix, Mary Sidney, Countess of Pembroke* [New York: Oxford University Press, 1990] 24 and passim).

82. For a description of these manuscripts, referred to as I and K, see M. Herbert, *Collected Works*, 2:317-22.

83. Ibid., 1:113, lines 8-11. See the discussion of this poem in the introduction to volume 2 (2:9).

84. The revised lines read:

> That heavens King may daigne his owne transform'd
> in substance no, but superficiall tire
> by thee put on; to praise, not to aspire
> To, those high Tons, so in themselves adorn'd,
> which Angells sing in their caelestiall Quire. (Rathmell,
> *The Psalms of Sir Philip Sidney*, 1:110, lines 8-12)

85. Despite these complaints, by the time of Pembroke's death in 1621, nearly 150 editions of Sternhold-Hopkins had been published (ibid., xiii). Sternhold-Hopkins remained unchallenged as the church's Psalter until the "New Version" of Tate and Brady in 1696.

86. Reprinted in Joseph Hall, *The Collected Poems of Joseph Hall, Bishop of Exeter and Norwich*, ed. A. Davenport (Liverpool, England: Cambridge University Press, 1949), 127. According to the second edition of the *Oxford English Dictionary*, Hall's title is the first recorded use of the word *metaphrase* ("a metrical translation") in the English language. Hall uses it again the following year in his dedicatory poem, "To Mr. Josuah Sylvester, of his Bartas Metaphrased," included in *Bartas His Devine Weekes and werkes*, trans. Josuah Sylvester (London, 1608), sig. B5v. The word is a variant on the term *metaphrasis*, which, according to the O.E.D., was first used by Roger Ascham in *The Scholemaster* (1568): "metaphrasis . . . is all one with *Paraphrasis*, save it is out of verse, either into prose, or into some other kind of meter, or else, out of prose into verse."

87. Hall, *Collected Poems*, 128.

88. From an epistle to M. Hugh Cholmley, reprinted in ibid., 270-71.

89. *A Preparation to the Psalter by George Wyther* (London, 1619), 9. Wither issued his own translation of the Psalms entitled "The Psalms of David, translated into Lyrick verse ac-

cording to the Scope of the Original . . . ," which was eventually published in Holland in 1632, following a series of protracted battles with the Stationers' Company. See Phillip von Rohr-Sauer, *English Metrical Psalms from 1600 to 1660: A Study in the Religious and Aesthetic Tendencies of That Period* (Freiburg: Universitätdruckerei Poppen & Ortman, 1938).

90. Wither, *A Preparation to the Psalter*, 68.

Chapter Four

1. *The Poems of John Donne*, ed. Herbert J. C. Grierson (Oxford: Clarendon Press, 1912), lines 37–44.

2. Louis Martz, *The Poetry of Meditation*, rev. ed. (New Haven, Conn.: Yale University Press, 1962), 7.

3. Barbara Lewalski, *Protestant Poetics and the Seventeenth-Century Devotional Lyric* (Princeton, N.J.: Princeton University Press, 1979), 13, 31.

4. Anne Ferry, *The "Inward" Language: Sonnets of Wyatt, Sidney, Shakespeare, Donne* (Chicago: University of Chicago Press, 1983), 227.

5. *The Prose Works of William Wordsworth*, ed. W. J. B. Owen and Jane Worthington Smyser, 3 vols. (Oxford: Clarendon Press, 1974), 1:126.

6. *The Sermons of John Donne*, ed. George R. Potter and Evelyn M. Simpson, 10 vols. (Berkeley: University of California Press, 1953–62), 7:61.

7. For an insightful account of recent debates surrounding the nature of the Laudian church, see Kenneth Fincham's introduction to Fincham, *The Early Stuart Church, 1603–42* (London: Macmillan, 1993).

8. Donne, *Sermons*, 2:167.

9. See Rom. 8:26: "we know not what we should pray for as we ought: but the Spirit itself maketh intercession for us with groanings which cannot be uttered." For the position that the reformers embraced St. Paul's Epistle to the Romans as the foundational text for English Protestantism, see John Coolidge, *The Pauline Renaissance* (Oxford: Oxford University Press, 1970) and A. G. Dickens, *The English Reformation* (New York: Schocken Books, 1974). Although Pauline theology certainly dominated many aspects of liturgical practice, I mean to show that this dismissal of human agency in generating prayers was not passively accepted, but instead actively and explicitly redressed through the imposition of formalized liturgical texts.

10. Samuel Hieron, *A Helpe unto Devotion, containing certain Moulds or Formes of Prayer*, 6th ed. (London, 1614).

11. Reprinted in George Wither, *The Hymnes and Songs of the Church*, with an introduction by Edward Farr (London: John Russell Smith, 1856), xii.

12. George Wither, *The Hymnes and Songs of the Church* (London, 1623?), sig. A2r–A3v.

13. Ibid., sig. P4v.

14. John Donne, *Letters to Severall Persons of Honor* (London, 1651), 28–29.

15. Izaak Walton, *The Lives of Dr. John Donne, Sir Henry Wotton, Mr. Richard Hooker, Mr. George Herbert*, 4th ed. (London, 1675), 54.

16. Izaak Walton, *The Life Of Mr. George Herbert*, printed in Herbert, *The Temple* (London, 1674), 9.

17. As Chana Bloch points out in her rich, book-length study of Herbert's use of the Psalms, the phrase "My God, My King" combines a series of David's addresses to God in

Psalms 5, 68, 84, and 145 (*Spelling the Word: George Herbert and the Bible* [Berkeley: University of California Press, 1985], 23).

18. There are only two surviving manuscripts of Herbert's poems: Tanner MS 307, known as the Bodleian Manuscript (or B); and Jones MS B 62, known as the Williams Manuscript (or W). W, which is in the author's hand, represents an earlier manuscript than B, which editors believe was copied sometime following Herbert's death from a lost authorial manuscript that contained the complete text of *The Temple*. For a detailed account of this history, see the introductions to both facsimile editions: *The Williams Manuscript of George Herbert's Poems: A Facsimile Reproduction with an Introduction by Amy M. Charles* (New York: Delmar, 1977), ix–xxxi and *The Bodleian Manuscript of George Herbert's Poems, A Facsimile of Tanner 307* (New York: Delmar, 1984).

19. Francis Bacon, *Translation Of Certaine Psalmes Into English Verse: By The Right Honourable, Francis Lo. Vervlam, Viscount St. Alban* (London, 1625), sig. A3.

20. Richard Crashaw, *Steps to the Temple* (London, 1646), sig. A3r.

21. Henry Vaughan, *Silex Scintillans: Sacred Poems and private Ejaculations* (London, 1655), sig. B2r.

22. Once again, the important exception to this general omission is John Wall's *Transformations of the Word: Spenser, Herbert, Vaughan* (Athens: University of Georgia Press, 1988), whose chapter on Herbert draws rich connections especially between Eucharist worship in the Prayer Book and the lyrics of *The Temple*. Wall's claim that the point of Herbert's poetry was to "promote the social agenda of the Church of England, to encourage participation in its worship" (160) accurately describes much of "The Church Porch," if not necessarily the majority of lyrics in "The Church." Although my focus falls more specifically on the forms of language that common prayer encouraged and that Herbert seems so deeply to admire, I am indebted to Wall's detailed study of the ways in which the Prayer Book's catechism, baptismal rites, and Communion service permeate *The Temple*. See in particular pp. 169–224.

23. Bloch, *Spelling by the Word*. See Coburn Freer, *Music for a King: George Herbert's Style and the Metrical Psalms* (Baltimore: Johns Hopkins University Press, 1972), which traces the formal and thematic affinities between Herbert's lyrics and the English metrical Psalms circulating in the late sixteenth and seventeenth centuries. See also Lewalski, *Protestant Poetics*.

24. Joseph Summers first identified the tendency among Herbert critics to choose between Herbert as a simple country parson and sophisticated lyric poet in his aptly named study, *George Herbert, His Religion and Art* (Cambridge, Mass.: Harvard University Press, 1954). In the decades following Summers's study, we have seen several significant manifestations of this critical division between devout and artful visions of Herbert. Richard Strier, for example, criticizes Helen Vendler for "attempt[ing] to distinguish the 'human' from the doctrinal content of Herbert's poetry," but draws his own opposition between Herbert's profound attachment to the Lutheran doctrine of justification by faith and his interest in the aesthetics of devotion (*Love Known: Theology and Experience in George Herbert's Poetry* [Chicago: University of Chicago Press, 1983], xxi; Vendler, *The Poetry of George Herbert* [Cambridge, Mass.: Harvard University Press, 1975]). See also Stanley Fish's influential vision of Herbert as committed to an Augustinian anti-aesthetic in *Self-Consuming Artifacts: The Experience of Seventeenth-Century Literature* (Berkeley: University of California Press, 1972).

25. All references to Herbert's poems and prose in this chapter are from *The Works of George Herbert*, ed. F. E. Hutchinson (Oxford: Oxford University Press, 1941) unless otherwise indicated.

26. Walton, *The Life of Mr. George Herbert*, 40.

27. Herbert, *Works*, 232–33.

28. See Wall's discussion of this stanza in *Transformations of the Word*, pp. 63–65, which highlights the didacticism embedded in Herbert's project. Indeed, Wall usefully refers here and elsewhere to Herbert's vocation as one of a "poet-homilist" (65, 221, and passim).

29. For the original version of this poem, see *The Williams Manuscript of George Herbert's Poems*, 48. Although "The Quidditie" distances the poet's art from all secular and courtly ambition, Michael Schoenfeldt has significantly complicated this vision of Herbert's relationship to the language of courtship in his accomplished and original study, *Prayer and Power: George Herbert and Renaissance Courtship* (Chicago: University of Chicago Press, 1991). Unlike many of his contemporary poets, whose poems were named by printers or publishers, Herbert appointed his own titles in both surviving documents. See Anne Ferry, "Titles in George Herbert's 'Little Book,'" *English Literary Renaissance* 23, no. 2 (1993): 314–44.

30. The choice of an altar as the subject for the first lyric of *The Temple* was not unproblematic. Although Herbert died before Laud officially began his campaign to rail altars in the east end of the church and to limit their access to the clergy, the use and position of altars were already matters of enormous controversy in the 1620s, and were by no means removed from Herbert's personal and professional worlds. For an extensive and thoughtful treatment of Herbert's ambiguous position in relation to the ceremonial innovations of the 1620s and early 1630s, see Achsah Guibbory, *Ceremony and Community from Herbert to Milton: Literature, Religion, and Cultural Conflict in Seventeenth-Century England* (Cambridge: Cambridge University Press, 1998), 44–78. For an informed account of the poem's offering of liturgical prayer in place of sacrifice, and its invocations of eucharistic worship, see Wall, *Transformations of the Word*, 200–204.

31. Strier, *Love Known*, 191–92.

32. Strier argues that the poem's "most extraordinary gesture occurs in the final line, when, just as the poem is attaining completion, Herbert uses the phrase, 'this *Altar*,' to refer away from the poem and back to the internal 'broken altar' of the opening" (ibid., 195).

33. Fish, *Self-Consuming Artifacts*, 207–15; Schoenfeldt, *Prayer and Power*, 164.

34. I am indebted to Annabel Patterson for this observation.

35. Diarmaid MacCulloch, *Thomas Cranmer, A Life* (New Haven, Conn.: Yale University Press, 1996), 331.

36. "Christmas" is in fact one of a handful of Herbert's poems for which we have found seventeenth-century musical settings. See Louise Schleiner, "Seventeenth-Century Settings of Herbert: Purcell's 'Longing,'" in *"Too rich to Clothe the Sunne": Essays on George Herbert*, ed. Ted-Larry Pebworth and Claude Summers (Pittsburgh: University of Pittsburgh Press, 1980), 195–207.

37. Hutchinson, *The Works of George Herbert*, xxxvii.

38. See Cristina Malcolmson's discussion of the limitations of the flower metaphor in relation to the processes of both sinfulness and "religious self-cultivation," in her rich and original study of Herbert's place within the economic and social changes of the mid-seventeenth century: *Heart-Work: George Herbert and the Protestant Ethic* (Stanford, Calif.: Stanford University Press, 1999), 147.

39. For a wonderfully nuanced discussion of the scriptural allusions to death in these final lines, see Fish, *Self-Consuming Artifacts*, 222–23.

40. See ibid., 221–22.

41. Herbert, *The Temple* (Cambridge: Cambridge University Press, 1633), ¶2v.

42. These works included Giles Fletcher the Elder's *Licia, or poems of love* (1593); Giles Fletcher the Younger's *Christ's victorie* (1610); and Phineas Fletcher's *The Locusts* (1627) and *Purple Island* (1633).

43. See Henry R. Plomer, *A Short History of English Printing* (London: Kegan Paul, Trench, Trubner and Co., 1900), 154.

44. Ibid., 168–69.

45. David McKitterick, *A History of Cambridge University Press*, 3 vols. (Cambridge: Cambridge University Press, 1992–) 1:116, 153–54.

46. Ibid., 167.

47. Cambridge's publications during the late Elizabethan and early Jacobean period include works of prominent non-conformists such as William Perkins, Andrew Willet, and Thomas Taylor.

48. *A Short-Title Catalogue of Books Printed in England, Scotland, & Ireland and of English Books Printed Abroad 1475–1640*, first compiled by A. W. Pollard and G. R. Redgrave, 3 vols., 2d ed. (London: The Bibliographical Society, 1986).

49. I am indebted to Gordon Teskey for information about use of the pilcrow in seventeenth-century printing. See Teskey, "Positioning Spenser's 'Letter to Ralegh,'" in *Craft and Tradition: Essays in Honour of William Blissett*, ed. H. B. de Groot and Alexander Leggatt (Calgary: University of Calgary Press, 1990), 41–42.

50. Cambridge University Press, for example, did not use pilcrows to separate poems or stanzas in either *The Locusts* or *Purple Island*, both roughly contemporaneous with Herbert's volume.

51. Cambridge's other publications of poetry, ranging from the volumes by Giles and Phineas Fletcher to commendatory verses in Latin published for the king, were issued in quarto or occasionally folio size.

Conclusion

1. Izaak Walton, *The Life Of Mr. George Herbert*, printed in *The Temple* (London, 1674), 56–57. Herbert's "inspired prophecy" about religion in America was ultimately no more sympathetic to the Puritans than it was to the church they left behind. After the two lines cited by Walton, "The Church Militant" continues:

> When height of malice, and prodigious lusts,
> Impudent sinning, witchcrafts, and distrusts
> (The mark of future bane) shall fill our cup
> Unto the brimme, and make our measure up . . .
> Then shall Religion to *America* flee:
> They have their times of Gospel, ev'n as we . . .
> Yet as the Church shall thither westward flie,
> So Sinne shall trace and dog her instantly:
> They have their period also and set times
> Both for their vertuous actions and their crimes.
> And where of old the Empire and the Arts
> Usher'd the Gospel ever in mens hearts,

Spain hath done one; when arts perform the other,
The Church shall come, and Sinne the Church shall smother. (235–65)

2. Under the category of "Octavo, &c.," in the first catalogue of the Harvard Library completed in 1723 we find the listing "Herbert, George, Temple, London, 1634" (*Catalogus Librorum Bibliothecae Collegii Harvardini Quod est Cantabrigiae in Nova Anglia* [Boston, 1723]). Also included in this catalogue are Hooker's *Lawes of Ecclesiastical Politie* (London, 1705); six volumes of Shakespeare's plays (London, 1709); Montaigne's *Essays* (London, 1613); and the Marot-Bèze Psalter. There is no poetry listed from Donne, Spenser, or Sidney. For a history of Harvard's library, see Samuel Eliot Morison, *The Founding of Harvard College* (Cambridge, Mass.: Harvard University Press, 1935).

3. John Winthrop, *The Journal of John Winthrop 1630–1649*, ed. Richard S. Dunn, James Savage, and Laetitia Yeandle (Cambridge, Mass.: The Belknap Press of Harvard University Press, 1996), 340–41.

4. And yet, as Judith Maltby has shown, these years also offer the finest testimony of the Prayer Book's strength among mainstream English Protestants, who fought bitterly against its repeal. See chapters 3–5 of her text for a detailed analysis of the petitions filed in favor of the Prayer Book before the Long Parliament (*Prayer Book and People in Elizabethan and Early Stuart England* [Cambridge: Cambridge University Press, 1998], 83–227).

5. According to the *Short-Title Catalogue*, The Book of Common Prayer was not printed between 1649 and 1660. (*A Short-Title Catalogue of Books Printed in England, Scotland, & Ireland and of English Books Printed Abroad 1475–1640*, first compiled by A. W. Pollard and G. R. Redgrave, 3 vols., 2d ed. [London: The Bibliographical Society, 1986].)

6. *An Ordinance of Parliament for the taking away of the Book of Common Prayer, January 3, 1644* (London, 1644), 44.

7. *A Directory for the Publique Worship of God Throughout the Three Kingdoms of England, Scotland, and Ireland* (1645; reprint, London, 1646), 3–4.

8. *An Ordinance of the Lords and Commons Assembled in Parliament for the More Effectual putting in execution the Directory for Public Worship, 23 August 1645* (London, 1645). The Directory saw its final printing in 1660, when the restoration of the monarchy brought with it the return of a revised Book of Common Prayer. The revised Prayer Book was published in 1662, following the Savoy Conference of 1661, which was held to hear the Puritans' complaints before reissuing the Prayer Book. Very few serious concessions were made.

9. John Cotton, *A Modest And Cleare Answer To Mr. Balls Discourse Of Set Formes Of Prayer* (London, 1642), 5.

10. *A Tryall Of The New-Church Way In New England And In Old . . . By that learned and godly Minister of Christ, John Ball, of Whitmore. Penned a little before his death, and sent over to the New England Ministers, Anno 1637. As a reply to an Answer of theirs in justification of the said Positions* (London, 1644), sig. A2.

11. Perry Miller, *The New England Mind: The Seventeenth Century* (New York: Macmillan Co., 1939), 298.

12. As Harry S. Stout has shown, there were many additional occasions for sermons: on fast days, election days, and so on. (*The New England Soul: Preaching and Religious Culture in Colonial New England* [Oxford: Oxford University Press, 1986], 28-29.)

13. See Edmund S. Morgan, *Visible Saints: The History of a Puritan Idea* (New York.: New York University Press, 1963) and Patricia Caldwell, *The Puritan Conversion Narrative: The Beginnings of American Expression* (Cambridge: Cambridge University Press, 1983).

14. The platform continues: "But whereas persons are of better abilities, there it is most

expedient, that they make their *relations*, & *confessions* personally with their own mouth, as David professeth of himself." Williston Walker, *The Creeds and Platforms of Congregationalism* (New York: Charles Scribner's Sons, 1893), 223. The issue of whether women ought to make their relations publicly was one of great debate. In John Fiske's *Notebook*, there is evidence that women were speaking before the congregation in the mid-1640s, but, according to the editor, Robert G. Pope, by the end of the 1650s it had become "common practice for a woman to stand silently while Fiske read her relation to the congregation" (*The Notebook of the Reverend John Fiske, 1644–1675*, ed. Robert G. Pope, Publications of the Colonial Society of Massachusetts, Collections 47 [Boston: Colonial Society of Massachusetts, 1974]). For a discussion of the debates over women's participation, see Mary Maples Dunn, "Saints and Sisters: Congregational and Quaker Women in the Early Colonial Period," *American Quarterly* 30 (winter 1978): 588–93 and passim.

15. Roger Clap, *Memoirs of Cap. Roger Clap* (Boston, 1731), 5. Reprinted in Daniel B. Shea, *Spiritual Autobiography in Early America* (Madison: University of Wisconsin Press, 1988), 121. See also Charles Cohen, *God's Caress: The Psychology of Puritan Religious Experience* (New York: Oxford University Press, 1986), 158–59.

16. Increase Mather, "Confutation of the Rev. Mr. Stoddard's Observations respecting the Lords Supper" (1680). Reprinted in *Proceedings of the American Antiquarian Society* no. 83, ed. Everett Emerson and Mason I. Lowance (Worcester, Mass., 1973), 63.

17. In *An Exact Collection of the Choicest Poems and Songs Relating to the late times, & Continued by the most Eminent Witts, from 1639 to 1661 Printed for Henry Brome* (London, 1662), 1–2. For a study of New England's opposition to organ playing and choir singing, see Percy A. Scholes, *The Puritans and Music in England and New England* (London: Oxford University Press, 1934).

18. The official title for this book was *The Whole Booke of Psalmes, Faithfully Translated into English Metre*.

19. John Cotton, *The Way Of The Churches Of Christ In New England, Or The Way Of Churches walking in Brotherly equalitie, or co-ordination, without Subjection of one Church to another* (London, 1645), 67.

20. The preface was originally considered the work of Richard Mather, but is now generally attributed to Cotton, following the thorough and detailed research of Zoltan Haraszti. For details of his analysis, see Haraszti, *The Enigma of the Bay Psalm Book* (Chicago: University of Chicago Press, 1956), 19–27.

21. *The Bay Psalm Book: A Facsimile Reprint of the First Edition of 1640*, ed. Zoltan Haraszti (Chicago: University of Chicago Press, 1956), sig. **2v.

22. The preface declares: "As for other objections taken from the difficulty of *Ainsworth's* tunes, and the corruptions in our common psalm books, we hope that they are answered in this new edition of psalms." (ibid., sig. **2r.)

23. *The Journal of John Winthrop, 1630–1649*, 283. As the editors note, Winthrop's reference to the Psalm Book in 1639, one year before it was printed, strongly suggests that many of these journal entries were written retrospectively.

24. Reprinted in George Parker Winship, *The Cambridge Press, 1638–1692: A Reexamination of the Evidence Concerning the Bay Psalm Book and the Eliot Indian Bible* (Philadelphia: University of Pennsylvania Press, 1945), 24. Cotton's *Magnalia* was first published in 1702.

25. According to Harold S. Jantz, Cotton Mather's version of these lines, which have been endlessly reprinted over the centuries, was not in fact accurate. Jantz argues that a handwritten copy of the verses from Cotton Mather's father, Increase Mather, contains a more authentic version:

you Roxborough poets take this in Time
see that you make a very good Rhyme
And eeke of Dorchester, when you the verses lengthen
see that you them with the words of the text doe strengthen.

(Jantz, *The First Century of New England Verse* [New York: Russell and Russell, 1962], 258.)

26. Haraszti, *The Enigma of the Bay Psalm Book*, 17. See pp. 12–18 for a discussion of the probable translators involved.

27. This was brought to my attention by Amy Robinson, whose forthcoming doctoral dissertation on Puritan poetics ("Poetry and Church Order in Seventeenth-Century Massachusetts," Cambridge University) has helped to elucidate many of the concerns in this chapter.

28. According to Wilberforce Eames's *A List of Editions of the Bay Psalm Book* (1885; reprint, New York: Burt Franklin, 1973), the first edition of the Bay Psalm Book was "small 8vo", and subsequent seventeenth-century editions were either "small 12mo" or simply "12mo." The price for these Psalters cannot easily be determined, but we do have evidence from a deposition made by the printer Steven Day in 1655, in a lawsuit brought against the president of Harvard University, Henry Dunster, that seventeen hundred copies of the Bay Psalm Book were printed, and they were "sold at 20 d. a poece [sic]"; the same deposition lists a subsequent edition, most likely of 1651, sold at "12d. a book to Mr. Usher [the leading bookseller], & 15d. the other 1000 [copies]." Two thousand copies were printed in all. Day's deposition is reprinted in Winship, *The Cambridge Press, 1638–1692*, 146–49. See pp. 129–45 for an extensive account of the suit against Dunster.

29. There were seventeen hundred copies of the first edition printed, and two thousand of the 1651 revised edition. Winship speculates, without much reliable information, that there may have been enough copies for each family in the settlements that were using the Bay Psalm Book (i.e., excluding Salem, Newbury, and Plymouth) to own its own copy, although he concedes that many would have had "neither the money nor the inclination to buy this book" (*The Cambridge Press, 1638–1692*, 34).

30. John Cotton, *Singing of Psalmes a Gospel Ordinance* (London, 1647), 62. For the argument that lining out was not practiced in New England until the last decades of the seventeenth century, see Horton Davies, *The Worship of the American Puritans 1629–1730* (New York: Peter Lang, 1990), 126 and Paul Westermeyer, "Religious Music and Hymnody," in *Encyclopedia of the American Religious Experience*, ed. Charles H. Lippy and Peter W. Williams (New York: Charles Scribner's Sons, 1988) 3:1285–1305.

31. Ball, *A Tryall Of The New-Church Way*, 6; Cotton, *A Modest and Cleare Answer*, 29.

32. Preface in Haraszti, *The Bay Psalm Book*, sig. *3v–4r.

33. Cotton, *Singing of Psalmes a Gospel Ordinance*, 55, 56; emphasis mine.

Index